Daily Devotions with William Barclay

365 Meditations on the Heart of the New Testament

COMPILED BY

Philip Law

WESTMINSTER
JOHN KNOX PRESS
LOUISVILLE · KENTUCKY

© 2008 Westminster John Knox Press

All extracts from *The New Daily Study Bible* © The William Barclay Estate, 1976, 2004.

The New Daily Study Bible originally published in 1959 as *The Daily Study Bible* by Saint Andrew Press, 121 George Street, Edinburgh EH2 4YN. Revised edition published in 1976. Third edition, fully revised and updated by Saint Andrew Press and published as *The New Daily Study Bible* in 2004.

2012 paperback edition
Originally published in hardback in the United States
by Westminster John Knox Press in 2008
Louisville, Kentucky

12 13 14 15 16 17 18 19 20 21—10 9 8 7 6 5 4 3 2 1

Book design by Sharon Adams
Cover design by Pam Poll Graphic Design

Library of Congress Cataloging-in-Publication Data

Barclay, William, 1907–1978.
    Daily devotions with William Barclay / compiled and edited by Philip Law.— 1st ed.
        p. cm.
    Includes index.
    ISBN 978-0-664-23270-2 (alk. paper)
    1. Bible. N.T.—Devotional literature.   2. Devotional calendars.   I. Law, Philip.   II. Title.
BS2341.3.B37   2009
242'.2—dc22   2008027986

ISBN: 978-0-664-23889-6 (paper edition)

♾ The paper used in this publication meets the minimum requirements of the American National Standard for Information Sciences—Permanence of Paper for Printed Library Materials, ANSI Z39.48-1992.

Contents

The Gift of God

The Beginning of the Story

Mark 1:1–4

Mark starts the story of Jesus a long way back. It did not begin with Jesus' birth; it did not even begin with John the Baptizer in the wilderness; it began with the dreams of the prophets long ago; that is to say, it began long, long ago in the mind of God.

There are things we may well learn here.

(1) It has been said that 'the thoughts of youth are long, long thoughts', and so are the thoughts of God. God is characteristically a God who is working his purposes out. History is not a random kaleidoscope of disconnected events; it is a process directed by the God who sees the end in the beginning.

(2) We are within that process, and because of that we can either help or hinder it. In one sense it is as great an honour to help in some great process as it is a privilege to see the ultimate goal. Life would be very different if, instead of yearning for some distant and at present unattainable goal, we did all that we could to bring that goal nearer. The goal will never be reached unless there are those who labour to make it possible.

The prophetic quotation which Mark uses is suggestive. 'I send my messenger before you and he will prepare your road for you.' This is from Malachi 3:1. In its original context it is a threat. In Malachi's day the priests were failing in their duty. The offerings were blemished and shoddy second-bests; the service of the Temple was a weariness to them. The messenger was to cleanse and purify the worship of the Temple before the Anointed One of God emerged upon the earth. So then the coming of Christ was a purification of life. And the world needed that purification. Seneca called Rome 'a cesspool of iniquity'. Juvenal spoke of her 'as the filthy sewer into which flowed the abominable dregs of every Syrian and Achaean stream'. Wherever Christianity comes it brings purification.

The Herald of the King

Mark 1:5–8

It is clear that the ministry of John was mightily effective, for they flocked out to listen to him and to submit to his baptism. Why was it that John made an impact such as this upon his nation?

(1) He was a man who lived his message. Not only his words, but also his whole life was a protest. There was the place in which he stayed — the wilderness. He was a man from the desert and from its solitudes and its desolations. He was a man who had given himself a chance to hear the voice of God. There were the clothes he wore — a garment woven of camel's hair and a leather belt about his waist. So did Elijah (2 Kings 1:8). To look at the man was to be reminded, not of the fashionable orators of the day, but of the ancient prophets who lived close to the great simplicities and avoided the soft and comfortable luxuries which kill the soul. There was the food he ate — locusts and wild honey. Many extol the blessings of poverty from comfortable homes. But in the case of John, the man was the message, and because of that people listened.

(2) His message was effective because he told people what in their heart of hearts they knew and brought them what in the depths of their souls they were waiting for.

(3) His message was effective because he was completely humble. His own verdict on himself was that he was not fit for the duty of a slave. Sandals were composed simply of leather soles fastened to the foot by straps passing through the toes. The roads were unsurfaced. In dry weather they were dust-heaps; in wet weather rivers of mud. To remove the sandals was the work and office of a slave. John asked nothing for himself but everything for the Christ whom he proclaimed. The man's obvious self-forgottenness, his patent yield-edness, his complete self-effacement, his utter lostness in his message compelled people to listen.

John's one aim was not to occupy the centre of the stage himself, but to try to connect men and women with the one who was greater and stronger than he; and they listened to him because he pointed, not to himself, but to the one whom we all need.

The Day of Decision

Mark 1:9–11

To any thinking person the baptism of Jesus presents a problem. John's baptism was a baptism of repentance, meant for those who were sorry for their sins and who wished to express their determination to have done with them. What had such a baptism to do with Jesus? Was he not the sinless one, and was not such a baptism unnecessary and quite irrelevant as far as he was concerned? For Jesus the baptism was four things.

(1) It was the moment of decision. For thirty years he had stayed in Nazareth. Faithfully he had done his day's work and discharged his duties to his home. For a long time he must have been conscious that the time for him to go out had to come. He must have waited for a sign. The emergence of John was that sign. This, he saw, was the moment when he had to launch out upon his task.

(2) It was the moment of identification. It is true that Jesus did not need to repent from sin, but here was a movement of the people back to God, and with that Godward movement he was determined to identify himself. It is possible to possess ease and comfort and wealth and still to identify with a movement to bring better things to the downtrodden and the poor and the ill-housed and the overworked and the underpaid. The really great identification is when people identify with a movement, not for their own sake, but for the sake of others.

(3) It was the moment of approval. No one lightly leaves home and sets out on an unknown way. He or she must be very sure that the decision is right. Jesus had decided on his course of action, and now he was looking for the seal of the approval of God.

(4) It was the moment of equipment. At that time the Holy Spirit descended upon him. There is a certain symbolism here. The Spirit descended as a dove might descend. The dove is the symbol of gentleness. He will conquer, but the conquest will be the conquest of love.

The Testing Time

Mark 1:12–13

In this life it is impossible to escape the assault of temptation, but one thing is sure—temptations are not sent to us to make us fall; they are sent to strengthen the nerve and the sinew of our minds and hearts and souls. They are not meant for our ruin, but for our good. They are meant to be tests from which we emerge better warriors and athletes of God.

Here we have the whole essence of the temptation story. Jesus had to decide how he was to do his work. He was conscious of a tremendous task and he was also conscious of tremendous powers. God was saying to him, 'Take my love to men and women; love them till you die for them; conquer them by this unconquerable love even if you finish up upon a cross.' Satan was saying to Jesus, 'Use your power to blast men and women; obliterate your enemies; win the world by might and power and bloodshed.' God said to Jesus, 'Set up a reign of love.' Satan said to Jesus, 'Set up a dictatorship of force.' Jesus had to choose that day between the way of God and the way of the Adversary of God.

Mark's brief story of the Temptations finishes with two vivid touches.

(1) The animals were his companions. In the desert there roamed the leopard, the bear, the wild boar and the jackal. This is usually taken to be a vivid detail that adds to the grim terror of the scene. But perhaps it is not so. Perhaps this is a lovely thing, for perhaps it means that the animals were Jesus' friends.

(2) The angels were helping him. There are always the divine reinforcements in the hour of trial. When Elisha and his servant were shut up in Dothan with their enemies pressing in upon them and no apparent way of escape, Elisha opened the young man's eyes, and all around he saw the horses and the chariots of fire which belonged to God (2 Kings 6:17). Jesus was not left to fight his battle alone—and neither are we.

The Witness of John

John 1:19–28

The deputation which came to interview John was composed of two kinds of people. First, there were the priests and the Levites. Their interest was very natural, for John was the son of Zacharias, and Zacharias was a priest (Luke 1:5). In Judaism, the only qualification for the priesthood was descent. If a man was not a descendant of Aaron, nothing could make him a priest; if he was a descendant of Aaron, nothing could stop him being one. Therefore, in the eyes of the authorities, John the Baptist was in fact a priest, and it was very natural that the priests should come to find out why he was behaving in such an unusual way.

Second, there were emissaries of the Pharisees. It may well be that behind them was the Sanhedrin. One of the functions of the Sanhedrin was to deal with anyone who was suspected of being a false prophet. John was a preacher to whom the people were flocking in hordes. The Sanhedrin may well have felt it their duty to check up on this man in case he was a false prophet.

The emissaries of the orthodox asked him who he was; his answer was that he was nothing but a voice bidding men and women prepare the way for the King. The quotation is from Isaiah 40:3. All the gospels cite it (Mark 1:3; Matthew 3:3; Luke 3:4). The idea behind it is this: The roads of Palestine were not surfaced and metalled. They were mere tracks. When a king was about to visit a province, when a conqueror was about to travel through his domains, the roads were smoothed and straightened out and put in order. We are to understand that by this time the baptism of Jesus had taken place at which John had recognized Jesus. So here John is saying again: 'The King is coming. And, for his coming, you need to be cleansed as much as any Gentile. Prepare yourself for the entry into history of the King.'

John is the great example of a man prepared to obliterate himself in order that Jesus Christ may be seen. He was only, as he saw it, a signpost pointing to Christ. God give us grace to forget ourselves and to remember only Christ.

The Coming of the Spirit

John 1:32–34

Here we can learn a great deal of what the word *baptism* means. The Greek verb *baptizein* means *to dip* or *to submerge*. It can be used of clothes being dipped in dye; it can be used of a ship submerged beneath the waves; it can be used of a person who is so drunk that he is soaked in drink. When John says that Jesus will baptize with the Holy Spirit, he means that Jesus can bring God's Spirit to us in such a way that we are saturated and our life and being are flooded with that Spirit.

Now what did this baptism mean for John? His own baptism meant two things.

(1) It meant cleansing. It meant being washed from the impurities that cling to us.

(2) It meant dedication. It meant going out to a new and a different and a better life.

But Jesus' baptism was a baptism of the Spirit. If we remember the Jewish conception of the Spirit, we can say that when the Spirit takes possession of us certain things happen.

(1) Our lives are enlightened. There comes to us the knowledge of God and God's will. We know what God's purpose is, what life means, where duty lies. Some of God's wisdom and light has come into us.

(2) Our lives are strengthened. Knowledge without power is a haunting and frustrating thing. But the Spirit gives us not only knowledge to know the right, but also strength and power to do it. The Spirit gives us a triumphant adequacy to cope with life.

(3) Our lives are purified. Christ's baptism with the Spirit was to be a baptism of fire (Matthew 3:11; Luke 3:16). The dross of evil things, the alloy of the lower things, the base admixture is burned away until we become clean and pure.

Often our prayers for the Spirit are a kind of theological and liturgical formality, but when we know that for which we are praying, these prayers become a desperate cry from the heart.

7

The First Disciples

John 1:35–39

Here we have the symbol of the divine initiative. It is always God who takes the first step. When the human mind begins to seek and the human heart begins to long, God comes to meet us far more than halfway. God does not leave us to search and search until we come to him; God comes out to meet us.

Jesus began by asking these two men the most fundamental question in life: 'What are you looking for?' It would be well if every now and again we were to ask ourselves: 'What am I looking for? What's my aim and goal? What am I really trying to get out of life?'

Some are searching for security. They would like a position which is safe, money enough to meet the needs of life and to put some past for the time when work is done, a material security which will take away the essential worry about material things. This is not a wrong aim, but it is a low aim, and an inadequate thing to which to direct all life; for, in the last analysis, there is no safe security in the chances and the changes of this life.

Some are searching for what they would call a career, for power, prominence, prestige, for a place to fit the talents and the abilities they believe themselves to have, for an opportunity to do the work they believe themselves capable of doing. If this is directed by motives of personal ambition it can be a bad aim; if it is directed by motives of the service of our neighbours it can be a high aim. But it is not enough, for its horizon is limited by time and by the world. Some are searching for some kind of peace, for something to enable them to live at peace with themselves, and at peace with God, and at peace with others. This is the search for God; this aim only Jesus Christ can meet and supply.

The answer of John's disciples was that they wished to know where Jesus stayed. They wished to linger long with him and talk out their problems and their troubles. Those who would be Jesus' disciples can never be satisfied with a passing word. They want to meet Jesus, not as an acquaintance in passing, but as a friend in their own homes.

The One Who Sees

John 1:40–42

When Andrew brought Peter to Jesus, Jesus looked at Peter. The word used of that look is *emblepein*. It describes a concentrated, intent gaze, the gaze which does not see only the superficial things that lie on the surface, but which reads a person's heart. When Jesus saw Simon, as he was then called, he said to him: 'Your name is Simon; but you are going to be called Cephas, which means a rock.'

In the ancient world, most people had two names. Greek was the universal language, and most people had a name in their own native tongue by which they were known to their friends and their family circle, and also a name in the Greek tongue by which they were known in the business and the commercial and the wider world. Sometimes one name was a translation of the other. *Peter* was the Greek and *Cephas* the Aramaic for a *rock*.

In the Old Testament, a change of name often denoted a new relationship with God. For instance, Jacob became Israel (Genesis 32:28), and Abram became Abraham (Genesis 17:5) when they entered into a new relationship with God. When a person entered into a new relationship with God, it was as if life began all over again and that person became new, so that a new name was needed.

But the great thing about this story is that it tells us how Jesus looks at us. He does not only see what we are; he also sees what we can become. He sees not only the actualities in us; he also sees the possibilities. Jesus looked at Peter and saw in him not only a Galilaean fisherman but one who had it in him to become the rock on which his Church would be built. Jesus sees us not only as we are, but as we can be; and he says: 'Give your life to me, and I will make you what you have it in you to be.'

Once someone came on Michelangelo chipping away with his chisel at a huge, shapeless piece of rock. He asked the sculptor what he was doing. 'I am releasing the angel imprisoned in this marble,' he answered. Jesus is the one who sees and can release the hidden potential in each of us.

The Surrender of Nathanael

John 1:43–51

Philip, like Andrew, could not keep the good news to himself. So Philip went and found his friend Nathanael. He told him that he believed that he had discovered the long-promised Messiah in Jesus, the man from Nazareth.

Nathanael was contemptuous. There was nothing in the Old Testament which foretold that God's chosen one should come from Nazareth. Philip was wise. He did not argue. He said simply: 'Come and see!' The only way to convince people of the supremacy of Christ is to confront them with Christ. On the whole, it is true to say that it is not argumentative and philosophical preaching and teaching which have won men and women for Christ; it is the presentation of the story of the cross.

There is a story which tells how, towards the end of the nineteenth century, Thomas Huxley, the great agnostic, was a member of a house party at a country house. Sunday came round, and most of the members prepared to go to church; but, very naturally, Huxley did not propose to go. Huxley approached a man known to have a simple and radiant Christian faith. He said to him: 'Suppose you don't go to church today. Suppose you stay at home and you tell me quite simply what your Christian faith means to you and why you are a Christian.' 'But', said the man, 'you could demolish my arguments in an instant. I'm not clever enough to argue with you.' Huxley said gently: 'I don't want to argue with you; I just want you to tell me simply what this Christ means to you.' The man stayed at home and told Huxley most simply of his faith. When he had finished there were tears in the great agnostic's eyes. 'I would give my right hand,' he said, 'if only I could believe that.'

It was not clever argument that touched Huxley's heart. He could have dealt efficiently and devastatingly with any argument that that simple, uncomplicated Christian was likely to have produced; but the simple presentation of Christ went straight to his heart. The best argument is to say to people: 'Come and see!' Of course, we have to know Christ ourselves before we can invite others to come to him.

The Searcher of Human Hearts

John 2:23–25

The question John is answering here is—if there were many who believed in Jesus right at the beginning, why did Jesus not there and then set up his standard and openly declare himself?

The answer is that Jesus knew human nature only too well. He knew that there were many whose interest in him would be short-lived. He knew that there were many who were attracted only by the sensational things he did. He knew that there were none who understood the way that he had chosen. He knew that there were many who would have followed him while he continued to produce miracles and wonders and signs, but who, if he had begun to talk to them about service and self-denial, if he had begun to talk to them about self-surrender to the will of God, if he had begun to talk to them about a cross and about carrying a cross, would have stared at him with blank incomprehension and left him on the spot.

It is a great characteristic of Jesus that he did not want followers unless they clearly knew and definitely accepted what was involved in following him. He refused to cash in on a moment's popularity. If he had entrusted himself to the mob in Jerusalem, they would have declared him Messiah there and then and would have waited for the kind of material action they expected the Messiah to take. But Jesus was a leader who refused to ask anyone ever to accept him until the full implications of that acceptance were understood. He insisted that people should know what they were doing.

Jesus knew human nature. He knew the fickleness and instability of human hearts. He knew that people can be swept away in a moment of emotion, and then back out when they discover what decision really means. He knew how human nature hungers for the spectacular. He wanted not a crowd cheering they knew not what, but a small company who knew what they were doing and who were prepared to follow to the end.

The Man Who Came by Night

John 3:1–6

When Nicodemus came to Jesus, he said that no one could help being impressed with the signs and wonders that he did. Jesus' answer was that it was not the signs and the wonders that were really important; the important thing was such a change in a person's inner life that it could only be described as a new birth.

When Jesus said that it was necessary to be born anew, Nicodemus misunderstood him, and the misunderstanding came from the fact that the word which the Revised Standard Version translates *anew*, the Greek word *anothen*, has three different meanings.

(1) It can mean *from the beginning, completely radically.*

(2) It can mean *again*, in the sense of *for the second time*.

(3) It can mean *from above*, and, therefore, *from God* (as in the New Revised Standard Version). It is not possible for us to get all these meanings into any English word; and yet all three of them are in the phrase *born anew*. To be born anew is to undergo such a radical change that it is like a new birth; it is to have something happen to the soul which can only be described as being born all over again; and the whole process is not a human achievement, because it comes from the grace and power of God.

What, then, does this rebirth mean for us? In the New Testament, and especially in the Fourth Gospel, there are four closely interrelated ideas. There is the idea of rebirth; there is the idea of the kingdom of heaven, into which people cannot enter unless they are reborn; there is the idea of being children of God; and there is the idea of eternal life. This idea of being reborn is not something which is peculiar to the thought of the Fourth Gospel. In Matthew, we have the same great truth put more simply and more vividly: 'Unless you change and become like children, you will never enter the kingdom of heaven' (Matthew 18:3). All these ideas have a common thought behind them.

Born Again

John 3:1–6

To those who believe, there is given the power to become God's children (John 1:12). But the very essence of being a child of God is necessarily obedience. 'They who have my commandments and keep them are those who love me' (John 14:21). The essence of this relationship is love; and the essence of love is obedience. We cannot with any reality say that we love a person and then do things which hurt and grieve that person's heart. This relationship is a privilege, but a privilege which is entered into only when full obedience is given. So then to be children of God and to be in the kingdom are one and the same thing. The children of God and the citizens of the kingdom are both people who have completely and willingly accepted the will of God.

Now let us take eternal life. It is far better to speak of eternal life than to speak of everlasting life. The main idea behind eternal life is not simply that of duration. It is quite clear that a life which went on forever could just as easily be hell as heaven. The idea behind eternal life is the idea of a certain quality of life. What kind? Eternal life is the kind of life that God lives; it is God's life. To enter into eternal life is to enter into possession of that kind of life which is the life of God. It is to be lifted up above merely human, transient things into that joy and peace which belong only to God. Clearly we can enter into this close fellowship with God only when we render to him that love, that reverence, that devotion and that obedience which truly bring us into fellowship with him.

Finally, in this passage, John lays down a great law. That which is born of the flesh is flesh, and that which is born of the Spirit is spirit. Human beings by themselves are flesh, and their power is limited to what the flesh can do. By themselves, they cannot be other than defeated and frustrated; that we know only too well; it is the universal fact of human experience. But the very essence of the Spirit is power and life which are beyond human power and human life; and when the Spirit takes possession of us, the defeated life of human nature becomes the victorious life of God.

The Duty to Know and the Right to Speak

John 3:7–13

There are any number of things in this world which we use every day without knowing how they work. Comparatively few of us know how electricity or radio or television works; but we do not deny that they exist because of that. Many of us drive a car with only the haziest notion of what goes on inside its engine; but our lack of understanding does not prevent us using and enjoying the benefits which a car confers. We may not understand how the Spirit works; but the effect of the Spirit on the lives of men and women is there for all to see. The unanswerable argument for Christianity is the Christian life. No one can disregard a faith which is able to make bad people good.

Jesus said to Nicodemus: 'I have tried to make things simple for you; I have used simple human pictures taken from everyday life; and you have not understood. How can you ever expect to understand the deep things if even the simple things are beyond you?' There is a warning here for every one of us. It is easy to sit in discussion groups, to sit in a study and to read books; it is easy to discuss the intellectual truth of Christianity; but the essential thing is to experience the power of Christianity. And it is fatally easy to start at the wrong end and to think of Christianity as something to be discussed, not as something to be experienced. It is certainly important to have an intellectual grasp of every aspect of Christian truth; but it is still more important to have a vital experience of the power of Jesus Christ.

When we undergo treatment from a doctor, when we have to have surgery, when we are given some medicine to take, we do not need to know the anatomy of the human body, the scientific effect of the anaesthetic, the way in which the drugs work on our bodies, in order to be cured. Ninety-nine out of every 100 accept the cure without being able to say how it was brought about. There is a sense in which Christianity is like that. At its heart there is a mystery, but it is not the mystery of intellectual appreciation; it is the mystery of redemption.

The Uplifted Christ

John 3:14–15

Eternal life is the very life of God himself. But let us ask this: if we possess eternal life, what do we have? If we enter into eternal life, what is it like? To have eternal life envelops every relationship in life with peace.

(1) It gives us peace with God. We are no longer cringing before a tyrannical king or seeking to hide from an austere judge. We are at home with our Father.

(2) It gives us peace with one another. If we have been forgiven, we must be forgiving. It enables us to see other people as God sees them. It makes us and all people into one great family joined in love.

(3) It gives us peace with life. If God is Father, God is working all things together for good. The eighteenth-century German dramatist G. E. Lessing used to say that if he had one question to ask the Sphinx, who knew everything, it would be: 'Is this a friendly universe?' When we believe that God is Father, we also believe that such a father's hand will never cause his child a needless tear. We may not understand life any better, but we will not resent life any longer.

(4) It gives us peace with ourselves. In the last analysis, we are more afraid of ourselves than of anything else. We know our own weaknesses; we know the force of our own temptations; we know our own tasks and the demands of our own lives. But now we know that we are facing it all with God. It is not we who live but Christ who lives in us. There is a peace founded on strength in his life.

(5) It makes us certain that the deepest peace on earth is only a shadow of the ultimate peace which is to come. It gives us a hope and a goal to which we may travel. It gives us a life of glorious wonder here and yet, at the same time, a life in which the best is yet to be.

The Love of God

John 3:16

All great men and women have had their favourite texts, but this has been called 'everybody's text'. Herein for every one of us is the very essence of the gospel. This text tells us certain great things.

(1) It tells us that the initiative in all salvation lies with God. Sometimes Christianity is presented in such a way that it sounds as if God had to be pacified, as if he had to be persuaded to forgive. Sometimes the picture is drawn of a stern, angry, unforgiving God and a gentle, loving, forgiving Jesus. Sometimes the Christian message is presented in such a way that it sounds as if Jesus did something which changed the attitude of God to men and women from condemnation to forgiveness. But this text tells us that it was with God that it all started. It was God who sent his Son, and he sent him because he loved the world he had created. At the back of everything is the love of God.

(2) It tells us that the mainspring of God's being is love. It is easy to think of God as looking at human beings in their heedlessness and their disobedience and their rebellion and saying: 'I'll break them: I'll discipline them and punish them and scourge them until they come back.' It is easy to think of God as seeking human allegiance in order to satisfy his own desire for power and for what we might call a completely subject universe. The tremendous thing about this text is that it shows us God acting not for his own sake but for ours; not to satisfy his desire for power, not to bring a universe to heel, but to satisfy his love.

(3) It tells us of the width of the love of God. It was the world that God so loved. It was not a nation; it was not the good people; it was not only the people who loved him; it was the world. The unlovable and the unlovely, the lonely who have no one else to love them, those who love God and those who never think of him, those who rest in the love of God and those who spurn it—all are included in this vast inclusive love of God. As St Augustine had it: 'God loves each one of us as if there was only one of us to love.'

Love and Judgment

John 3:17–21

Here we are faced with one of the apparent paradoxes of the Fourth Gospel —
the paradox of love and judgment. We have just been thinking of the love of
God, and now suddenly we are confronted with judgment and condemnation
and conviction. John has just said that it was because God so loved the world
that he sent his Son into the world. Later he will go on to show us Jesus saying: 'I came into this world for judgment' (9:39). How can both things be true?

We may take our friends to see some great masterpiece of art; we may take
them to listen to the most eloquent of preachers; we may give them a great
book to read; we may take them to gaze upon some beauty. Their reactions
are a judgment; if they find no beauty and no thrill, we know that there is a
blind spot in their souls. A visitor was being shown round an art gallery by
one of the attendants. In that gallery there were certain masterpieces beyond
all price, possessions of eternal beauty and unquestioned genius. At the end
of the tour, the visitor said: 'Well, I don't think much of your old pictures.'
The attendant answered quietly: 'Sir, I would remind you that these pictures
are no longer on trial, but those who look at them are.' All that the man's reaction had done was to show his own pitiable blindness.

This is so with regard to Jesus. If when people are confronted with Jesus
their souls respond to that wonder and beauty, they are on the way to salvation. But if when they are confronted with Jesus they see nothing lovely, they
stand condemned. Their reaction has condemned them. God sent Jesus in
love. He sent him for the salvation of those people; but that which was sent
in love has become a condemnation. It is not God who has condemned them;
God only loved them; the people have condemned themselves.

By our reaction to Jesus Christ, we stand revealed and our souls are laid
bare. If we regard Christ with love, even with wistful yearning, there is hope
for us; but if in Christ we see nothing attractive, we have condemned ourselves. The one who was sent in love has become our judge.

The One from Heaven

John 3:31–36

If we want information, we have to go to the person who possesses that information. If we want information about a family, we will get it at firsthand only from a member of that family. If we want information about a town, we will get it at firsthand only from someone who comes from that town. So, if we want information about God, we will get it only from the Son of God; and if we want information about heaven and heaven's life, we will get it only from him who comes from heaven.

John goes on: we can believe what Jesus says, because on him God poured out the Spirit in full measure, keeping nothing back. Even the Jews themselves said that the prophets received from God a certain measure of the Spirit. The full measure of the Spirit was reserved for God's own chosen one. Now, in Hebrew thought the Spirit of God had two functions — first, the Spirit revealed God's truth to men and women; and, second, the Spirit enabled them to recognize and understand that truth when it came to them. So to say that the Spirit was on Jesus in the completest possible way is to say that he perfectly knew and perfectly understood the truth of God. To put that in another way — to listen to Jesus is to listen to the very voice of God.

Finally, John again sets before us the eternal choice — life or death. All through history, this choice had been set before Israel. Deuteronomy records the words of Moses: 'See, I have set before you today life and prosperity, death and adversity. . . . I call heaven and earth to witness against you today that I have set before you life and death, blessings and curses. Choose life so that you and your descendants may live' (Deuteronomy 30:15–20). The challenge was reiterated by Joshua: 'Choose this day whom you will serve' (Joshua 24:15).

It has been said that all life concentrates upon a man or woman at the crossroads. Once again, John returns to his favourite thought. What matters is the reaction people have to Christ. If that reaction is love and longing, they will know life. If it is indifference or hostility, they will know death. It is not that God sends his wrath upon them; it is that they bring that wrath upon themselves.

Breaking Down the Barriers

John 4:1–9

Few stories in the gospel record show us so much about the character of Jesus.

(1) It shows us the reality of his humanity. Jesus was weary from the journey, and he sat by the side of the well exhausted. It is very significant that John, who stresses the sheer deity of Jesus Christ more than any other of the gospel writers, also stresses his humanity to the full. John does not show us a figure freed from the tiredness and the struggle of our humanity. He shows us one for whom life was an effort as it is for us.

(2) It shows us the warmth of his sympathy. From one of the orthodox religious leaders of the day, the Samaritan woman would have fled in embarrassment. If by any unlikely chance he had spoken to her, she would have met him with an ashamed and even a hostile silence. But it seemed the most natural thing in the world to talk to Jesus. She had at last met someone who was not a critic but a friend, one who did not condemn but who understood.

But there was still another way in which Jesus was taking down the barriers. The Samaritan was a woman. The strict Rabbis forbade a Rabbi to greet a woman in public. A Rabbi might not even speak to his own wife or daughter or sister in public. There were even Pharisees who were called 'the bruised and bleeding Pharisees' because they shut their eyes when they saw a woman on the street and so walked into walls and houses! For a Rabbi to be seen speaking to a woman in public was the end of his reputation—and yet Jesus spoke to this woman. Not only was she a woman; she was also a woman of notorious character. No decent man, let alone a Rabbi, would have been seen in her company, or even exchanging a word with her—and yet Jesus spoke to her.

To a Jew, this was an amazing story. Here was the Son of God, tired and weary and thirsty. Here was the holiest of men, listening with understanding to a sorry story. Here was Jesus breaking through the barriers of nationality and orthodox Jewish custom. Here is the beginning of the universality of the gospel; here is God so loving the world, not in theory, but in action.

The Living Water

John 4:10–15

Jesus was not using terms that were bound to be misunderstood; he was using terms that anyone with spiritual insight should have understood. The promise was that the chosen people would draw water with joy from the wells of salvation (Isaiah 12:3). The psalmist spoke of his soul being thirsty for the living God (Psalm 42:1). God's promise was: 'I will pour water on the thirsty land' (Isaiah 44:3). The summons was that everyone who was thirsty should come to the waters and freely drink (Isaiah 55:1).

Sometimes the Rabbis identified this living water with the wisdom of the law; sometimes they identified it with nothing less than the Holy Spirit of God. All Jewish pictorial religious language was full of this idea of the thirst of the soul which could be quenched only with the living water which was the gift of God.

At the heart of all this, there is the fundamental truth that in the human heart there is a thirst for something that only Jesus Christ can satisfy. In one of his books, the American novelist Sinclair Lewis draws a picture of a respectable little businessman who kicked over the traces. He is talking to the girl he loves. She says to him: 'On the surface we seem quite different; but deep down we are fundamentally the same. We are both desperately unhappy about something—and we don't know what it is.' In each of us, there is this nameless unsatisfied longing, this vague discontent, this something lacking, this frustration.

In his novel *Sorrell and Son*, Warwick Deeping tells of a conversation between Sorrell and his son. The boy is talking about life. He says that it is like groping in an enchanted fog. The fog breaks for a moment; you see the moon or a girl's face; you think you want the moon or the face; and then the fog comes down again and leaves you groping for something, you don't quite know what. Augustine talks about 'our hearts being restless till they find rest in thee'.

Part of the human situation is that we cannot find happiness out of the things that the human situation has to offer. We are never safe from the longing for eternity which God has put into the human soul. There is a thirst which only Jesus Christ can satisfy.

The True Worship

John 4:16–26

There are many people whose religion is founded on a kind of vague fear of what might happen if they leave God out of the reckoning. But real religion is founded not on fear but on the love of God and gratitude for what God has done.

Jesus pointed to the true worship. God, he said, is spirit. Immediately we grasp that, a new floodlight breaks over us. If God is spirit, God is not confined to things; and therefore idol-worship is not only an irrelevance, it is an insult to the very nature of God. If God is spirit, God is not confined to places; and therefore to limit the worship of God to Jerusalem or to any other spot is to set a limit to that which by its nature exceeds all limits. If God is spirit, our gifts to God must be gifts of the spirit. Animal sacrifices and all things of our own creating become inadequate. The only gifts that befit the nature of God are the gifts of the spirit—love, loyalty, obedience and devotion.

The spirit is the highest part of a human being. That is the part which lasts when the physical part has vanished. That is the part which dreams the dreams and sees the visions which, because of the weakness and faultiness of the body, may never be carried out. It is this spirit which is the source of our highest dreams and thoughts and ideals and desires. The true worship is when each of us, through that spirit, attains to friendship and intimacy with God. Genuine worship does not consist in coming to a certain place, nor in going through a certain ritual or liturgy, nor even in bringing certain gifts. True worship is when the spirit, the immortal and invisible part within us, speaks to and meets with God, himself immortal and invisible.

This passage closes with a great declaration. There had opened before this Samaritan woman a vista which bewildered and staggered her. Here were things beyond her understanding, things full of wonder. All that she could say was: 'When the Messiah, the Christ, the Anointed One of God comes, then we will know all about it.' Jesus said to her: 'I who am speaking to you am he.' It is as if Jesus said that this is not a dream of the truth; this is the truth itself.

Sharing the Wonder

John 4:27–30

The woman was on her way back to the village without her water pot. The fact that she left her water pot showed two things. It showed that she was in a hurry to share this extraordinary experience, and it showed that she never dreamed of doing anything else but come back. Her whole action has much to tell us of real Christian experience.

(1) Her experience began with being compelled to face herself and to see herself as she was. Our Christian experience will often begin with a humiliating wave of self-disgust. It usually happens that the last thing people see is themselves. And it often happens that the first thing Christ does for people is to compel them to do what they have spent their lives refusing to do—look at themselves.

(2) The Samaritan woman was staggered by Christ's ability to see into her inmost being. She was amazed at his intimate knowledge of the human heart, and of her heart in particular. The psalmist was awed by that same thought. 'You discern my thoughts from far away. . . . Even before a word is on my tongue, O Lord, you know it completely' (Psalm 139:1–4). It is told that once a small girl heard a sermon by C. H. Spurgeon, and whispered to her mother at the end of it: 'Mother, how does he know what goes on in our house?' There are no wrappings and disguises which are protection against the gaze of Christ. It is his power to see into the depths of the human heart. It is not that he sees only the evil there; he sees also the potential for great things in the soul of every one of us. He is like the surgeon who sees the diseased part, but who also sees the health which will follow when that part is taken away.

(3) The first instinct of the Samaritan woman was to share her discovery. Having found this amazing person, she was compelled to share her find with others. The Christian life is based on the twin pillars of discovery and communication. No discovery is complete until the desire to share it fills our hearts; and we cannot communicate Christ to others until we have discovered him for ourselves.

The Most Satisfying Food

John 4:31–34

The great keynote of Jesus' life is submission to the will of God. His uniqueness lies in the very fact that he was the only person who ever was or who ever will be perfectly obedient to God's will. It can be truly said that Jesus is the only person in all the world who never did what he liked but always what God liked.

He was God-sent. Again and again, the Fourth Gospel speaks of Jesus being *sent* by God. There are two Greek words used in the Fourth Gospel for this sending. There is *apostellein*, which is used seventeen times, and *pempein*, which is used twenty-seven times. That is to say, no fewer than forty-four times the Fourth Gospel speaks, or shows us Jesus speaking, about his being sent by God.

Then once Jesus had come, again and again he spoke of the work that was given him to do. In John 5:36 he speaks of the works which his Father has given him to do. In 17:4 his only claim is that he has finished the work his Father gave him to do. When he speaks of taking up and laying down his life, of living and of dying, he says: 'I have received this command from my Father' (10:18). He speaks continually, as he speaks here, of the will of God. 'I have come down from heaven,' he says, 'not to do my own will, but the will of him who sent me' (6:38). 'I always do', he says, 'what is pleasing to him' (8:29). In 14:23 he lays it down, out of his personal experience and on his personal example, that the only proof of love lies in the keeping of the commandments of the one a person claims to love. This obedience of Jesus was not, as it is with us, a spasmodic thing. It was the very essence and being, the mainspring and the core, the dynamic and the moving power of his life.

It is his great desire that we should be as he was. To do the will of God is the only way to peace. There can be no peace when we are at variance with the King of the universe.

The Saviour of the World

John 4:39–42

The Samaritans discovered in Christ the Saviour of the world. It is not likely that they themselves put it exactly that way. John was writing years afterwards, and was putting the discovery of the Samaritans into his own words, words which enshrine a lifetime's living with and thinking about Jesus Christ. It is only in John that we find this tremendous title. We find it here and in 1 John 4:14. To him it was the title par excellence for Christ. John did not invent the title. In the Old Testament, God had often been called the God of Salvation, the Saviour, the Saving God. Many of the Greek gods had acquired this title. At the time John was writing, the Roman emperor was invested with the title 'Saviour of the world'. It is as if John said: 'All that you have dreamed of has at last in Jesus come true.'

We do well to remember this title. Jesus was not simply a prophet who came with a message in words from God. He was not simply an expert psychologist with an uncanny faculty for seeing into the human mind. True, he showed that very skill in the case of the Samaritan woman, but he showed more than that. He was not simply an example. He did not come simply to show men and women the way in which life ought to be lived. A great example can be merely heartbreaking and frustrating when we find ourselves powerless to follow it.

Jesus was Saviour. He rescued people from the evil and hopeless situations in which they found themselves; he broke the chains that bound them to the past and gave them a power which enabled them to meet the future. The Samaritan woman is in fact the great example of his saving power. The town where she stayed would no doubt have labelled her a character beyond reformation; and she herself would no doubt have agreed that a respectable life was beyond her. But Jesus came and doubly rescued her; he enabled her to break away from the past and he opened a new future to her. There is no title adequate to describe Jesus except Saviour of the world.

The Father and the Son

John 5:19–20

This is the beginning of Jesus' answer to the Jews' charge that he was making himself equal to God. He lays down three things about his relationship with God.

He lays down his identity with God. The salient truth about Jesus is that in him we see God. If we wish to see how God feels to human beings, if we wish to see how God reacts to sin, if we wish to see how God regards the human situation, we must look at Jesus. The mind of Jesus is the mind of God; the words of Jesus are the words of God; the actions of Jesus are the actions of God.

This identity is based not so much on equality as on complete obedience. Jesus never did what he wanted to do but always what God wanted him to do. It is because his will was completely submitted to God's will that we see God in him. Jesus is to God as we must be to Jesus.

This obedience is not based on submission to power; it is based on love. The unity between Jesus and God is a unity of love. We speak of two minds having only a single thought and two hearts beating as one. In human terms, that is a perfect description of the relationship between Jesus and God. There is such complete identity of mind and will and heart that Father and Son are one.

But this passage has something still more to tell us about Jesus.

(1) It tells us of his complete confidence. On purely human grounds, the one thing Jesus might reasonably expect was death. The forces of Jewish orthodoxy were gathering against him and the end was already sure. But Jesus was quite certain that the future was in the hands of God and that what God had sent him to do could not be stopped by any human means.

(2) It tells of his complete fearlessness. That he would be misunderstood was certain. That his words would inflame the minds of his hearers and endanger his own life was beyond argument. He would make his claim and speak his truth no matter what people might threaten to do. To him, it was much more important to be true to God than to fear human actions.

Life, Judgment and Honour

John 5:21–23

Here we see three great functions which belong to Jesus Christ as the Son of God.

(1) He is the giver of life. John meant this in a double sense. He meant it in time. We are not fully alive until Jesus Christ enters into us and we enter into Jesus Christ. When we make the discovery of the realm of music or of literature or of art or of travel, we sometimes speak of a new world opening out to us. People into whose lives Jesus Christ has entered find life made new. They are changed people; their personal relationships are changed; their conception of work and duty and pleasure is changed; their relationship to God is changed. He meant it in eternity. After this life is ended, for those who have accepted Jesus Christ there opens life still more full and still more wonderful; while for those who have refused Jesus Christ, there comes that death which is separation from God. Jesus Christ gives life both in this world and in the world to come.

(2) He is the bringer of judgment. John says that God committed the whole process of judgment to Jesus Christ. What he means is this—our judgment depends on our reaction to Jesus. If we find in Jesus the one person to be loved and followed, we are on the way to life. If we see in Jesus an enemy, we have condemned ourselves. Jesus is the touchstone by which all are tested; reaction to him is the test by which all are divided.

(3) He is the receiver of honour. The most uplifting thing about the New Testament is its unquenchable hope and its unconquerable certainty. It tells the story of a crucified Christ and yet never has any doubt that at the end all people will be drawn to that crucified figure and that all people will know him and acknowledge him and love him. Amid persecution and disregard, in spite of smallness of numbers and poverty of influence, in the face of failure and disloyalty, the New Testament and the early Church never doubted the ultimate triumph of Christ.

When we are tempted to despair, we would do well to remember that human salvation is the purpose of God and that nothing, in the end, can frustrate his will. The evil will of men and women may delay God's purpose; it cannot defeat it.

Acceptance Means Life

John 5:24

What does it mean to listen to Jesus' word and to believe in the Father who sent him? To put it at its briefest, it means three things.

(1) It means to believe that God is as Jesus says he is; that he is love; and so to enter into a new relationship with him in which fear is banished.

(2) It means to accept the way of life that Jesus offers us, however difficult it may be and whatever sacrifices it may involve, certain that to accept it is the ultimate way to peace and to happiness, and to refuse it the ultimate way to death and judgment.

(3) It means to accept the help that the risen Christ gives and the guidance that the Holy Spirit offers, and so to find strength for all that the way of Christ involves.

When we do that, we enter into three new relationships.

(1) We enter into a new relationship with God. The judge becomes the father, the distant becomes the near, strangeness becomes intimacy and fear becomes love.

(2) We enter into a new relationship with our neighbours. Hatred becomes love, selfishness becomes service and bitterness becomes forgiveness.

(3) We enter into a new relationship with ourselves. Weakness becomes strength, frustration becomes achievement and tension becomes peace.

To accept the offer of Jesus Christ is to find life. Everyone in one sense may be said to be alive; but there are few who can be said to know life in the real sense of the term. When Sir Wilfred Grenfell was writing to a nursing sister about her decision to come out to Labrador to help in his work there, he told her that he could not offer her much money, but that if she came she would discover that in serving Christ and the people of the country she would have the time of her life.

The person who accepts the way of Christ has passed from death to life. In this world, life becomes new and thrilling; in the world to come, eternal life with God becomes a certainty.

January 27

Death and Life

John 5:25–29

In this passage, John seems to use the word *dead* in two senses.

(1) He uses it of those who are spiritually dead; to them, Jesus will bring new life. What does it mean?

(a) To be spiritually dead is to have stopped trying. It is to have come to look on all faults as ineradicable and all virtues as unattainable. But the Christian life cannot stand still; it must either go on or slip back; and to stop trying is therefore to slip back to death.

(b) To be spiritually dead is to have stopped feeling. There are many people who at one time felt intensely in face of the sin and the sorrow and the suffering of the world; but slowly they have become insensitive. They can look at evil and feel no indignation; they can look at sorrow and suffering and feel no answering sword of grief and pity pierce their heart. When compassion goes, the heart is dead.

(c) To be spiritually dead is to have stopped thinking. The day when the desire to learn leaves us, the day when new truth, new methods, new thought become simply a disturbance with which we cannot be bothered, is the day of our spiritual death.

(d) To be spiritually dead is to have stopped repenting. The day when someone is able to sin in peace is the day of that person's spiritual death; and it is easy to slip into that frame of mind. The first time we do a wrong thing, we do it with fear and regret. If we do it a second time, it is easier to do it. If we do it a third time, it is easier still. If we go on doing it, the time comes when we scarcely give it a thought.

(2) John also uses the word *dead* literally. Jesus teaches that the resurrection will come and that what happens to someone in the afterlife is inextricably bound up with what that person has done in this life. The awful importance of this life is that it determines eternity. All through it, we are fitting or unfitting ourselves for the life to come, making ourselves fit or unfit for the presence of God.

The Witness of God

John 5:37–43

The Jewish authorities searched the law and yet failed to recognize Christ when he came. What was wrong? The best Bible students in the world, people who meticulously and continuously read Scripture, rejected Jesus. How could that happen?

One thing is clear—they read Scripture in the wrong way.

(1) They read it with a shut mind. They read it not to search for God but to find arguments to support their own positions. They did not really love God; they loved their own ideas about him. Water has as much chance of getting into concrete as the word of God had of getting into their minds. They did not humbly learn a theology from Scripture; they used Scripture to defend a theology which they themselves had produced. There is still danger that we should use the Bible to prove our beliefs and not to test them.

(2) They made a still bigger mistake—they regarded God as having given a written revelation. The revelation of God is a revelation in history. It is not God speaking, but God acting. The Bible itself is not his revelation; it is the record of his revelation. But they worshipped the Bible's words. There is only one proper way to read the Bible—to read it as all pointing to Jesus Christ. Then many of the things which puzzle us, and sometimes distress us, are clearly seen as stages on the way, a pointing forward to Jesus Christ, who is the supreme revelation and by whose light all other revelation is to be tested. The Jewish authorities worshipped a God who wrote rather than a God who acted, and therefore when Christ came they did not recognize him. The function of the Scriptures is not to give life but to point to him who can.

In verse 34, Jesus had said the purpose of his words was 'that you may be saved'. There is something tremendous here. When people oppose us and we argue back, what is our main feeling? Wounded pride? The conceit that hates any kind of failure? Annoyance? A desire to cram our opinions down other people's throats? Jesus talked as he did only because he loved men and women. His voice might be stern, but in the sternness there was still the accent of yearning love; his eyes might flash fire, but the flame was the flame of love.

The Bread of Life

John 6:35–40

This is one of the great passages of the Fourth Gospel, and indeed of the New Testament. In it there are two great lines of thought that we must try to analyse.

First, what did Jesus mean when he said: 'I am the bread of life'? Let us analyse it step by step. Bread sustains life. It is that without which life cannot go on. But what is life? Clearly by life is meant something far more than mere physical existence. What is this new spiritual meaning of life? Real life is the new relationship with God, that relationship of trust and obedience and love. That relationship is made possible only by Jesus Christ. Apart from him, no one can enter into it. That is to say, without Jesus there may be existence, but not life.

Therefore, if Jesus is the essential of life, he may be described as the bread of life. The hunger of the human situation is ended when we know Christ and through him know God. The restless soul is at rest; the hungry heart is satisfied.

Second, this passage opens out to us the stages of the Christian life. We see Jesus. We see him in the pages of the New Testament, in the teaching of the Church, sometimes even face to face. Having seen him, we come to him. We regard him not as some distant hero and pattern, not as a figure in a book, but as someone accessible. We believe in him. That is to say, we accept him as the final authority on God, on all humanity, on life. This process gives us life. It puts us into a new and lovely relationship with God, wherein he becomes an intimate friend; we are now at home with the one whom we feared or never knew. The possibility of this is free and universal. The invitation is to everyone. The bread of life is ours for the taking. The only way to that new relationship is through Jesus. Without him, it would never have been possible. No searching of the human mind or longing of the human heart can fully find God apart from Jesus.

At the back of the whole process is God. It is those whom God has given him who come to Christ. God not only provides the goal; he moves in the human heart to awaken desire for him. We could never even have sought him unless he had already found us.

His Body and His Blood

John 6:51–59

To most of us, this is a very difficult passage. It speaks in language and moves in a world of ideas which are quite strange to us and which may seem even fantastic and grotesque. But to those who heard it first, it was moving among familiar ideas which went back to the very childhood of the race.

Jesus said we must drink his blood. In Jewish thought, the blood stands for the life. It is easy to understand why. As the blood flows from a wound, life ebbs away; and to the Jews, the blood belonged to God. When Jesus said we must drink his blood, he meant that we must take his life into the very core of our hearts.

What does that mean? Think of it this way. Here in a bookcase is a book which you never read. It may be the glory and the wonder of the tragedies of Shakespeare; but as long as it remains unread upon your bookshelves, it is external to you. One day, you take it down and read it. You are thrilled and fascinated and moved. The story sticks to you; the great lines remain in your memory; now when you want to, you can take that wonder out from inside yourself and remember it and think about it and feed your mind and your heart upon it. Once the book was outside you. Now it is inside you and you can feed upon it. It is that way with any great experience in life. It remains external until we take it within ourselves.

It is so with Jesus. As long as he remains a figure in a book, he is external to us; but when he enters into our hearts, we can feed upon the life and the strength and the dynamic vitality that he gives to us. Jesus said that we must drink his blood. He is saying: 'You must stop thinking of me as a subject for theological debate; you must take me into you, and you must come into me; and then you will have real life.'

When he told us to eat his flesh and drink his blood, he was telling us to feed our hearts and souls and minds on his humanity, and to revitalize our lives with his life until we are filled with the life of God.

The All-Important Spirit

John 6:59–65

The real difficulty of Christianity is twofold. It demands an act of surrender to Christ, an acceptance of him as the final authority; and it demands a moral standard of the highest level. The disciples were well aware that Jesus had claimed to be the very life and mind of God come down to earth; their difficulty was to accept that as true, with all its implications. To this day many refuse Christ, not because he puzzles intellect, but because he challenges their lives.

Jesus goes on, not to try to prove his claim, but to state that some day events will prove it. What he is saying is this: 'You find it difficult to believe that I am the bread, the essential of life, which came down from heaven. Well then, you will have no difficulty in accepting that claim when some day you see me ascending back to heaven.' It is a forecast of the ascension. It means that the resurrection is the guarantee of the claims of Jesus. He was not one who lived nobly and died gallantly for a lost cause; he was the one whose claims were vindicated by the fact that he rose again.

Jesus goes on to say that the all-important thing is the life-giving power of the Spirit; the flesh is of no help. We can put that very simply in a way which will give us at least something of its meaning—the most important thing is the spirit in which any action is done. It has been put this way: 'All human things are trivial if they exist for nothing beyond themselves.' The real value of anything depends on its aim. If we eat simply for the sake of eating, we become gluttons, and it is likely to do us far more harm than good; if we eat to sustain life, to do our work better, to maintain the fitness of our body at its highest peak, food has a real significance. If people spend a great deal of time on sport simply for the sake of sport, they are at least to some extent wasting their time. But if they spend that time in order to keep their bodies fit and thereby to do their work for God and for others better, sport ceases to be trivial and becomes important. The things of the flesh all gain their value from the spirit in which they are done.

The Heavenly Teacher

Without Honour in His Own Country

Luke 4:16–30

The synagogue was the centre of religious life in Palestine. There was only one Temple; but the law said that wherever there were ten Jewish families there must be a synagogue; and so in every town and village it was in the synagogue that the people met to worship. There were no sacrifices in the synagogue. The Temple was designed for sacrifice; the synagogue was for teaching. But how could Jesus gain an entry into the synagogue and how could he, a layman, the carpenter from Nazareth, deliver his message there?

In the synagogue service there were three parts.

(1) The worship part in which prayer was offered.

(2) The reading of the Scriptures. Seven people from the congregation read. As they read, the ancient Hebrew, which was no longer widely understood, was translated by the Targumist into Aramaic or Greek, in the case of the law, one verse at a time, in the case of the prophets, three verses at a time.

(3) The teaching part. In the synagogue there was no professional ministry nor any one person to give the address; the president would invite any distinguished person present to speak, and discussion and talk would follow. That is how Jesus got his chance. The synagogue and its platform were open to him at this stage.

It was not a book that Jesus took, for at this time everything was written on scrolls. It was from Isaiah 61 that he read. Verse 20 says that Jesus sat down. That gives us the impression that he was finished. In point of fact it means that he was about to start, because the speaker gave the address seated and Rabbis taught sitting down.

What angered the people was the apparent compliment that Jesus paid to Gentiles. The Jews were so sure that they were God's people that they tended to look down on all others. And here was this young Jesus, whom they all knew, preaching as if the Gentiles were specially favoured by God. It was beginning to dawn upon them that there were things in this new message the like of which they had never dreamed.

The Guest of an Outcast

Luke 5:18–26

Of all people in Palestine the tax collectors were the most hated. Palestine was a country subject to the Romans; tax collectors had taken service under the Roman government; therefore they were regarded as renegades and traitors. There were two types of taxes. First, there were stated taxes. Second, there were all kinds of duties. A tax was payable for using the main roads, the harbours, the markets. A tax was payable on a cart, on each wheel of it, and on the animal which pulled it. There was purchase tax on certain articles, and there were import and export duties. A tax collector could bid a man stop on the road and unpack his bundles and charge him well-nigh what he liked. If a man could not pay, sometimes the tax collector would offer to lend him money at an exorbitant rate of interest and so get him further into his clutches. Robbers, murderers and tax collectors were classed together. A tax collector was barred from the synagogue. Yet Jesus chose Matthew the tax collector to be an apostle.

(1) The first thing Matthew did was to invite Jesus to a feast—he could well afford it—and to invite his fellow tax collectors and their outcast friends to meet him. Matthew's first instinct was to share the wonder he had found. John Wesley once said, 'No man ever went to Heaven alone; he must either find friends or make them.' It is a Christian duty to share the blessedness that we have found.

(2) The scribes and Pharisees objected. The Pharisees—the separated ones—would not even let the skirt of their robe touch the likes of Matthew. Jesus gave the perfect answer. Once the Greek philosopher Epictetus called his teaching 'the medicine of salvation'. Jesus pointed out that it is only sick people who need doctors; and people like Matthew and his friends were the very people who needed him most.

It would be well if we were to regard the sinner not as a criminal but as someone who is ill; and if we were to look on the person who has made a mistake not as someone deserving contempt and condemnation but as someone needing love and help to find the right way.

The Happy Company

Luke 5:33–35

What amazed and shocked the scribes and the Pharisees was the normality of the followers of Jesus. The orthodox Jews had an idea that people were not being religious unless they were uncomfortable.

They had systematized their religious observances. They fasted on Mondays and Thursdays; and often they whitened their faces so that no one could fail to see that they were fasting. Even prayer was systematized. It was to be offered two or three times daily, at morning and evening and sometimes at noon.

Jesus was opposed radically to religion by rule. He used a vivid picture. When two young people married in Palestine they did not go away for a honeymoon; they stayed at home, and for a week kept open house. They dressed in their best; sometimes they even wore crowns; for that week they were king and queen and their word was law. The daily routine of life was hard and they would never again have a week like that. And the favoured guests who shared this festive week were called the children of the bride chamber.

(1) It is extremely significant that more than once Jesus likened the Christian life to a wedding feast. Joy is a primary Christian characteristic. It was said of a famous American teacher by one of her students, 'She made me feel as if I was bathed in sunshine.' Far too many people think of Christianity as something which compels them to do all the things they do not want to do and hinders them from doing all the things they do want to do. Laughter has become a sin, instead of—as a famous philosopher called it—'a sudden glory'.

(2) At the same time Jesus knew there would come a day when the bridegroom would be taken away. He was not caught unawares by death. Ahead he saw the cross; but even on the way to the cross he knew the joy that no one can take away, because it is the joy of the presence of God.

The Increasing Opposition

Luke 6:1–5

Jesus and his disciples were passing along one of the paths which intersected the corn fields. The fact that the disciples plucked the ears of corn was in itself no crime. One of the merciful laws of the Old Testament laid it down that anyone passing through a corn field was free to pluck the corn as long as a sickle was not put into it (Deuteronomy 23:25). On any other day there would have been no complaint; but this was the Sabbath. Four of the forbidden kinds of work were reaping, threshing, winnowing and preparing food; and technically the disciples had broken every one of them.

This passage contains a great general truth. Jesus said to the Pharisees, 'Have you not read what David did?' The answer of course was, 'Yes' — but they had never seen what it meant. It is possible to read Scripture meticulously, to know the Bible inside out from cover to cover, to be able to quote it verbatim and to pass any examination on it — and yet completely miss its real meaning. Why did the Pharisees miss the meaning — and why do we so often miss it?

(1) They did not bring to Scripture an open mind. They came to Scripture not to learn God's will but to find proof texts to buttress up their own ideas. Far too often people take their theology to the Bible instead of finding their theology in the Bible.

(2) They did not bring a needy heart. The person who comes with no sense of need always misses the deepest meaning of Scripture. When need awakens, the Bible is a new book. When Bishop Butler was dying he was troubled. 'Have you forgotten, my lord,' said his chaplain, 'that Jesus Christ is a Saviour?' 'But,' said the dying bishop, 'how can I know that he is a Saviour for me?' 'It is written,' said the chaplain, 'him that cometh unto me I will in nowise cast out.' And Butler answered, 'I have read these words a thousand times and I never saw their meaning until now. Now I die in peace.' The sense of need unlocked for him the treasury of Scripture.

When we read God's book we must bring to it the open mind and the needy heart — and then to us also it will be the greatest book in the world.

February 5

Jesus Chooses the Twelve

Luke 6:12–19

Here we see Jesus choosing the Twelve. It is interesting and salutary to see why he chose them, because it is for the same reasons that he still wants and needs men and women.

(1) Mark 3:14 tells us that he chose them that they might be with him. He chose them to be his friends. It is amazing that Jesus needed human friendship. It is of the very essence of the Christian faith that we can say in all reverence and humility that God cannot be happy without men and women.

(2) Jesus chose them to be his disciples. The word *disciple* means *a learner*. They were to be those who were always learning more and more about him. Christians spend their whole lives learning about that Lord whom they will some day meet face to face and will then know even as they are known.

(3) Jesus chose them to be his apostles. The Greek word *apostolos* means *someone who is sent out*. It can be used for an envoy or an ambassador. They were to be his ambassadors to men and women. Christians are sent to be ambassadors for Christ, not only by their words but by their lives and deeds.

About the Twelve themselves we may note two things.

(1) They were very ordinary men. There was not a wealthy, nor a famous, nor an influential man among them. It is as if Jesus said, 'Give me twelve ordinary men and I will change the world.' The work of Jesus is not in the hands of those whom the world calls great, but in the hands of ordinary people like ourselves.

(2) They were a strange mixture. To take but two of them—Matthew was a tax collector, and, therefore, a traitor and a renegade. Simon was a Zealot, and the Zealots were fanatical nationalists, who were sworn to assassinate every traitor and every Roman they could. It is one of the miracles of the power of Christ that Matthew the tax collector and Simon the Zealot could live at peace in the close company of the apostolic band. When people are really Christian the most diverse and divergent types can live at peace together.

The End of the World's Values

Luke 6:20–26

Luke's Sermon on the Plain and Matthew's Sermon on the Mount (Matthew, chapters 5–7) closely correspond. Both start with a series of beatitudes. There are differences between the versions of Matthew and Luke, but this one thing is clear—they are a series of bombshells. It may well be that we have read them so often that we have forgotten how revolutionary they are.

They take the accepted standards and turn them upside down. The people whom Jesus called happy the world would call wretched; and the people Jesus called wretched the world would call happy. Just imagine anyone saying, 'Happy are the poor, and, Woe to the rich!' To talk like that is to put an end to the world's values altogether.

Where then is the key to this? It comes in verse 24. There Jesus says, 'Woe to you who are rich because you have all the comfort you are going to get.' The word Jesus uses for *have* is the word used for receiving payment in full of an account. What Jesus is saying is this, 'If you set your heart and bend your whole energies to obtain the things which the world values, you will get them—but that is all you will ever get.' In the expressive phrase, literally, *you have had it!* But if on the other hand you set your heart and bend all your energies to be utterly loyal to God and true to Christ, you will run into all kinds of trouble; you may by the world's standards look unhappy, but much of your payment is still to come; and it will be joy eternal.

We are here face to face with an eternal choice which begins in childhood and never ends till life ends. Will you take the easy way which yields immediate pleasure and profit? Or will you take the hard way which yields immediate toil and sometimes suffering? Will you seize on the pleasure and the profit of the moment? Or are you willing to look ahead and sacrifice them for the greater good? Will you concentrate on the world's rewards? Or will you concentrate on Christ?

If you take the world's way, you must abandon the values of Christ. If you take Christ's way, you must abandon the values of the world.

The Golden Rule

Luke 6:27–38

In Greek there are three words for 'to love'. There is *eran*, which describes passionate love, the love between the sexes. There is *philein*, which describes our love for our nearest and dearest, the warm affection of the heart. Neither of these two words is used here; the word used here is *agapan*, which needs a whole paragraph to translate it.

Agapan describes an active feeling of benevolence towards other people; it means that no matter what others do to us we will never allow ourselves to desire anything but their highest good; and we will deliberately and of set purpose go out of our way to be good and kind to them. This is most suggestive. We cannot love our enemies as we love our nearest and dearest. To do so would be unnatural, impossible and even wrong. But we can see to it that, no matter what others do to us, even if they insult, ill-treat and injure us, we will seek nothing but their highest good.

This passage has in it two great facts about the Christian ethic.

(1) The Christian ethic is positive. It does not consist in not doing things but in doing them. Jesus gave us the Golden Rule, which bids us do to others as we would have them do to us. That rule exists in many writers of many creeds in its negative form. It is not unduly difficult to keep yourself from such action; but it is a very different thing to go out of your way to do to others what you would want them to do to you. The very essence of Christian conduct is that it consists, not in refraining from bad things, but in actively doing good things.

(2) The Christian ethic is based on the extra thing. Jesus described the common ways of sensible conduct and then dismissed them with the question, 'What special grace is in that?' So often people claim to be just as good as their neighbours. Very likely they are. But the question of Jesus is, 'How much *better* are you than the ordinary person?' It is not our neighbour with whom we must compare ourselves; we may well stand that comparison very adequately; it is God with whom we must compare ourselves; and in that comparison we are all in default.

The King's Honesty to His Messengers

Matthew 10:16–23

No one can read this passage without being deeply impressed with the honesty of Jesus. He never hesitated to tell people what they might expect, if they followed him. It is as if he said: 'Here is my task for you—at its grimmest and at its worst—do you accept it?' In his commentary, Plummer comments: 'This is not the world's way to win adherents.' The world will offer people roses, roses all the way, comfort, ease, advancement and the fulfilment of their worldly ambitions. Jesus offered his followers hardship and death. And yet the proof of history is that Jesus was right. In their heart of hearts, people love a call to adventure.

After the siege of Rome in 1849, the Italian statesman Garibaldi issued the following proclamation to his followers: 'Soldiers, all our efforts against superior forces have been unavailing. I have nothing to offer you but hunger and thirst, hardship and death; but I call on all who love their country to join with me'—and they came in their hundreds. During the Second World War, after Dunkirk, the British Prime Minister Winston Churchill offered his country 'blood, toil, sweat and tears'.

When Sir Ernest Shackleton proposed his march to the South Pole, he asked for volunteers for that trek through the blizzards across the polar ice. He expected to have difficulty, but he was inundated with letters from young and old, rich and poor, from every part of society, all desiring to share in that great adventure.

It may be that the Church must learn again that we will never attract men and women to an easy way; it is the call of the heroic which ultimately speaks to people's hearts.

The King's Messenger
and the King's Sufferings

Matthew 10:24–25

Jesus warns his disciples that they must expect what happened to him to happen to them. This sentence was well known to the Jews: 'It is enough for the slave to be as his master.' In the later days, they were to use it in a special way. In AD 70, Jerusalem was destroyed, and destroyed so completely that a plough was drawn across the devastation. The Temple of God and the holy city were in ruins. The Jews were dispersed throughout the world, and many of them mourned and lamented the terrible fate which had befallen them personally. It was then that the Rabbis said to them: 'When God's Temple has been destroyed, how can any individual Jew complain about his personal misfortunes?'

In this saying of Jesus, there are two things.

(1) There is a warning. There is the warning that, as Christ had to carry a cross, so also the individual Christian must carry a cross. The word that is used for *members of a household* is the one Greek word *oikiakoi*. This word has a technical use: it means the members of the household of a government official, that is to say, the official's *staff*. It is as if Jesus said: 'If I, the leader and commander, must suffer, you who are the members of my staff cannot escape.' Jesus calls us not only to share his glory but to share his warfare and his agony; and we do not deserve to share the fruits of victory if we refuse to share the struggle of which these fruits are the result.

(2) There is the statement of a privilege. To suffer for Christ is to share the work of Christ; to have to sacrifice for the faith is to share the sacrifice of Christ. When Christianity is hard, we can say to ourselves not only: 'We are treading where the saints have trod'; we can also say: 'We are treading where the feet of Christ have trod.'

When Christianity costs something, we are closer than we ever were to the fellowship of Jesus Christ; and if we know the fellowship of his sufferings, we shall also know the power of his resurrection.

The Reward of Those Who Welcome the King's Messenger

Matthew 10:40–42

In this passage, there is something very lovely for every simple and humble individual.

(1) We cannot all be prophets, and preach and proclaim the word of God; but those who give God's messenger the simple gift of hospitality will receive no less a reward than that prophet. There are many who have been great public figures; there are many whose voices have kindled the hearts of thousands of people; there are many who have carried an almost intolerable burden of public service and public responsibility, all of whom would gladly have borne witness that they could never have survived the effort and the demands of their task, were it not for the love and the care and the sympathy and the service of someone at home, who was never in the public eye at all.

When true greatness is measured up in the sight of God, it will be seen again and again that those who greatly moved the world were entirely dependent on someone else who, as far as the world is concerned, remained unknown. Even prophets must eat and be clothed. Let those who have the often thankless task of making a home, cooking meals, washing clothes, shopping for household necessities or caring for children never think of it as a dreary and weary chore. It is God's greatest task; and they will be far more likely to receive the prophet's reward than those whose days are filled with committees and whose homes are comfortless.

(2) We cannot all be shining examples of goodness; we cannot all stand out in the world's eye as righteous; but those who help such people in their work will receive equal reward. The great beauty of this passage is its stress on simple things. The Church and Christ will always need their great orators, their great shining examples of sainthood, their great teachers, those whose names are household words; but the Church and Christ will also always need those in whose homes there is hospitality, on whose hands there is all the service which makes a home, and in whose hearts there is the caring which is Christian love; and, as Robert Browning wrote in 'Pippa Passes', 'All service ranks the same with God.'

The Accent of Sorrowful Rebuke

Matthew 11:16–19

Jesus was saddened by the sheer perversity of human nature. To him, men and women seemed to be like children playing in the village square. One group said to the other: 'Come on and let's play at weddings,' and the others said: 'We don't feel like being happy today.' Then the first group said: 'All right; come on and let's play at funerals,' and the others said: 'We don't feel like being sad today.' They were what the Scots call contrary. No matter what was suggested, they did not want to do it; and no matter what was offered, they found a fault in it. John came, living in the desert, fasting and despising food, isolated from the society of others; and they said of him: 'The man is mad to cut himself off from human society and human pleasures like that.' Jesus came, mixing with all kinds of people, sharing in their sorrows and their joys, keeping company with them in their times of joy; and they said of him: 'He is a socialite; he is a party-goer; he is the friend of outsiders with whom no decent person would have anything to do.' They called John's self-denial madness; and they called Jesus' sociability laxness of morals. They could find grounds for criticism either way.

The plain fact is that when people do not want to listen to the truth, they will easily enough find an excuse for not listening to it. They do not even try to be consistent in their criticisms; they will criticize the same person, and the same institution, from quite opposite grounds. If people are determined to make no response, they will remain stubbornly unresponsive no matter what invitation is made to them. Grown men and women can be very like spoiled children who refuse to play no matter what the game is.

Then comes Jesus' final sentence in this section: 'Wisdom is shown to be right by her deeds.' The ultimate verdict lies not with the cantankerous and perverse critics but with events. The Jews might criticize John for his lonely isolation, but John had moved the hearts of men and women to God as they had not been moved for centuries; the Jews might criticize Jesus for mixing too much in ordinary life and with ordinary people, but in him people were finding a new life and a new goodness and a new power to live as they ought and a new access to God.

The Accent of Heartbroken Condemnation

Matthew 11:20–24

We must be careful to catch the accent in Jesus' voice as he said these words. The Revised Standard Version has it: 'Woe to you, Chorazin! Woe to you, Bethsaida!' The Greek word for *woe* is *ouai*; and *ouai* expresses *sorrowful pity* at least as much as it does anger. This is not the accent of one who is in a temper because his self-esteem has been touched; it is not the accent of one who is blazing with anger because he has been insulted. It is the accent of sorrow, the accent of one who offered men and women the most precious thing in the world and saw it disregarded. Jesus' condemnation of sin is holy anger, but the anger comes not from outraged pride but from a broken heart. What then was the sin of Chorazin, of Bethsaida, of Capernaum, the sin which was worse than the sin of Tyre and Sidon, and of Sodom and Gomorrah?

(1) It was the sin of the people who forgot the responsibilities of privilege. To the cities of Galilee had been given a privilege which had never come to Tyre and Sidon, or to Sodom and Gomorrah, for the cities of Galilee had actually seen and heard Jesus. We cannot condemn people who never had the chance to know any better; but if those who have had every chance to know the right do the wrong, then they stand condemned.

(2) It was the sin of indifference. These cities did not attack Jesus Christ; they did not drive him from their gates; they did not seek to crucify him; they simply disregarded him. Neglect can kill as much as persecution can. An author writes a book; it is sent out for review. Some reviewers may praise it, others may damn it; it does not matter so long as it is noticed. The one thing which will kill a book stone dead is if it is never noticed at all for either praise or blame.

(3) And so we are face to face with one great threatening truth — it is also a sin to do nothing. There are sins of action, sins of deed; but there is also a sin of inaction, and of absence of deeds. The sin of Chorazin, of Bethsaida and of Capernaum was the sin of doing nothing. Many people's defence is: 'But I never did anything.' That defence may be in fact their condemnation.

45

The Accent of Compassion

Matthew 11:28–30

Jesus spoke to people desperately trying to find God and desperately trying to be good, who were finding the tasks impossible and who were driven to weariness and to despair. He says: 'Come to me all you who are exhausted.' It is Jesus' claim that the weary search for God ends in Jesus himself. The way to know God is not by mental search, but by giving attention to Jesus Christ, for in him we see what God is like.

He says: 'Come to me all you who are weighted down beneath your burdens.' For orthodox Jews, religion was a thing of burdens. Jesus said of the scribes and Pharisees: 'They tie up heavy burdens, hard to bear, and lay them on the shoulders of others' (Matthew 23:4). They must listen forever to a voice which said: 'You shall not.'

Jesus invites us to take his yoke upon our shoulders. The Jews used the phrase *the yoke* for *entering into submission to*. He says: 'My yoke is easy.' The word *easy* is in Greek *chrestos*, which can mean *well-fitting*. In Palestine, ox-yokes were made of wood; the ox was brought, and the measurements were taken. The yoke was then roughed out, and the ox was brought back to have the yoke tried on. The yoke was carefully adjusted, so that it would fit well, and not chafe the neck of the patient animal.

There is a legend that Jesus made the best ox-yokes in all Galilee, and that from all over the country people came to him to buy the best yokes that skill could make. It may well be that Jesus is here using a picture from the carpenter's shop in Nazareth where he had worked throughout the silent years.

Jesus says: 'My yoke fits well.' What he means is: 'The life I give you is not a burden to cause you pain; your task is made to measure to fit you.' Whatever God sends us is made to fit our needs and our abilities exactly.

Jesus says: 'My burden is light.' It is not that the burden is easy to carry; but it is laid on us in love; it is meant to be carried in love; and love makes even the heaviest burden light.

The Final Proof

Luke 7:18–29

John sent emissaries to Jesus to ask if he really was the Messiah or if they must look for someone else.

(1) This incident has worried many because they have been surprised at the apparent doubt in the mind of John. Various explanations have been advanced.

(a) It is suggested that John took this step, not for his own sake, but for the sake of his disciples. He was sure enough; but they had their qualms and he desired that they should be confronted with proof unanswerable.

(b) It is suggested that John wished to hurry Jesus on because he thought it was time Jesus moved towards decisive action.

(c) The simplest explanation is the best. Think what was happening to John. John, the child of the desert and of the wide-open spaces, was confined in a dungeon cell in the castle of Machaerus. Shut in his cell, choked by the narrow walls, John asked his question because his cruel captivity had put tremors in his heart.

(2) Note the proof that Jesus offered. He pointed at the facts. The sick and the suffering and the humble poor were experiencing the power and hearing the word of the good news. Here is a point which is seldom realized—this is not the answer John expected. If Jesus was God's Anointed One, John would have expected him to say, 'My armies are massing. Caesarea, the headquarters of the Roman government, is about to fall. The sinners are being obliterated. And judgment has begun.' He would have expected Jesus to say, 'The wrath of God is on the march,' but Jesus said, 'The mercy of God is here.'

Let us remember that where pain is soothed and sorrow turned to joy, where suffering and death are vanquished, there is the kingdom of God.

Human Perversity

Luke 7:30–35

This passage has two great warnings in it.

(1) It tells of the perils of free will. The scribes and the Pharisees had succeeded in frustrating God's purpose for themselves. The tremendous truth of Christianity is that the coercion of God is not of force but of love. It is precisely there that we can glimpse the sorrow of God. It is always love's greatest tragedy to look upon some loved one who has taken the wrong way and to see what might have been, what could have been and what was meant to have been. That is life's greatest heartbreak. God's tragedy, too, is the 'might have been' of life. As G. K. Chesterton said, 'God had written not so much a poem, but rather a play; a play he had planned as perfect, but which had necessarily been left to human actors and stage managers, who had since made a great mess of it.' God save us from making shipwreck of life and bringing heartbreak to himself by using our free will to frustrate his purposes.

(2) It tells of human perversity. John had come, living with a hermit's austerity, and the scribes and Pharisees had said that he was a mad eccentric and that some demon had taken his wits away. Jesus had come, living life to the full and entering into every kind of activity, and they had taunted him with loving earth's pleasures far too much. We all know the days when a child will complain at anything and the moods when nothing will please us. The human heart can be lost in a perversity in which any appeal God may make will be met with wilful and childish discontent.

(3) But there are the few who answer; and God's wisdom is in the end justified by those who are his children. We may misuse our free will to frustrate God's purposes; in our perversity we may be blind and deaf to all his appeal. Had God used the force of coercion and laid on us the iron bonds of a will that could not be denied, there would have been a world of automata and a world without trouble. But God chose the dangerous way of love, and love in the end will triumph.

A Sinner's Love

Luke 7:36–50

In the Middle East the guests did not sit, but reclined, at table. They lay on low couches, resting on the left elbow, leaving the right arm free, with the feet stretched out behind; and during the meal the sandals were taken off. That explains how the woman was standing beside Jesus' feet.

Simon was a Pharisee, one of the separated ones. Why should such a man invite Jesus to his house at all? There are three possible reasons.

(1) It is just possible that he was an admirer and a sympathizer, for not all the Pharisees were Jesus' enemies (cf. Luke 13:31). But the whole atmosphere of discourtesy makes that unlikely.

(2) It could be that Simon had invited Jesus with the deliberate intention of enticing him into some word or action which might have been made the basis of a charge against him. Simon may have been an agent provocateur. Again it is not likely, because in verse 40 Simon gives Jesus the title Rabbi.

(3) Most likely, Simon was a collector of celebrities; and with a half-patronizing contempt he had invited this startling young Galilaean to have a meal with him. That would best explain the strange combination of a certain respect with the omission of the usual courtesies. Simon was a man who tried to patronize Jesus.

The story demonstrates a contrast between two attitudes of mind and heart.

(1) Simon was conscious of no need and therefore felt no love, and so received no forgiveness. Simon's impression of himself was that he was a good man in the sight of others.

(2) The woman was conscious of nothing else than a burning need, and therefore was overwhelmed with love for him who could supply it, and so received forgiveness. The one thing which shuts us off from God is self-sufficiency. And the strange thing is that the better we are, the more keenly we feel our sin.

It is true to say that the greatest of sins is to be conscious of no sin; but a sense of need will open the door to the forgiveness of God, because God is love, and love's greatest glory is to be needed.

On the Road

Luke 8:1–3

Jesus was on the road. The synagogues were not now open to him, as once they had been. He had begun, as it were, in the church, where anyone with a message from God might expect to find a responsive and receptive audience. Instead of a welcome he had found opposition; so now he took to the open road and the hillside and the lakeshore.

(1) This passage lists a little group of women who served him out of their resources. It was always considered to be a pious act to support a Rabbi, and the fact that the devoted followers of Jesus helped him in this way was in direct line with ordinary practice. But, as with the disciples, so with these women, we cannot fail to see how mixed a company they were. There was Mary Magdalene, that is, Mary from the town of Magdala, out of whom he had cast seven devils. Clearly she had a dark and terrible past. There was Joanna. She was the wife of Chuza, Herod's *epitropos*. A king had many entitlements and much private property; his *epitropos* was the official who looked after the king's financial interests. There could be no more trusted and important official. It is an amazing thing to find Mary Magdalene, with the dark past, and Joanna, the lady of the court, in the one company.

(2) In this list of women we have a group whose help was practical. Being women, they would not be allowed to preach; but they gave the gifts they had. There was an old shoemaker who once had wished to become a minister but the way had never opened up. He was the friend of a young divinity student; and when the young man one day was called to his first church the old man asked him for a favour. He asked to be allowed always to make his shoes so that he might feel the preacher was wearing his shoes in that pulpit into which he could never go himself.

It is not always the person in the foreground who is doing the greatest work. Many who occupy public positions could not sustain their place for one week without support from home! There is no gift which cannot be used in the service of Christ. Many of his greatest servants are in the background, unseen but essential to his cause.

The Sin beyond Forgiveness

Matthew 12:31–33

Let us try to understand what Jesus meant by the sin against the Holy Spirit. One thing is necessary. We must grasp the fact that Jesus was not speaking about the Holy Spirit in the full Christian sense of the term. He could not have been, for Pentecost had to come before the Holy Spirit came upon men and women in all his power and light and fullness. This must be interpreted in the light of the Jewish conception of the Holy Spirit.

According to Jewish teaching, the Holy Spirit had two supreme functions. First, the Holy Spirit brought God's truth to men and women; second, the Holy Spirit enabled them to recognize and to understand that truth when they saw it. So people, as the Jews saw it, needed the Holy Spirit, both to receive and to recognize God's truth.

If we shut our eyes and ears to God's way for long enough, if we turn our backs upon the messages which God is sending us, if we prefer our own ideas to the ideas which God is seeking to put into our minds, in the end we come to a stage when we cannot recognize God's truth and God's beauty and God's goodness when we see them. We come to a stage when our own evil seems to us good, and when God's good seems to us evil.

Why should that sin be unforgivable? What differentiates it so terribly from all other sins? The answer is simple. When anyone reaches that stage, repentance is impossible. If people cannot recognize the good when they see it, they cannot desire it. If they do not recognize evil as evil, they cannot be sorry for it and wish to depart from it. And if they cannot, in spite of failures, love the good and hate the evil, then they cannot repent; and if they cannot repent, they cannot be forgiven, for repentance is the only condition of forgiveness.

It would save much heartbreak if people would realize that the very people who cannot have committed the sin against the Holy Spirit are those who fear that they have, for the sin against the Holy Spirit can be truly described as the loss of all sense of sin.

Hearts and Words

Matthew 12:34–37

It is little wonder that Jesus chose to speak here about the awful responsibility of words. The scribes and Pharisees had just spoken the most terrible words. They had looked on the Son of God and called him the ally of the devil. Such words were dreadful words indeed. So Jesus laid down two laws.

(1) The state of our hearts can be seen through the words we speak. That which is in the heart can come to the surface only through the lips.

(2) Jesus laid it down that people would specially render account for their idle words. Jesus was saying something which is profoundly true. There are in fact two great truths here.

(a) It is the words which we speak without thinking, the words which we utter when the conventional restraints are removed, which really show what we are like. As A. Plummer, commenting on this passage, puts it: 'The carefully spoken words may be a calculated hypocrisy.' When we are consciously on our guard, we will be careful what we say and how we say it; but when we are off guard, our words reveal our character. It is quite possible for a person's public utterances to be fine and noble, and for the private conversation of that person to be coarse and obscene. In public, words are carefully chosen; in private, the guard is down, and any word leaves the gateway of that person's lips.

(b) It is often these words which cause the greatest damage. We may say in anger things we would never have said if we were in control of ourselves. We may say afterwards that we never meant what we said; but that does not free us from the responsibility of having said it; and the fact that we have said it often leaves a wound that nothing will cure, and erects a barrier that nothing will take away. People may say in relaxed moments a coarse and questionable thing that they would never have said in public—and that very thing may lodge in someone's memory and stay there unforgotten.

Once the hurting word or the offensive word is spoken, nothing will bring it back; and it pursues a course of damage wherever it goes.

True Kinship

Matthew 12:46–50

It was one of the great human tragedies of Jesus' life that, during his lifetime, his nearest and dearest never understood him. 'For not even his brothers', says John, 'believed in him' (John 7:5). Mark tells us that when Jesus set out on his public mission, his friends tried to restrain him, for they said that he was mad (Mark 3:21). He seemed to them to be busily engaged in throwing his life away in a kind of insanity. It has often been the case that, when men and women embarked on the way of Jesus Christ, their nearest and dearest could not understand them, and were even hostile to them.

True friendship and true love are founded on certain things without which they cannot exist.

(1) Friendship is founded on a common ideal. People who are very different in their background, their mental capacity and even their methods can be firm friends if they have a common ideal for which they work and towards which they press.

(2) Friendship is founded on a common experience and on the memories which come from it. It is when two people have together passed through some great experience and when they can together look back on it that real friendship begins.

(3) True love is founded on obedience. 'You are my friends', said Jesus, 'if you do what I command you' (John 15:14). There is no way of showing the reality of love unless by the spirit of obedience.

For all these reasons, true kinship is not always a matter of a flesh-and-blood relationship. It remains true that blood is a tie that nothing can break and that many people find their delight and their peace in the circle of their family. But it is also true that sometimes our nearest and dearest are the people who understand us least, and that we find our true fellowship with those who work for a common ideal and who share a common experience.

This certainly is true—even if Christians find that those who should be closest to them are those who are most out of sympathy with them, there remains for them the fellowship of Jesus Christ and the friendship of all who love the Lord.

Three Verdicts on Jesus

Mark 6:14–15

In this passage, we have three verdicts upon Jesus.

(1) There is the verdict of a guilty conscience. Herod had been guilty of allowing the execution of John the Baptizer, and now he was haunted by what he had done. Whenever people commit evil acts, the whole world becomes their enemy. Inwardly, they cannot command their thoughts; and, whenever they allow themselves to think, their thoughts return to the wicked things that they have done. We cannot avoid living with ourselves; and when we are filled with self-accusations, life becomes intolerable. Outwardly, we live in the fear that we will be found out and that some day the consequences of our evil deeds will catch up with us.

(2) There is the verdict of the nationalist. Some thought that this Jesus was Elijah come again. The Jews waited for the Messiah. There were many ideas about the Messiah, but the commonest of all was that he would be a conquering king who would first give the Jews back their liberty and who would then lead them on a triumphant campaign throughout the world. This is the verdict of those who desire to find in Jesus the realization of their own ambitions. They think of Jesus not as someone to whom they must submit and whom they must obey; they think of Jesus as someone they can use. Such people think more of their own ambitions than of the will of God.

(3) There is the verdict of those who are waiting for the voice of God. There were those who saw in Jesus a prophet. In those days, the Jews were only too well aware that for 300 years the voice of prophecy had been silent. They had listened to the arguments and the legal disputations of the Rabbis; they had listened to the moral lectures of the synagogue; but it was three long centuries since they had listened to a voice which proclaimed, 'Thus says the Lord.' People in those days were listening for the authentic voice of God—and in Jesus they heard it.

It is true that Jesus was more than a prophet. He did not bring only the voice of God. He brought the very power and the very life and the very being of God.

An Evil Woman's Revenge

Mark 6:16–29

There is something to learn from every character in this story.

(1) Herod stands revealed before us.

(a) He was an odd mixture. At one and the same time he feared John and respected him. At one and the same time he dreaded John's tongue and yet found pleasure in listening to him. There is nothing in this world so strange a mixture as a human being.

(b) Herod was a man who acted on impulse. He made his reckless promise to Salome without thinking. It may well be that he made it when he was more than a little drunk and bloated with wine. Let us take care. Let us think before we speak. Let us never by self-indulgence get into a state when we lose our powers of judgment and are liable to do things for which afterwards we will be very sorry.

(c) Herod feared what others might say. He kept his promise to Salome because he had made it in front of his cronies and was unwilling to break it. He feared their jeers, their laughter; he feared that they would think him weak. Many have done things they afterwards bitterly regretted because they had not the moral courage to do the right. Many have made themselves far worse than they might otherwise have been because they feared the laughter of their so-called friends.

(2) Herodias shows us what an embittered person can do. The trouble with Herodias was that she wished to eliminate the one man who had the courage to confront her with her sin. She wished to do as she liked with no one to remind her of the moral law. She murdered John that she might sin in peace. She forgot that while she need no longer meet John, she still had to meet God.

(3) John the Baptizer stands revealed before us. He stands as the man of courage. He was a child of the desert and of the wide-open spaces, and to imprison him in the dark dungeons of Machaerus must have been the last refinement of torture. But John preferred death to falsehood. He lived for the truth and he died for it.

The Pathos of the Crowd

Mark 6:30–34

When the disciples came back from their mission, they reported to Jesus all that they had done. The demanding crowds were so insistent that they had no time even to eat; so Jesus told them to come with him to a lonely place on the other side of the lake that they might have peace and rest for a little time.

Here we see what might be called the rhythm of the Christian life. The Christian life is a continuous going into the presence of God from the presence of men and women and coming out into the presence of men and women from the presence of God. It is like the rhythm of sleep and work. We cannot work unless we have our time of rest; and sleep will not come unless we have worked until we are tired.

There are two dangers in life.

First, there is the danger of a too constant activity. We cannot work without rest; and we cannot live the Christian life unless we give ourselves time with God. It may well be that the whole trouble in our lives is that we give God no opportunity to speak to us, because we do not know how to be still and to listen; we give God no time to recharge us with spiritual energy and strength, because there is no time when we wait upon him. How can we bear life's burdens if we have no contact with him who is the Lord of all good life? How can we do God's work unless in God's strength? And how can we receive that strength unless we seek in quietness and in loneliness the presence of God?

Second, there is the danger of too much withdrawal. Devotion that does not issue in action is not real devotion. Prayer that does not issue in work is not real prayer. We must never seek God's fellowship in order to avoid human fellowship but in order to fit ourselves better for it. The rhythm of the Christian life is the alternate meeting with God in the secret place and serving one another in the market place.

Clean and Unclean

Mark 7:1–4

Originally, for a Jew, the law meant two things: it meant, first and foremost, the Ten Commandments, and, second, the first five books of the Old Testament, or, as they are called, the Pentateuch. Now it is true that the Pentateuch contains a certain number of detailed regulations and instructions; but, in the matter of moral questions, what is laid down is a series of great moral principles which individuals must interpret and apply for themselves.

For a long time, the Jews were content with that. But in the fourth and fifth centuries before Christ, there came into being a class of legal experts whom we know as the scribes. They were not content with great moral principles; they had what can only be called a passion for definition. They wanted these great principles amplified, expanded and broken down until they issued in thousands and thousands of little rules and regulations governing every possible action and every possible situation in life. These rules and regulations were not written down until long after the time of Jesus. They are what is called the oral law; these rules make up the tradition of the elders.

The word *elders* does not mean, in this phrase, the officials of the synagogue; rather it means *the ancients*, the great legal experts of the old days, like Hillel and Shammai. Much later, in the third century after Christ, a summary of all these rules and regulations was made and written down, and that summary is known as the Mishnah.

To the scribes and Pharisees, these rules and regulations were the essence of religion. To observe them was to please God; to break them was to sin. This was their idea of goodness and of the service of God. In the religious sense, Jesus and these people spoke different languages. It was precisely because he had no use for all these regulations that they considered him a bad man.

There is a fundamental split here—that between those who see religion as ritual, ceremonial, rules and regulations, and those who see in religion loving God and loving their fellow men and women. The next passage will develop this; but it is clear that Jesus' idea of religion and that of the scribes and Pharisees had nothing in common at all.

God's Laws and Human Rules

Mark 7:5–8

Jesus accused the scribes and Pharisees of two things.

(1) He accused them of *hypocrisy*. The word *hupokrites* has an interesting and revealing history. It begins by meaning simply *one who answers*; it goes on to mean one who answers in a set dialogue or a set conversation, that is to say, *an actor*; and finally it means, not simply an actor on the stage, but one whose whole life is a piece of acting without any sincerity behind it at all. Anyone to whom religion is a legal thing, anyone to whom religion means carrying out certain external rules and regulations, anyone to whom religion is entirely connected with the observation of a certain ritual and the keeping of a certain number of tabus is in the end bound to be, in this sense, a hypocrite. The reason is this—such people believe that they are good if they carry out the correct acts and practices, no matter what their hearts and their thoughts are like.

There is no greater religious peril than that of identifying religion with outward observance. There is no commoner religious mistake than to identify goodness with certain so-called religious acts. Church-going, Bible-reading, careful financial giving, even timetabled prayer do not make us good. The fundamental question is, how are our hearts towards God and towards others? And if in our hearts there are enmity, bitterness, grudges and pride, not all the outward religious observances in the world will make us anything other than hypocrites.

(2) The second accusation that Jesus implicitly levelled against these legalists was that they substituted the efforts of human ingenuity for the laws of God. For their guidance for life they did not depend on listening to God; they depended on listening to the clever arguments and debates, the fine-spun niceties, the ingenious interpretations of the legal experts.

Cleverness can never be the basis of true religion. It must always come, not from their ingenious discoveries, but from the simple listening to and accepting the voice of God.

An Iniquitous Regulation

Mark 7:9–13

The exact meaning of this passage is very difficult to discover. It hinges on the word *Corban*, which seems to have undergone two stages of meaning in Jewish usage.

(1) The word meant a *gift*. It was used to describe something which was specially dedicated to God. A thing which was *Corban* was as if it had already been laid upon the altar. If a man wished to dedicate some of his money or his property to God, he declared it *Corban*, and thereafter it might never again be used for any ordinary or secular purpose.

(2) There came a time when *Corban* became a much more generalized oath. When a person declared anything *Corban* he entirely alienated it from the person to whom he was talking. A man might say, '*Corban* that by which I might be profited by you,' and, in so doing, he bound himself never to touch, taste, have or handle anything possessed by the person so addressed. Or he might say, '*Corban* that by which you might be profited by me,' and, in so saying, he bound himself never to help or to benefit the person so addressed by anything that belonged to himself. If that is the use here, the passage means that, at some time, perhaps in a fit of anger or rebellion, a man had said to his parents, '*Corban* anything by which you may ever be helped by me,' and that afterwards, even if he repented from his rash vow, the scribal legalists declared that it was unbreakable and that he might never again render his parents any assistance.

Whichever is the case—and it is not possible to be certain—this much is sure, that there were cases in which the strict performance of the scribal law made it impossible to carry out the law of the Ten Commandments.

Jesus was attacking a system which put rules and regulations before the claim of human need. Jesus was quite sure that any regulation which prevented anyone from giving help where help was needed was nothing less than a contradiction of the law of God.

We must take care that we never allow rules to paralyse the claims of love. Nothing that prevents us helping another person can ever be a rule approved by God.

February 27

The Real Defilement

Mark 7:14–23

Although it may not seem so now, this passage, when it was first spoken, was well-nigh the most revolutionary passage in the New Testament. Jesus has been arguing with the legal experts about different aspects of the traditional law. He has shown the irrelevance of the elaborate hand-washings. He has shown how rigid adherence to the traditional law can actually mean disobedience to the law of God. But here he says something more startling yet. He declares that nothing that goes into a person can possibly cause defilement, for it is received only into the body, which rids itself of it in the normal, physical way.

No Jew ever believed that, and orthodox Jews do not believe it even now. Leviticus 11 has a long list of animals that are unclean and may not be used for food. Against this, Jesus made his revolutionary statement that nothing that goes into a person can make that person unclean. He was wiping out at one stroke the laws for which Jews had suffered and died. No wonder the disciples were amazed.

In effect, Jesus was saying that things cannot be either unclean or clean in any real religious sense of the term. Only persons can be really defiled; and what defiles people are their own actions, which are the product of their own hearts. This was shatteringly new doctrine. Jews had, and still have, a whole system of things which are clean and unclean. With one sweeping pronouncement, Jesus declared the whole thing irrelevant and that uncleanness has nothing to do with what people take into their bodies but everything to do with what comes out of their hearts.

It is a truly terrible list which Jesus cites of the things that come from the human heart. When we examine it, a shudder surely passes over us. Nonetheless it is a summons, not to a fastidious shrinking from such things, but to an honest self-examination of our own hearts.

The Dangerous Leaven

Matthew 16:5–12

To the Jewish mind, leaven was always symbolic of evil. It is fermented dough; the Jews identified fermentation with putrefaction; leaven stood for all that was rotten and bad. Leaven has the power to permeate any mass of dough into which it is inserted. Therefore leaven stood for an evil influence liable to spread through life and to corrupt it.

What would be in Jesus' mind when he warned against the evil influence of the teaching of the Pharisees and Sadducees? That is something which we can only surmise; but we do know the characteristics of the minds of the Pharisees and Sadducees.

(1) The Pharisees saw religion in terms of laws and commandments and rules and regulations. They saw religion in terms of outward ritual and outward purity. So Jesus is saying: 'Take care that you do not make your religion a series of "you shall nots" in the way the Pharisees do. Take care that you do not identify religion with a series of outward actions and forget that what matters is the state of a person's heart.' This is a warning against living in legalism and calling it religion; it is a warning against a religion which looks on a person's outward actions and forgets the inner state of the heart.

(2) The Sadducees had two characteristics, which were closely connected. They were wealthy and aristocratic, and they were deeply involved in politics. So Jesus may well have been saying: 'Take care that you never identify the kingdom of heaven with outward goods, and that you never pin your hopes of bringing it into political action.' This may well be a warning against giving material things too high a place in our scheme of values and against thinking that people can be reformed by political action. Jesus may well have been reminding the disciples that material prosperity is far from being the highest good, and that political action is far from producing the most important results.

The true blessings are the blessings of the heart; and the true change is not the change of outward circumstances but the change of human hearts.

The Road to the Cross

The Great Discovery

Luke 9:18–22

This is one of the most crucial moments in the life of Jesus. He asked this question when he was already turning his face to go to Jerusalem (Luke 9:51). He well knew what awaited him there, and the answer to his question was of supreme importance. He knew that he was going to a cross to die; he wanted to know before he went if there was anyone who had really discovered who he was. The right answer would make all the difference. If instead there was dull incomprehension, all his work would have gone for nothing. If there was any realization, however incomplete, it meant that he had lit such a flame in human hearts as time would never put out.

How Jesus' heart must have lifted when Peter's sudden discovery rushed to his lips—'You are the Anointed One of God!' When Jesus heard that, he knew he had not failed. Not only had the Twelve to discover the fact; they had also to discover what the fact meant. They had grown up against a background of thought which expected from God a conquering king who would lead them to world dominion. Peter's eyes would blaze with excitement when he said this. But Jesus had to teach them that God's Anointed One had come to die upon a cross. He had to take their ideas of God and of God's purposes and turn them upside down; and from this time that is what he set himself to do. They had discovered who he was; now they had to learn what that discovery meant.

Jesus began by asking what people were saying about him; and then, suddenly, he flashes the question at the Twelve, 'Who do you say that I am?' It is never enough to know what other people have said about Jesus. It might be possible to pass any examination on what has been said and thought about Jesus, or to read every book about Christology written in every language upon earth, and still not be a Christian.

Jesus must always be our own personal discovery. Paul did not say, 'I know what I have believed'; he said, 'I know the one in whom I have put my trust' (2 Timothy 1:12). Christianity does not mean reciting a creed; it means knowing a person.

The Conditions of Service

Luke 9:23–27

Here Jesus lays down the conditions of service for those who would follow him.

(1) They are called to self-denial. What does that mean? It is to treat the self as if it did not exist. Usually we treat ourselves as if our self was by far the most important thing in the world. If we are to follow Jesus, we must forget that self exists.

(2) They are called to take up a cross. Jesus knew what crucifixion meant. When he was a young boy of about eleven years of age, Judas the Galilaean had led a rebellion against Rome. He had raided the royal armoury at Sepphoris, which was only four miles from Nazareth. The Roman vengeance was swift and sudden. Sepphoris was burned to the ground; its inhabitants were sold into slavery; and 2,000 of the rebels were crucified on crosses which were set in lines along the roadside that they might be a dreadful warning to others tempted to rebel. To take up our cross means to be prepared to face things like that for loyalty to Jesus; it means to be ready to endure the worst that anyone can do to us for the sake of being true to him.

(3) They are called to spend life, not hoard it. The whole gamut of the world's standards must be changed. The questions are not, 'How much can I get?' but, 'How much can I give?' Not, 'What is the safe thing to do?' but, 'What is the right thing to do?' Not, 'What is the minimum permissible in the way of work?' but, 'What is the maximum possible?' Christians must realize that life is given, not to keep for themselves but to spend for others; not to nurture its flame but to burn it out for Christ and for others.

(4) Loyalty to Jesus will have its reward, and disloyalty its punishment. If we are true to him in time, he will be true to us in eternity. If we seek to follow him in this world, in the next he will point to us as one of his people. But if by our lives we disown him, even though with our lips we confess him, the day must come when he cannot do other than disown us.

March 3

The Mountaintop of Glory

Luke 9:28–36

There is a vivid sentence here. It says of the three apostles, 'When they were fully awake they saw his glory.' In life we miss so much because our minds are asleep. There are certain things which are liable to keep our minds asleep.

(1) There is prejudice. We may be so set in our ideas that our minds are shut. A new idea knocks at the door but we are like sleepers who will not awake.

(2) There is mental lethargy. There are so many who refuse the strenuous struggle of thought. 'The unexamined life', said Socrates, 'is the life not worth living.' How many of us have really thought things out and thought them through?

(3) There is the love of ease. There is a kind of defence mechanism in us that makes us automatically shut the door against any disturbing thought.

We can drug ourselves mentally until our minds are sound asleep. But life is full of things designed to waken us.

(1) There is sorrow. Once, the English composer Sir Edward Elgar said of a young singer, who was technically perfect, but quite without feeling and expression, 'She will be great when something breaks her heart.' Often sorrow can rudely awaken us, but in that moment, through the tears, we will see the glory.

(2) There is love. Robert Browning tells of two people who fell in love. She looked at him; he looked at her—'and suddenly life awoke'. Real love is an awakening to horizons we never dreamed were there.

(3) There is the sense of need. It is easy enough to live the routine of life half-asleep; then all of a sudden there comes some completely insoluble problem, some quite unanswerable question, some overwhelming temptation, some summons to an effort which we feel is beyond our strength. In that day there is nothing left to do but to 'cry, clinging heaven by the hems'. And that sense of need awakens us to God. We would do well to pray, 'Lord, keep me always awake to you.'

66

The Mind of a Child

Matthew 18:1–4

There are many lovely characteristics in children—the power to wonder, before they have become deadeningly used to the wonder of the world; the power to forgive and to forget, even when adults and parents treat them unjustly as they so often do. No doubt Jesus was thinking of these things; but, wonderful as they are, they are not the main things in his mind. Children have three great qualities which make them the symbol of those who are citizens of the kingdom.

(1) First and foremost, there is the quality which is the keynote of the whole passage—the child's humility. Children do not wish to push themselves forward; rather, they wish to fade into the background. They do not wish for prominence; they would rather be left in obscurity. It is only as they grow up, and begin to be initiated into a competitive world, with its fierce struggle and scramble for prizes and for first places, that this instinctive humility is left behind.

(2) There is the child's dependence. To children, a state of dependence is perfectly natural. They never think that they can face life by themselves. They are perfectly content to be utterly dependent on those who love them and care for them. If men and women would accept the fact of their dependence on God, a new strength and a new peace would enter their lives.

(3) There is the child's trust. Children are instinctively dependent, and just as instinctively they trust their parents that their needs will be met. When we are children, we cannot buy our own food or our own clothes, or maintain our own home; yet we never doubt that we will be clothed and fed, and that there will be shelter and warmth and comfort waiting for us when we come home. When we are children, we set out on a journey with no means of paying the fare, and with no idea of how to get to our journey's end, and yet it never enters our heads to doubt that our parents will bring us safely there.

The child's humility is the pattern of the behaviour of Christians to their neighbours, and the child's dependence and trust are the pattern of the Christian attitude towards God, the Father of all.

Christ and the Child

Matthew 18:5–7, 10

The phrase *in my name* can mean one of two things.

(1) It can mean *for my sake*. The care of children is something which is carried out for the sake of none other than Jesus Christ.

(2) It can mean *with a blessing*. It can mean receiving the child, and, as it were, naming the name of Jesus over that child. Anyone who brings Jesus and the blessing of Jesus to a child is doing a Christ-like work.

To receive the child is also a phrase which is capable of bearing more than one meaning.

(1) It can mean, not so much to receive a child, as to receive a person who has this childlike quality of humility. In this highly competitive world, it is very easy to pay most attention to the person who is belligerent and aggressive and self-assertive and full of self-confidence. It is easy to pay most attention to the person who, in the worldly sense of the term, has made a success of life. Jesus may well be saying that the most important people are not the thrusters and those who have climbed to the top of the tree by pushing everyone else out of the way, but the quiet, humble, ordinary people, who have the heart of a child.

(2) It can mean simply to welcome the child, to give that child the care and the love and the teaching required to create a good human being. To help a child to live well and to know God better is to help Jesus Christ.

(3) But this phrase can have another and very wonderful meaning. It can mean to see Christ in the child. To teach unruly, disobedient, restless little children can be a wearing job. To satisfy the physical needs of children, to wash their clothes and tend their cuts and soothe their bruises and cook their meals may often seem a very unromantic task; the cooker and the sink and the first-aid kit have not much glamour; but there is no one in all this world who helps Jesus Christ more than the teacher of the little child and the harassed, hard-pressed parent in the home.

All who take on these tasks will find a glory in the grey, and discover wonder in the ordinary, if in the child they sometimes glimpse none other than Jesus himself.

Two Lessons in Tolerance

Luke 9:49–56

The direct way from Galilee to Jerusalem led through Samaria; but most Jews avoided it. There was a centuries-old quarrel between the Jews and the Samaritans (John 4:9).

The Samaritans in fact did everything they could to hinder and even to injure any bands of pilgrims who attempted to pass through their territory. For Jesus to take that way to Jerusalem was unusual; and to attempt to find hospitality in a Samaritan village was still more unusual. When he did this he was extending a hand of friendship to a people who were enemies. In this case not only was hospitality refused but the offer of friendship was spurned. No doubt, therefore, James and John believed they were doing a praiseworthy thing when they offered to call in divine aid to blot out the village. But Jesus would not permit them.

The conviction that our beliefs and our methods alone are correct has been the cause of more tragedy and distress in the Church than almost any other thing. Oliver Cromwell wrote once to the intransigent Scots, 'I beseech you by the bowels of Christ, think it possible that you may be mistaken.' And we do well to note another saying, 'Remember that whatever your hand finds to do, someone thinks differently!' There are many ways to God. He has his own secret stairway into every heart. He fulfils himself in many ways; and no individual or church has a monopoly of his truth.

But—and this is intensely important—our tolerance must be based not on indifference but on love. We ought to be tolerant not because we could not care less; but because we look at the other person with eyes of love. When Abraham Lincoln was criticized for being too courteous to his enemies and reminded that it was his duty to destroy them, he gave the great answer, 'Do I not destroy my enemies when I make them my friends?'

Even if someone is utterly mistaken, that person must never be regarded as an enemy to be destroyed but as a strayed friend to be recovered by love.

March 7

The Honesty of Jesus

Luke 9:57–62

Here we have the words of Jesus to three would-be followers.

(1) To the first man, his advice was, 'Before you follow me, count the cost.' No one can ever claim to have been induced to follow Jesus under false pretences. Jesus has paid us the compliment of pitching his demands so high that they cannot be higher. It may well be that we have done great hurt to the Church by letting people think that church membership need not make so very much difference. We ought to tell them that it should make all the difference in the world. We might have fewer people; but those we have would be really pledged to Christ.

(2) Jesus' words to the second man sound harsh, but they need not be so. In all probability the man's father was not dead, and not even nearly dead. His saying most likely meant, 'I will follow you after my father has died.' The story is told of a very brilliant young Arab who was offered a scholarship to Oxford or Cambridge. His answer was, 'I will take it after I have buried my father.' At the time his father was not much more than forty years of age.

The point Jesus was making is that in everything there is a crucial moment; if that moment is missed the thing most likely will never be done at all. The man in the story had stirrings in his heart to get out of his spiritually dead surroundings; if he missed that moment he would never get out. Psychologists tell us that every time we have a fine feeling and do not act on it, the less likely we are to act on it at all. The emotion becomes a substitute for the action.

(3) His words to the third man state a truth which no one can deny. No ploughman ever ploughed a straight furrow looking back over his shoulder. There are some whose hearts are in the past. They walk forever looking backwards and thinking wistfully of the good old days. The watchword of the kingdom is not 'Backwards!' but 'Forwards!' To this man Jesus did not say either 'Follow!' or 'Return!' He said, 'I accept no lukewarm service,' and left the man to make his own decision.

70

March 8

The Clash of Temperaments

Luke 10:38–42

It would be hard to find more vivid character drawing in greater economy of words than we find in these verses.

(1) They show us the clash of temperaments. We have never allowed enough for the place of temperament in religion. Some people are naturally dynamos of activity; others are naturally quiet. It is hard for the active person to understand the person who sits and contemplates. And the person who is devoted to quiet times and meditation is apt to look down on the person who would rather be active.

(2) These verses show us something more—they show us the wrong type of kindness. Think where Jesus was going when this happened. He was on his way to Jerusalem—to die. His whole being was taken up with the intensity of the inner battle to bend his will to the will of God. When Jesus came to that home in Bethany it was a great day; and Martha was eager to celebrate it by laying on the best the house could give. So she rushed and fussed and cooked; and that was precisely what Jesus did not want. All he wanted was quiet. With the cross before him and with the inner tension in his heart, he had turned aside to Bethany to find an oasis of calm away from the demanding crowds if only for an hour or two; and that is what Mary gave him and what Martha, in her kindness, did her best to destroy. 'One thing is necessary'—quite possibly this means, 'I don't want a big spread; one course, the simplest meal is all I want.' It was simply that Mary understood and that Martha did not.

Here is one of the great difficulties in life. So often we want to be kind to people—but we want to be kind to them in our way; and should it happen that our way is not the necessary way, we sometimes take offence and think that we are not appreciated. If we are trying to be kind the first necessity is to try to see into the heart of the person we desire to help—and then to forget all our own plans and to think only of what he or she needs. Jesus loved Martha and Martha loved him, but when Martha set out to be kind, it had to be her way of being kind which was really being unkind to him whose heart cried out for quiet. Jesus loved Mary and Mary loved him, and Mary understood.

71

March 9

Suffering and Sin

Luke 13:1–5

We have here references to two disasters about which we have no definite information and can only speculate.

But there is far more than a historical problem in this passage. The Jews rigidly connected sin and suffering. Eliphaz had long ago said to Job, 'Who that was innocent ever perished?' (Job 4:7). This was a cruel and a heart-breaking doctrine, as Job knew well, and Jesus utterly denied it in the case of the individual. As we all know very well, it is often the greatest saints who have to suffer most.

But Jesus went on to say that if his hearers did not repent they too would perish. What did he mean? One thing is clear—he foresaw and foretold the destruction of Jerusalem, which happened in AD 70 (cf. Luke 21:21–24). He knew well that if the Jews went on with their intrigues, their rebellions, their plottings and their political ambitions, they were simply going to commit national suicide; he knew that in the end Rome would step in and obliterate the nation; and that is precisely what happened. So what Jesus meant was that if the Jewish nation kept on seeking an earthly kingdom and rejecting the king-dom of God they could come to only one end. To put the matter like that leaves, at first sight, a paradoxical situation. It means that we cannot say that individ-ual suffering and sin are inevitably connected, but we can say that national sin and suffering are so connected. The nation which chooses the wrong ways will in the end suffer for it. But the individual is in a very different position. An individual is not an isolated unit, but is bound up in the bundle of life.

Often he or she may object, and object violently, to the course the nation is taking; but when the consequence of that course comes, it is not possible to escape being involved in it. Individuals are often caught up in situations which are not of their making, suffering often through no fault of their own; but the nation is a unit and chooses its own policy and reaps the fruit of it. It is always dangerous to attribute human suffering to human sin; but always safe to say that the nation which rebels against God is on the way to disaster.

72

How Much Do You Want Goodness?

Mark 10:17–22

Never did any story so lay down the essential Christian truth that respectability is not enough. Jesus quoted the commandments which were the basis of the decent life. Without hesitation the man said he had kept them all. Note one thing—with one exception they were all negative commandments, and that one exception operated only in the family circle. In effect the man was saying, 'I never in my life did anyone any harm.' That was perfectly true. But the real question is, 'What good have you done?' And the question to this man was even more pointed, 'With all your possessions, with your wealth, with all that you could give away, what positive good have you done to others? How much have you gone out of your way to help and comfort and strengthen others as you might have done?' Respectability, on the whole, consists in not doing things; Christianity consists in doing things. That was precisely where this man—like so many of us—fell down.

So Jesus confronted him with a challenge. In effect he said, 'Get out of this moral respectability. Stop looking at goodness as consisting in not doing things. Take yourself and all that you have, and spend everything on others. Then you will find true happiness in time and in eternity.' The man could not do it. He had great possessions, which it had never entered his head to give away; and when it was suggested to him, he could not. True, he had never stolen, and he had never defrauded anyone—but neither had he ever been, nor could he compel himself to be, positively and sacrificially generous.

It may be respectable never to take away from anyone. It is Christian to give to someone. In reality, Jesus was confronting this man with a basic and essential question: 'How much do you want real Christianity? Do you want it enough to give your possessions away?' And the man had to answer in effect, 'I want it—but I don't want it as much as all that.' It was the failing of not wanting enough which meant tragedy for the man who came running to Jesus.

It is the failing from which most of us suffer. We all want goodness, but so few of us want it enough to pay the price.

March 11

The Peril of Riches

Mark 10:23–27

No one ever saw the dangers of prosperity and of material things more clearly than Jesus did. What are these dangers?

(1) Material possessions tend to fix our hearts to this world. We have so large a stake in it, we have so great an interest in it, that it is difficult for us to think beyond it, and it is specially difficult for us to contemplate leaving it. Dr Johnson was once shown round a famous castle and its lovely grounds. After he had seen it all, he turned to his friends and said, 'These are the things that make it difficult to die.' The danger of possessions is that they fix our thoughts and interests to this world.

(2) If our main interest is in material things, we will think in terms of price and not in terms of value. We will think in terms of what money can get. And we may well forget that there are values in this world far beyond money, that there are things which have no price, and that there are precious things that money cannot buy. It is fatal to begin to think that everything worth having has a monetary value.

The reaction of the disciples was that if what Jesus was saying was true, to be saved at all was well-nigh impossible. Then Jesus stated the whole doctrine of salvation in a nutshell. 'If', he said, 'salvation depended on a person's own efforts it would be impossible for anyone. But salvation is the gift of God and all things are possible to him.'

Those who trust in themselves and in their possessions can never be saved. Those who trust in the saving power and the redeeming love of God can enter freely into salvation.

Christ Is No One's Debtor

Mark 10:28–31

Peter had just seen a man deliberately refuse Jesus' 'Follow me!' He had just heard Jesus say in effect that that man by his action had shut himself out from the kingdom of God. Peter could not help drawing the contrast between that man and himself and his friends. Just as the man had refused Jesus' 'Follow me!' he and his friends had accepted it, and Peter with that almost crude honesty of his wanted to know what he and his friends were to get out of it.

Jesus said that no one ever gave up anything for the sake of himself and of his good news without getting it back a hundredfold. It so happened that in the early Church that was literally true. A person's Christianity might involve the loss of home and friends and loved ones, but entry into the Christian Church brought with it a family far greater and wider than the one left behind — a new spiritual family.

When Egerton Young first preached the gospel to the Native Americans in Saskatchewan, the idea of the fatherhood of God fascinated people who had hitherto seen God only in the thunder and the lightning and the storm blast. An old chief said to Young, 'Did I hear you say to God "Our Father"?' 'I did,' said Young. 'God is your Father?' asked the chief. 'Yes,' said Young. 'And', continued the chief, 'he is also my Father?' 'He certainly is,' said Young. Suddenly the chief's face lit up with a new radiance. His hand went out. 'Then,' he said with the tone of someone making a dazzling discovery, 'you and I are brothers.' Becoming a Christian may mean sacrificing ties that are very dear, but anyone who does so becomes a member of a family as wide as earth and heaven.

Then Jesus added one warning epigram — 'Many who are first shall be last, and the last first.' What Jesus was saying was, 'The final standard of judgment is with God. Many may stand well in the judgment of the world, but the judgment of God may upset the world's judgment. Still more — many may stand well in their own judgment, and find that God's evaluation of them is very different.'

The Request Made out of Ambition

Mark 10:35–40

This is a very revealing story. It tells us something of Jesus' standard of greatness. It was the custom at a royal banquet for the king to hand the cup to his guests. The cup therefore became a metaphor for the life and experience that God handed out to men and women. 'My cup overflows,' said the psalmist (Psalm 23:5), when he spoke of a life and experience of happiness given to him by God. 'In the hand of the Lord there is a cup,' said the psalmist (Psalm 75:8), when he was thinking of the fate in store for the wicked and the disobedient. Isaiah, thinking of the disasters which had come upon the people of Israel, describes them as having drunk 'at the hand of the Lord the cup of his wrath' (Isaiah 51:17). The cup speaks of the experience allotted to men and women by God.

The other phrase which Jesus uses is actually misleading in the literal English version. He speaks of the *baptism* with which he was *baptized*. The Greek verb *baptizein* means *to dip*. Its past participle (*bebaptismenos*) means *submerged*, and it is regularly used of being submerged in any experience. For instance, a spendthrift is said to be submerged in debt. A drunk person is said to be submerged in drink. A grief-stricken person is said to be submerged in sorrow. A pupil before a cross-examining teacher is said to be submerged in questions. The word is regularly used for a ship that has been wrecked and submerged beneath the waves. The metaphor is very closely related to a metaphor which the psalmist often uses. In Psalm 42:7 we read, 'All your waves and your billows have gone over me.' In Psalm 124:4 we read, 'Then the flood would have swept us away, the torrent would have gone over us.' The expression, as Jesus used it here, had nothing to do with technical baptism. What he is saying is, 'Can you bear to go through the terrible experience which I have to go through? Can you face being submerged in hatred and pain and death, as I have to be?'

He was telling these two disciples that without a cross there can never be a crown. The standard of greatness in the kingdom is the standard of the cross.

March 14

The Price of Salvation

Mark 10:41–45

Jesus had come, he said, to give his life *a ransom for many*. This is one of the great phrases of the gospel, and yet it has been sadly mishandled and maltreated.

It was not long before people were asking to whom this ransom of the life of Christ had been paid. Origen asked the question, 'To whom did he give his life a ransom for many? It was not to God. Was it not then to the evil one? For the devil was holding us fast until the ransom should be given to him, even the life of Jesus.'

In the fourth century, Gregory of Nyssa saw the flaw in that theory, namely, that it really puts the devil on an equality with God. It allows him to make a bargain with God on equal terms. So Gregory conceived of the extraordinary idea of a trick played by God. The devil was tricked by the seeming weakness of the incarnation. He mistook Jesus for a mere man. He tried to exert his authority over him and, by trying to do so, lost it.

Another 200 years passed and Gregory the Great took up the idea. He used a fantastic metaphor. The incarnation was a divine stratagem to catch the great Leviathan. The deity of Christ was the hook, his flesh was the bait. When the bait was dangled before Leviathan, the devil, he swallowed it, and tried to swallow the hook, too, and so was overcome forever.

Finally, in the twelfth century, Peter the Lombard brought this idea to its most grotesque and repulsive. 'The cross', he said, 'was a mousetrap to catch the devil, baited with the blood of Christ.' All this simply shows what happens when a lovely and precious picture is taken and attempts are made to make a cold theology out of it.

Suppose we say, 'Sorrow is the price of love' — we mean that love cannot exist without the possibility of sorrow, but we never even think of trying to explain to whom that price is paid. Suppose we say that freedom can be obtained only at the price of blood, toil, tears and sweat — we never think of investigating to whom that price is paid. This saying of Jesus is a simple and pictorial way of saying that it cost the life of Jesus to bring men and women back from their sin into the love of God. Beyond that we cannot go, and beyond that we do not need to go.

77

March 15

The Guest of the Man
Whom Everyone Despised

Luke 19:1–10

Zacchaeus was a man who had reached the top of his profession; and he was the most hated man in the district. There are three stages in his story.

(1) Zacchaeus was wealthy but he was not happy. Inevitably he was lonely, for he had chosen a way that made him an outcast. He had heard of this Jesus who welcomed tax collectors and sinners, and he wondered if he would have any word for him. Despised and hated by all, Zacchaeus was reaching after the love of God.

(2) Zacchaeus was determined to see Jesus, and would let nothing stop him. For Zacchaeus to mingle with the crowd at all was a courageous thing to do, for many would take the chance to get a nudge, or kick, or push at the little tax collector. It was an opportunity not to be missed. Zacchaeus would be black and blue with bruises that day. He could not see—the crowd took an ill delight in making sure of that. So he ran on ahead and climbed a fig-mulberry tree. Things were not easy for Zacchaeus, but the little man had the courage of desperation.

(3) Zacchaeus took steps to show all the community that he was a changed man. When Jesus announced that he would stay that day at his house, and when he discovered that he had found a new and wonderful friend, immediately Zacchaeus made a decision. He decided to give half of his goods to the poor; the other half he did not intend to keep to himself but to use to make restitution for the frauds of which he had been self-confessedly guilty.

(4) The story ends with the great words that the Son of Man came to seek and to save that which was lost. We must always be careful how we take the meaning of this word *lost*. In the New Testament it does not mean damned or doomed. It simply means *in the wrong place*. A thing is lost when it has got out of its own place into the wrong place; and when we find such a thing, we return it to the place it ought to occupy. A person is lost when he or she has wandered away from God; and is found when once again that person occupies the rightful place as an obedient child in the household and the family of the Father.

The Entry of the King

Luke 19:28–40

From Jerusalem to Jericho was only seventeen miles, and now Jesus had almost reached his goal. Jerusalem, journey's end, lay just ahead. The prophets had a regular custom of which they made use again and again. When words were of no effect, when people refused to take in and understand the spoken message, they resorted to some dramatic action which put their message into a picture which none could fail to see. It was just such a dramatic action which Jesus planned now. He proposed to ride into Jerusalem in a way that would be an unmistakable claim to be the Messiah, God's anointed king. We have to note certain things about this entry into Jerusalem.

(1) It was carefully planned. It was no sudden, impulsive action. He had his arrangement with the owners of the colt.

(2) It was an act of glorious defiance and of superlative courage. By this time there was a price on Jesus' head (John 11:57). It would have been natural that, if he must go into Jerusalem at all, he should have slipped in unseen and hidden away in some secret place in the back streets. But he entered in such a way as to focus the whole limelight upon himself and to occupy the centre of the stage. It is a breathtaking thing to think of a man with a price upon his head, an outlaw, deliberately riding into a city in such a way that every eye was fixed upon him. It is impossible to exaggerate the sheer courage of Jesus.

(3) It was a deliberate claim to be king, a deliberate fulfilling of the picture in Zechariah 9:9. But even in this Jesus underlined the kind of kingship which he claimed. The donkey in Palestine was not the lowly beast that it is in this country. It was noble. Only in war did kings ride upon a horse; when they came in peace they came upon a donkey. So Jesus by this action came as a king of love and peace, and not as the conquering military hero whom the tumultuous crowds expected and awaited.

(4) It was one last appeal. In this action Jesus came, as it were, with pleading hands outstretched, saying, 'Even now, will you not take me as your king?' Before human hatred engulfed him, once again he confronted people with love's invitation.

March 17

The Pity and the Anger of Jesus

Luke 19:41–48

Why did Jesus, who was the very incarnation of love, act with such violence to the moneychangers and the sellers of animals in the Temple courts?

First, let us look at the moneychangers. Every male Jew had to pay a Temple tax every year of half a shekel, and it must be remembered that a half-shekel was equal to nearly two days' pay for a workingman. A month before the Passover, booths were set up in all the towns and villages and it could be paid there; but by far the greater part was actually paid by the pilgrims in Jerusalem when they came to the Passover Feast. In Palestine all kinds of currencies were in circulation, and, for ordinary purposes, they were all—Greek, Roman, Tyrian, Syrian, Egyptian—equally valid. But this tax had to be paid either in exact half-shekels of the sanctuary or in ordinary Galilaean shekels. That is where the moneychangers came in. To change a coin of exact value they charged a commission. If a larger coin was tendered then commission was charged for the requisite half-shekel and again for the giving of change. By this means the moneychangers made an annual profit equivalent to many thousands of pounds. It was a deliberate swindle, and an imposition on poor people, who could least of all afford it.

Second, let us look at the sellers of animals. Victims could be bought outside at very reasonable prices; but the Temple authorities had appointed inspectors, for a victim must be without spot or blemish. It was, therefore, far safer to buy victims from the booths officially set up in the Temple. But there were times when inside the Temple a pair of doves would cost as much as ten or fifteen times more than they would cost outside. Again it was a deliberately planned victimization of the poor pilgrims, nothing more or less than legalized robbery.

Jesus cleansed the Temple with such violence because its traffic was being used to exploit helpless men and women. It was not simply that the buying and selling interfered with the dignity and solemnity of worship; it was that the very worship of the house of God was being used to exploit the worshippers. It was the passion for social justice which burned in Jesus' heart when he took this drastic step.

March 18

The Fountain of Living Water

John 7:37–44

In this passage, there is a startling thing. The Authorized Version and the Revised Standard Version tone it down, but in the best Greek manuscript (reflected in the translation of the New Revised Standard Version) there is the strange statement in verse 39: 'For as yet there was no Spirit.' What is the meaning of that? Think of it this way. A great power can exist for years and even centuries without anyone being able to tap it.

To take a very relevant example—there has always been atomic power in this world; it is not a human invention. But only in our own time have we tapped and used it. The Holy Spirit has always existed; but people never really enjoyed his full power until after Pentecost. As it has been finely said, 'There could be no Pentecost without Calvary.' It was only when men and women had known Jesus that they really knew the Spirit. Before that, the Spirit had been a power; but now he is a person, for he has become to us nothing other than the presence of the risen Christ always with us. In this apparently startling sentence, John is not saying that the Spirit did not exist; but that it took the life and death of Jesus Christ to open the floodgates for the Spirit to become real and powerful to all people.

We must notice how this passage finishes. Some people thought that Jesus was the prophet whom Moses had promised (Deuteronomy 18:15). Some thought that he was the Anointed One of God; and there followed a wrangle about whether or not the Anointed One of God must come from Bethlehem. Here is tragedy. A great religious experience had ended in the aridity of a theological wrangle.

That is what above all we must avoid. Jesus is not someone about whom to argue; he is someone to know and love and enjoy. If we have one view of him and someone else has another, it does not matter so long as both of us find him Saviour and accept him as Lord. Even if we explain our religious experience in different ways, that should never divide us, for it is the experience that is important, and not our explanation of it.

Wretchedness and Pity

John 7:53–8:11

This passage shows us two things about the attitude of the scribes and the Pharisees.

(1) It shows us their conception of authority. The scribes and the Pharisees were the legal experts of the day; problems were taken to them for decision. It is clear that to them authority was characteristically critical, censorious and condemnatory. That authority should be based on sympathy, that its aim should be to reclaim the criminal and the sinner, never entered their heads.

There are still those who regard a position of authority as giving them the right to condemn and the duty to punish. They think that such authority as they have has given them the right to be moral watchdogs trained to tear the sinner to pieces; but all true authority is founded on sympathy. When the Methodist evangelist George Whitefield saw the criminal on the way to the gallows, he uttered the famous sentence: 'There, but for the grace of God, go I.' The first duty of authority is to try to understand the force of the temptations which drove the sinner to sin and the seductiveness of the circumstances in which sin became so attractive. No one can pass judgment on another unless some attempt has been made to understand what the other has come through. The second duty of authority is to seek to reclaim the wrongdoer. Any authority which is solely concerned with punishment is wrong; any authority which, in its exercise, drives a wrongdoer either to despair or to resentment is a failure.

(2) This incident shows vividly and cruelly the attitude of the scribes and Pharisees to people. They were not looking on this woman as a person at all; they were looking on her only as a thing, an instrument whereby they could formulate a charge against Jesus. They were using her, as a person might use a tool, for their own purposes.

God uses his authority to love us into goodness; to God no person ever becomes a thing. We must use such authority as we have always to understand and always at least to try to mend the person who has made the mistake; and we will never even begin to do that unless we remember that every man and woman is a person, not a thing.

March 20

The Light That People Failed to Recognize

John 8:12–20

We often speak of following Jesus; we often urge others to do so. What do we mean? The Greek for *to follow* is *akolouthein*; and its meanings combine to shed a flood of light on what it means to follow Jesus. *Akolouthein* has five different but closely connected meanings.

(1) It is often used of a soldier following his captain. On the long route marches, into battle, in campaigns in strange lands, the soldier follows wherever the captain may lead. Christians are the soldiers whose commander is Christ.

(2) It is often used of a slave accompanying his master. Wherever the master goes, the slave is in attendance upon him, always ready to spring to his service and to carry out the tasks he gives him to do. He is literally at his master's beck and call. Christians are the slaves whose joy it is always to serve Christ.

(3) It is often used of accepting a wise counsellor's opinion. When people are in doubt they go to the expert, and if they are wise they accept the judgment they receive. Christians are people who guide their lives and conduct by the counsel of Christ.

(4) It is often used of giving obedience to the laws of a city or a state. To be useful members of any society or citizens of any community, we must agree to abide by its laws. Christians, being citizens of the kingdom of heaven, accept the law of the kingdom and of Christ as the law which governs their lives.

(5) It is often used of following a teacher's line of argument, or of following the gist of someone's speech. Christians are people who have understood the meaning of the teaching of Christ. They have not listened in dull incomprehension or with slack inattention. They take the message into their minds and understand, receive the words into their memories and remember, and hide them in their hearts and obey.

To be followers of Christ is to give body, soul and spirit into the obedience of the Master; and to follow him is to walk in the light.

March 21

The True Discipleship

John 8:31–32

Few New Testament passages have such a complete picture of discipleship as this.

(1) Discipleship begins with belief. Its beginning is the moment when we accept what Jesus says as true—all that he says about the love of God, all that he says about the terror of sin, all that he says about the real meaning of life.

(2) Discipleship means constantly remaining in the word of Jesus. It involves constant listening to the word of Jesus. It involves constant learning from Jesus. It involves constant penetrating into the truth which the words of Jesus bear. It involves constant obeying of the word of Jesus. The disciple is the learner who learns in order to do. The truth which Jesus brought is designed for action.

(3) Discipleship issues in knowledge of the truth. To learn from Jesus is to learn the truth. 'You will know the truth,' said Jesus. What is that truth? There are many possible answers to that question, but the most comprehensive way to put it is that the truth which Jesus brings shows us the real values of life. The fundamental question to which everyone has consciously or unconsciously to give an answer is: 'To what am I to give my life? To a career? To the amassing of material possessions? To pleasure? To the service of God?' In the truth of Jesus, we see what things are really important and what are not.

(4) Discipleship results in freedom. 'The truth will make you free.' 'In his service is perfect freedom.' It brings us freedom from fear. It brings freedom from self. It brings freedom from other people. It brings freedom from sin.

Many people have come to the stage when they sin, not because they want to, but because they cannot help it. Their sins have so taken over their lives that, try as they will, they cannot break away from them. Discipleship breaks the chains which bind us to them and enables us to be the persons we know we ought to be.

84

Caesar and God

Mark 12:13–17

Never did anyone lay down a more influential principle. At one and the same time these words asserted the rights of the state and the liberty of conscience.

On the whole the New Testament lays down three great principles with regard to the individual Christian and the state.

(1) The state is ordained by God. Without the laws of the state life would be chaos. Human beings cannot live together unless they agree to obey the laws of living together. Without the state there are valuable services that no one could enjoy. Individuals could not have their own water supply, their own sewage system, their own transport system, their own social security organization. The state is the origin of many of the things which make life livable.

(2) No one can accept all the benefits which the state gives and then opt out of all the responsibilities. It is beyond question that the Roman government brought to the ancient world a sense of security it never had before. For the most part, except in certain notorious areas, the seas were cleared of pirates and the roads of brigands, civil wars were changed for peace and capricious tyranny for Roman impartial justice.

It is still true that people cannot honourably receive all the benefits which living in a state confers upon them and then opt out of all the responsibilities of citizenship.

(3) But there is a limit. E. A. Abbott, the New Testament scholar, has a suggestive thought. The coin had Caesar's image upon it, and therefore belonged to Caesar. Human beings have God's image upon them—God created them in his own image (Genesis 1:26–27)—and therefore belong to God. The inevitable conclusion is that if the state remains within its proper boundaries and makes its proper demands, individuals must give it their loyalty and their service; but in the last analysis both state and human beings belong to God, and, therefore, should their claims conflict, loyalty to God comes first. But it remains true that, in all ordinary circumstances, our Christianity should make us better citizens.

The Wrong Idea of the Life to Come

Mark 12:18–27

This passage may seem to deal with a matter which is recondite and remote. It is an argument on terms which are out of the orbit of our experience. In spite of that, two eternally valid truths emerge.

(1) The Sadducees made the mistake of creating heaven in the image of earth. That has always been a human failing. The Native Americans, who were by nature hunters, conceived of a heaven which was a happy hunting-ground. The Vikings, who were by nature warriors, thought of a Valhalla where they would fight all day, where at night the dead would be raised and the wounded made whole again, and they would spend the evening in banquets, drinking wine from cups made from the skulls of their conquered foes.

There has always been a tendency to create in thought a heaven to suit human desires. But we do well to remember that Paul was right (1 Corinthians 2:9) when he took the words of the prophet (Isaiah 64:4) and made them his own: 'What no eye has seen, nor ear heard, nor the human heart conceived, what God has prepared for those who love him.' The life of the heavenly places will be greater than any conception this life can supply.

(2) In the end, Jesus based his conviction of the resurrection on the fact that the relationship between God and a good man or a good woman is one that nothing can break. God was the friend of Abraham, Isaac and Jacob when they lived. That friendship could not cease with death. 'God', as the French theologian Alfred Loisy said, 'cannot cease to be the God of those who served him and loved him.' As the psalmist said, 'I am continually with you; you hold my right hand. You guide me with your counsel, and afterward you will receive me [to glory]' (Psalm 73:23–24). It is inconceivable that that relationship with God can ever be broken.

In a word, there is only one immortal thing—and that is love.

Love for God and Love for Neighbour

Mark 12:28–34

The expert who asked Jesus this question was asking about something which was a living issue in Jewish thought and discussion.

For his answer Jesus took two great commandments and put them together.

(1) 'Hear, O Israel: The Lord is our God, the Lord alone.' That single sentence is the real creed of Judaism (Deuteronomy 6:4). It had three uses. It is called *the Shema*. *Shema* is the imperative of the Hebrew verb *to hear*, and it is so called from the first word in the sentence.

(2) 'You shall love your neighbour as yourself.' That is a quotation from Leviticus 19:18. Jesus did one thing with it. In its original context it has to do only with fellow Jews. It would not have included the Gentiles, whom it was quite permissible to hate. But Jesus quoted it without qualification and without limiting boundaries. He took an old law and filled it with a new meaning.

The scribe willingly accepted this, and went on to say that such a love was better than all sacrifices. In that, he was in line with the highest thought of his people. Long, long ago Samuel had said, 'Has the Lord as great delight in burnt offerings and sacrifices, as in obeying the voice of the Lord? Surely, to obey is better than sacrifice, and to heed than the fat of rams' (1 Samuel 15:22). Hosea had heard God say, 'I desire steadfast love and not sacrifice' (Hosea 6:6).

But it is always easy to let ritual take the place of love. It is always easy to let worship become a matter of the church building instead of a matter of the whole life. The priest and the Levite could pass by the wounded traveller because they were eager to get on with the ritual of the Temple. This scribe had risen beyond his contemporaries, and that is why he found himself in sympathy with Jesus.

There must have been a look of love in Jesus' eyes, and a look of appeal as he said to him, 'You have gone so far. Will you not come further and accept my way of things? Then you will be a true citizen of the kingdom.'

The Greatest Gift

Mark 12:41–44

Between the Court of the Gentiles and the Court of the Women there was the Gate Beautiful. It may well be that Jesus had gone to sit quietly there after the argument and the tension of the Court of the Gentiles and the discussions in the cloisters. In the Court of the Women there were thirteen collecting boxes called 'The Trumpets', because they were so shaped. Many people threw in quite considerable contributions. Then came a widow. She flung in two mites. The coin so called was a *lepton*, which literally means *a thin one*. It was the smallest of all coins. And yet Jesus said that her tiny contribution was greater than all the others.

Here is a lesson in giving:

(1) Real giving must be sacrificial. The amount of the gift never matters so much as its cost to the giver; not the size of the gift, but the sacrifice. Real generosity gives until it hurts. For many of us it is a real question if ever our giving to God's work is any sacrifice at all. Few people will do without their pleasures to give a little more to the work of God. There can be few of us who read this story without shame.

(2) Real giving has a certain recklessness in it. The woman might have kept one coin. It would not have been much but it would have been something, yet she gave everything she had. There is a great symbolic truth here. It is our tragedy that there is so often some part of our lives, some part of our activities, some part of ourselves which we do not give to Christ. Somehow there is nearly always something we hold back. We rarely make the final sacrifice and the final surrender.

(3) It is a strange and lovely thing that the person whom the New Testament and Jesus hand down to history as a pattern of generosity was a person who gave a gift of so little value in monetary terms. We may feel that we have not much in the way of material gifts or personal gifts to give to Christ, but if we put all that we have and are at his disposal, he can do things with it and with us that are beyond our imaginings.

March 26

The Things to Come

Mark 13

The gospel writers had a way of collecting Jesus' sayings on any subject. It was a wise way to write and excellent for teaching purposes. Here Mark, as it were, collects Jesus' sayings about the future.

(1) There are prophecies of the destruction of Jerusalem. We get them in verses 1–2 and 14–20. Jesus foresaw the end of the holy city. The Temple was destroyed and the most terrible things happened.

(2) There is warning of persecution to come. We get that in verses 9–13. Jesus foresaw that his followers would have to go through the most heart-breaking and soul-searing experiences, and he warned them in advance.

(3) There are warnings of the dangers of the last days. We get them in verses 3–6 and 21–22. Jesus wished to defend his people in advance from the here-sies and lies which would invade the Church.

(4) There are warnings of the second coming. Now, these warnings of the second coming are dressed in the language which has to do with the day of the Lord. We get them in verses 7–8 and 24–27. The imagery of the day of the Lord and of the second coming are not meant to be taken literally. They are meant as impressionistic pictures, as a seer's visions, designed to impress upon people the greatness of that event when it should come.

(5) There are warnings of the necessity to be on the watch. We get them in verses 28–37. If men and women live in the shadow of eternity, if they live with the constant possibility of the intervention of God, if they live with the prospect of the consummation of the coming of Christ always before them, there is the necessity always to be ready.

We are like those who know that their master will come, but who do not know when. We live in the shadow of eternity. That is no reason for fearful and hysterical expectation. But it means that day by day our work must be completed. It means that we must so live that it does not matter when he comes. It gives us the great task of making every day fit for him to see and being at any moment ready to meet him face to face.

Love's Extravagance

Mark 14:3–9

The poignancy of this story lies in the fact that it tells us of almost the last kindness that Jesus had done to him. This story shows the action of love.

(1) Jesus said that it was a *lovely* thing the woman had done. In Greek there are two words for *good*. There is *agathos*, which describes a thing which is morally good; and there is *kalos*, which describes a thing which is not only good but *lovely*. A thing might be *agathos*, and yet be hard, stern, austere, unattractive. But a thing which is *kalos* is captivating and lovely, with a certain bloom of charm upon it. Love does not do only good things. Love does lovely things.

(2) If love is true, there must always be a certain extravagance in it. It does not nicely calculate the less or more. It is not concerned to see how little it can decently give. If it gave all it had, the gift would still be too little. There is a recklessness in love which refuses to count the cost.

(3) Love can see that there are things, the chance to do which comes only once. It is one of the tragedies of life that often we are moved to do something fine and do not do it. It may be that we are too shy and feel awkward about it. It may be that second thoughts suggest a more prudent course. It occurs in the simplest things—the impulse to send a letter of thanks, the impulse to tell someone of our love or gratitude, the impulse to give some special gift or speak some special word. The tragedy is that the impulse is so often strangled at birth. This world would be so much lovelier if there were more people like this woman, who acted on her impulse of love because she knew in her heart of hearts that if she did not do it then she would never do it at all. How that last extravagant, impulsive kindness must have uplifted Jesus' heart.

(4) Once again we see the invincible confidence of Jesus. The cross loomed close ahead now, but he never believed that it would be the end. He believed that the good news would go all round the world. And with the good news would go the story of this lovely thing, done with reckless extravagance, done on the impulse of the moment, done out of a heart of love.

The Shepherd and His Sheep

John 10:1–6

The Palestinian shepherd had different ways of doing things from the shepherds of our country; and, to get the full meaning of this picture, we must look at the shepherd and the way in which he worked.

The relationship between sheep and shepherd is quite different in Palestine. In Britain, the sheep are largely kept for killing, but in Palestine largely for their wool. It thus happens that in Palestine the sheep are often with the shepherd for years, and often they have names by which the shepherd calls them. Usually these names are descriptive, for instance, 'Brown-leg', 'Black-ear'. In Palestine, the shepherd goes in front and the sheep follow. The shepherd goes first to see that the path is safe, and sometimes the sheep have to be encouraged to follow. A traveller tells how he saw a shepherd leading his flock come to a ford across a stream. The sheep were unwilling to cross. The shepherd finally solved the problem by carrying one of the lambs across. When its mother saw her lamb on the other side she crossed too, and soon all the rest of the flock had followed her. It is strictly true that in this part of the world the sheep know and understand the shepherd's voice, and that they will never answer to the voice of a stranger.

H. V. Morton tells of a scene that he saw in a cave near Bethlehem. Two shepherds had sheltered their flocks in the cave during the night. How were the flocks to be sorted out? One of the shepherds stood some distance away and gave his peculiar call, which only his own sheep knew, and soon his whole flock had run to him, because they knew his voice. They would have come for no one else, but they knew the call of their own shepherd. An eighteenth-century traveller actually tells how Palestinian sheep could be made to dance, quick or slow, to the peculiar whistle or the peculiar tune on the flute of their own shepherd.

Every detail of the shepherd's life lights up the picture of the good shepherd whose sheep hear his voice and whose constant care is for his flock.

Love's Choice

John 10:17–18

Few passages in the New Testament tell us so much about Jesus in so short a compass.

(1) It tells us that Jesus saw his whole life as an act of obedience to God. God had given him a task to do, and he was prepared to carry it out to the end, even if it meant death. He was in a unique relationship to God which we can describe only by saying that he was the Son of God. But that relationship did not give him the right to do what he liked; it depended on his doing always, cost what it may, what God liked. Sonship for him, and our relationship to God, could never be based on anything except obedience.

(2) It tells us that Jesus always saw the cross and the glory together. He never doubted that he must die; and equally he never doubted that he would rise again. The reason was his confidence in God; he was sure that God would never abandon him. All life is based on the fact that anything worth getting is hard to get. There is always a price to be paid.

(3) It tells us in a way that we cannot possibly mistake that Jesus' death was entirely voluntary. He was not the victim of circumstance. He was not like some animal, dragged unwillingly and without understanding to the sacrifice. Jesus laid down his life because he chose to do so.

It is told that in the First World War there was a young French soldier who was seriously wounded. His arm was so badly smashed that it had to be amputated. He was a fine-looking young man, and the surgeon was grieved that he must go through life maimed. So he waited beside his bedside to tell him the bad news when he recovered consciousness. When the young man's eyes opened, the surgeon said to him: 'I am sorry to tell you that you have lost your arm.' 'Sir,' said the young man, 'I did not lose it; I gave it—for France.'

Jesus was not helplessly caught up in a mesh of circumstances from which he could not break free. Apart from any divine power he might have called in, it is quite clear that to the end he could have turned back and saved his life. He did not lose his life; he gave it. The cross was not thrust upon him: he willingly accepted it—for us.

The Amazing Paradox

John 12:20–26

What was this amazing paradox which Jesus was teaching? He was saying three things, which are all variations of one central truth and all at the heart of the Christian faith and life.

(1) He was saying that only by death comes life. The grain of wheat was ineffective and unfruitful as long as it was preserved, as it were, in safety and security. It was when it was thrown into the cold ground, and buried there as if in a tomb, that it bore fruit. It was by the death of the martyrs that the Church grew. In the famous phrase: 'The blood of the martyrs was the seed of the Church.'

It is always because men and women have been prepared to die that the great things have lived. But it becomes more personal than that. It is sometimes only when we bury our personal aims and ambitions that we begin to be of real use to God. By death comes life. By the loyalty which was true to death there have been preserved and born the most precious things which humanity possesses. By the death of personal desire and personal ambition we become servants of God.

(2) He was saying that only by spending life do we retain it. Those who love their lives are moved by two aims — by selfishness and by the desire for security. Not once or twice but many times, Jesus insisted that those who hoarded their lives must in the end lose them, and those who spent their lives must in the end gain them.

We have only to think of what this world would have lost if there had not been men and women prepared to forget their personal safety, security, selfish gain and selfish advancement. The world owes everything to people who recklessly spent their strength and gave themselves to God and to others. No doubt we will exist longer if we take things easily, if we avoid all strain, if we sit at the fire and cosset life, if we look after ourselves as hypochondriacs look after their health. No doubt we will exist longer — but we will never live.

The Inescapable Judgment

John 12:44–50

Jesus makes the claim which is the basis of his whole life, that in him men and women are confronted with God. To listen to him is to listen to God; to see him is to see God. In him God meets human beings, and human beings meet God. That confrontation has two results, and both have in them the core of judgment.

(1) Once again, Jesus returns to a thought that is never far away in the Fourth Gospel. He did not come into the world to condemn; he came to save. It was not the wrath of God which sent Jesus to us; it was his love. Yet the coming of Jesus inevitably involves judgment. Why should that be? Because by our attitude to Jesus we show what we are and therefore judge ourselves. If we find in Jesus an infinite magnetism and attraction, even if we never succeed in making our lives what we know we ought to make them, we have felt the tug of God upon our hearts; and therefore we are safe. If on the other hand we see in Jesus nothing lovely and our hearts remain completely untouched in his presence, it means that we are impervious to God; and we have therefore judged ourselves. Always in the Fourth Gospel there is this essential paradox; Jesus came in love, yet his coming is a judgment. We can in perfect, unmixed love offer people some great experience, and find that they see nothing in it; the experience offered in love has become a judgment. Jesus is God's touchstone. By our attitude to him we stand revealed.

(2) Jesus said that at the last day the words which these people had heard would be their judges. That is one of the great truths of life. We cannot blame people for not knowing. But if they know the right and do the wrong, their condemnation is all the more serious. Therefore every wise thing that we have heard, and every opportunity we have had to know the truth, will in the end be a witness against us.

The Willing Sacrifice

The Traitor

Mark 14:10–11

There is always a shudder of the heart as we think of Judas. Mark tells the story with such economy of words that he leaves us no material for speculation. But at the back of Judas's action we can distinguish certain things.

(1) There was covetousness. Matthew 26:15 actually tells us that Judas went to the authorities and asked what price they were prepared to pay and drove a bargain with them for thirty pieces of silver.

(2) There was ambition. Again and again we see how the Twelve thought of the kingdom in earthly terms and dreamed of high position in it. Judas must have been like that. It may well be that, while the others still clung to them, he came to see how far wrong these dreams were and how little chance they ever had of any earthly fulfilment. And it may well be that in his disillusionment the love he once bore to Jesus turned to hate.

Both Luke and John say quite simply that the devil entered into Judas (Luke 22:3; John 13:27). In the last analysis that is what happened. Judas wanted Jesus to be what he wanted him to be and not what Jesus wanted to be. In reality Judas attached himself to Jesus, not so much to become a follower as to use Jesus to work out the plans and desires of his own ambitious heart. So far from surrendering to Jesus, he wanted Jesus to surrender to him; and when Jesus took his own way, the way of the cross, Judas was so incensed that he betrayed him. The essence of sin is pride; the core of sin is independence; the heart of sin is the desire to do what we like and not what God likes. That is what the devil, Satan, the evil one stands for. That is the spirit which was incarnate in Judas.

We shudder at Judas. But let us think again—covetousness, ambition, the dominant desire to have our own way of things. Are we so very different? These are the things which made Judas betray Jesus, and these are the things which still make people betray him.

Love's Last Appeal

Mark 14:17–21

This is a poignant passage. All the time, there was a text running in Jesus' head. 'Even my bosom friend in whom I trusted, who ate of my bread, has lifted the heel against me' (Psalm 41:9). These words were in his mind all the time. We can see certain great things here.

(1) Jesus knew what was going to happen. That is his supreme courage, especially in the last days. It would have been easy for him to escape, and yet undeterred he went on. Homer relates how the great warrior Achilles was told that if he went out to his last battle he would surely be killed. His answer was, 'Nevertheless I am for going on.' With a full knowledge of what lay ahead, Jesus was for going on.

(2) Jesus could see into the heart of Judas. The curious thing is that the other disciples seem to have had no suspicions. If they had known what Judas was engaged in, it is certain that they would have stopped him even by violence. Here is something to remember. There may be things we succeed in hiding from other people, but we cannot hide them from Jesus Christ. He is the searcher of human hearts.

(3) In this passage, we see Jesus offering two things to Judas.

(a) He is making love's last appeal. It is as if he is saying to Judas, 'I know what you are going to do. Will you not stop even now?'

(b) He is offering Judas a last warning. He is telling him in advance of the consequences of the thing that it is in his heart to do. But we must note this, for it is of the essence of the way in which God deals with us—there is no compulsion. Without a doubt, Jesus could have stopped Judas. All he had to do was tell the other eleven what Judas was planning, and Judas would never have left that room alive.

Here is the whole human situation. God has given us wills that are free. His love appeals to us. His truth warns us. But there is no compulsion. We hold the awful responsibility that we can spurn the appeal of God's love and disregard the warning of his voice. In the end, there is no one but ourselves responsible for our sins.

The Symbol of Salvation

Mark 14:22–26

What did Jesus mean when he said that the cup stood for a new covenant? The word *covenant* is a common word in the Jewish religion. The basis of that religion was that God had entered into a covenant with Israel. The word means something like an arrangement, a bargain, a relationship. The acceptance of the old covenant is set out in Exodus 24:3–8; and from that passage we see that the covenant was entirely dependent on Israel keeping the law. If the law was broken, the covenant was broken and the relationship between God and the nation shattered. It was a relationship entirely dependent on law and on obedience to law. God was judge. And since no one can keep the law, the people were always in default.

But Jesus says, 'I am introducing and ratifying a new covenant, a new kind of relationship between God and human beings. And it is not dependent on law, it is dependent on the blood that I will shed.' That is to say, it is dependent solely on love. The new covenant was a relationship between human beings and God, dependent not on law but on love. In other words Jesus says, 'I am doing what I am doing to show you how much God loves you.' Men and women are no longer simply under the law of God. Because of what Jesus did, they are forever within the love of God. That is the essence of what the sacrament says to us.

We note one thing more. In the last sentence we see again the two things we have so often seen. Jesus was sure of two things. He knew he was to die, and he knew his kingdom would come. He was certain of the cross, but just as certain of the glory. And the reason was that he was just as certain of God's love as he was of human sin; and he knew that in the end that love would conquer that sin.

The Royalty of Service

John 13:1–17

There is more in the background of this passage than even John tells us. If we turn to Luke's account of the last meal together, we find the tragic sentence: 'A dispute also arose among them as to which one of them was to be regarded as the greatest' (Luke 22:24). Even within sight of the cross, the disciples were still arguing about matters of precedence and prestige.

It may well be that this very argument produced the situation which made Jesus act as he did. The roads of Palestine were unsurfaced and uncleaned. In dry weather they were inches deep in dust, and in wet they were liquid mud. The shoes ordinary people wore were sandals, which were simply soles held on to the foot by a few straps. They gave little protection against the dust or the mud of the roads. For that reason, there were always great water pots at the door of a house; and a servant was there with a ewer and a towel to wash the soiled feet of the guests as they came in. Jesus' little company of friends had no servants. The duties which servants would carry out in wealthier circles they must have shared among themselves. It may well be that on the night of this last meal together they had got themselves into such a state of competitive pride that not one of them would accept the duty of seeing that the water and the towels were there to wash the feet of the company as they came in; and Jesus mended their omission in the most vivid and dramatic way. He himself did what none of them was prepared to do.

There is only one kind of greatness, the greatness of service. The world is full of people who are standing on their dignity when they ought to be kneeling at the feet of their brothers and sisters. In any society, it may happen that someone is given a quite unintentional slight and either explodes in anger or broods in sulkiness for days afterwards. When we are tempted to think of our dignity, our prestige or our rights, let us see again the picture of the Son of God, wrapped around with a towel, kneeling at his disciples' feet.

April 5

The Way, the Truth and the Life

John 14:4–6

Jesus said: 'I am the way.' What did he mean? Suppose we are in a strange town and ask for directions. Suppose the person asked says: 'Take the first to the right, and the second to the left. Cross the square, go past the church, take the third on the right and the road you want is the fourth on the left.' The chances are that we will be lost before we get halfway. But suppose the person we ask says: 'Come. I'll take you there.' In that case, the person to us is the way, and we cannot miss it. That is what Jesus does for us. He does not only give advice and directions. He takes us by the hand and leads us; he strengthens us and guides us personally every day. He does not tell us about the way; he is the way.

Jesus said: 'I am the truth.' The psalmist said: 'Teach me your way, O Lord, that I may walk in your truth' (Psalm 86:11). Many people have told us the truth, but no one ever embodied it. There is one all-important thing about moral truth. A person's character does not really affect the teaching of geometry or astronomy or Latin verbs. But if someone proposes to teach moral truth, that person's character makes all the difference in the world. Moral truth cannot be conveyed solely in words; it must be conveyed in example. And that is precisely where the greatest human teacher must fall down. No teacher has ever embodied the truth that he or she taught—except Jesus. Many could say: 'I have taught you the truth.' Only Jesus could say: 'I am the truth.' The tremendous thing about Jesus is not simply that the statement of moral perfection finds its peak in him; it is that the fact of moral perfection finds its realization in him.

Jesus said: 'I am the life.' The writer of the Proverbs said: 'Whoever heeds instruction is on the path to life' (Proverbs 10:17). 'You show me the path of life,' said the psalmist (Psalm 16:11). In the last analysis, what we are always seeking for is life. Our search is not for knowledge for its own sake, but for what will make life worth living. Robert Browning tells of two people who have fallen in love. One says: 'I never knew what life was until I saw it in your eyes.' Love had brought life. That is what Jesus does. Life with Jesus is life indeed.

The Vision of God

John 14:7–11

Jesus insists that the things he said and the things he did came not from his own initiative or his own power or his own knowledge but from God. His words were God's voice speaking to us. His deeds were God's power flowing through him to us. He was the channel by which God came to us.

It was not a self-chosen expedition to the world which Jesus made. He did not do it to soften a hard heart in God. He came because God sent him, because God so loved the world. Jesus went on to make a claim and to offer a test, based on two things: his words and his works.

(1) He claimed to be tested by what he said. It is as if Jesus said: 'When you listen to me, can you not realize at once that what I am saying is God's own truth?' The words of any genius are always self-evidencing. When we read great poetry, we cannot for the most part say why it is great and grips our hearts. We may analyse the vowel sounds and so on, but in the end there is something which defies analysis, but nevertheless is easily and immediately recognizable. It is so with the words of Jesus. When we hear them, we cannot help saying: 'If only the world would live on these principles, how different it would be! If only I would live on these principles, how different I would be!'

(2) He claimed to be tested by his deeds. He said to Philip: 'If you cannot believe in me because of what I say, surely you will allow what I can do to convince you.' That was the same answer as Jesus sent back to John when he sent his messengers to ask whether Jesus was the Messiah, or if they must look for another. 'Go back,' he said, 'and tell John what is happening—and that will convince him' (Matthew 11:1–6). Jesus' proof is that no one else ever succeeded in making bad people good.

Jesus said in effect to Philip: 'Listen to me! Look at me! And believe!' Still the way to Christian belief is not to argue about Jesus but to listen to him and to look at him. If we do that, the sheer personal impact will compel us to believe.

The Promised Helper

John 14:15–17

Jesus does not leave us to struggle with the Christian life alone. He would send us another *Helper*. The Greek word is *parakletos*, which is really untranslatable. The Authorized Version renders it *Comforter*, which, although hallowed by time and usage, is not a good translation. Moffatt translates it as *Helper*. It is only when we examine this word *parakletos* in detail that we catch something of the riches of the doctrine of the Holy Spirit. It really means *someone who is called in*; but it is the reason why the person is called in which gives the word its distinctive associations.

The Greeks used the word in a wide variety of ways. A *parakletos* might be a person called in to give witness in a law court in someone's favour, or an advocate called in to plead the cause of someone under a charge which would issue in a serious penalty; an expert called in to give advice in some difficult situation, or a person called in when, for example, a company of soldiers were depressed and dispirited to put new courage into their minds and hearts. Always a *parakletos* is *someone called in to help* in time of trouble or need.

Comforter was once a perfectly good translation. It actually goes back to John Wyclif, the first person to use it, who did so in his translation made in the fourteenth century. But in his day it meant much more than it means now. The word comes from the Latin *fortis*, which means *brave*; and a comforter was someone who enabled some dispirited creature to be brave. Nowadays comfort has to do almost solely with sorrow; and a comforter is someone who sympathizes with us when we are sad. Beyond a doubt the Holy Spirit does that, but to limit his work to that function is sadly to belittle him. We often talk of being able to cope with things. That is precisely the work of the Holy Spirit. He takes away our inadequacies and enables us to cope with life. The Holy Spirit substitutes victorious for defeated living.

The Holy Spirit gatecrashes no one's heart; he waits to be received. So when we think of the wonderful things which the Holy Spirit can do, surely we will set apart some time amid the bustle and the rush of life to wait in silence for his coming.

April 8

The Bequests of Christ

John 14:25–31

This is a passage closely packed with truth. In it, Jesus speaks of five things.

(1) He speaks of his ally, the Holy Spirit, and says two basic things about him.

(a) The Holy Spirit will teach us all things. To the end of the day, Christians must be learners, for to the end of the day the Holy Spirit will be leading them deeper and deeper into the truth of God.

(b) The Holy Spirit will remind us of what Jesus has said. Nearly all of us have this sort of experience in life. We are tempted to do something wrong and are on the very brink of doing it, when back into our mind comes a saying of Jesus, the verse of a psalm, the picture of Jesus, words of someone we love and admire, teaching we received when very young. In the moment of danger, these things flash unbidden into our minds. That is the work of the Holy Spirit.

(2) He speaks of his gift, and his gift is peace. In the Bible, the word for *peace, shalom,* never means simply the absence of trouble. It means everything which makes for our highest good. The peace which the world offers us is the peace of escape, the peace which comes from the avoidance of trouble and from refusing to face things. The peace which Jesus offers us is the peace of conquest. No experience of life can ever take it from us, and no sorrow, no danger, no suffering can ever make it less.

(3) He speaks of his destination. He is going back to his Father; and he says that if his disciples really loved him, they would be glad that it was so. He was being released from the limitations of this world; he was being restored to his glory.

(4) He speaks of his struggle. The cross was the final battle of Jesus with the powers of evil. But he was not afraid of it, for he knew that evil had no ultimate power over him. He went to his death in the certainty, not of defeat, but of conquest.

(5) He speaks of his vindication. At the time, people saw in the cross only his humiliation and his shame; but the time would come when they would see in it his obedience to God and his love for men and women.

April 9

The Vine and the Branches

John 15:1–10

Suppose in a moment of weakness we have fallen to temptation; we have made a mess of things; we are on the way down to degeneracy of mind and heart and mental strength. Now suppose that we have friends of a strong and lovely and loving nature, who rescue us from our degraded situation. There is only one way in which we can retain our reformation and keep ourselves on the right way. We must keep contact with our friends. If we lose that contact, all the chances are that our weakness will overcome us; the old temptations will rear their heads again; and we will fall. Our salvation lies in continual contact with the strength of our friends.

When the writer Charles Kingsley was asked the secret of his life, referring to the theologian and Christian Socialist F. D. Maurice, he said: 'I had a friend.' The contact with loveliness made him lovely.

Abiding in Christ means something like that. The secret of the life of Jesus was his contact with God; again and again he withdrew into a solitary place to meet him. We must keep contact with Jesus. We cannot do that unless we deliberately take steps to do it. To take but one example—to pray in the morning, even if it is for only a few moments, is to have an antiseptic for the whole day; for we cannot come out of the presence of Christ to touch the evil things. For a few of us, abiding in Christ will be a mystical experience which is beyond words to express. For most of us, it will mean a constant contact with him. It will mean arranging life, arranging prayer, arranging silence in such a way that there is never a day when we give ourselves a chance to forget him.

Finally, we must note that here there are two things laid down about good disciples. First, they enrich their own lives; their contact makes them fruitful branches. Second, they bring glory to God; the sight of their lives turns the thoughts of others to the God who made them like that. God is glorified when we bear much fruit and show ourselves to be disciples of Jesus. The greatest glory of the Christian life is that by our life and conduct we can bring glory to God.

The Life of Jesus' Chosen People

John 15:11–17

The central words of this passage are those in which Jesus says that his disciples have not chosen him, but he has chosen them. It was not we who chose God, but God who, in his grace, approached us with a call and an offer made out of his love.

Out of this passage, we can compile a list of things for which we are chosen and to which we are called.

(1) We are chosen for joy. However hard the Christian way is, it is, both in the travelling and in the goal, the way of joy. There is always a joy in doing the right thing. Christians are men and women of joy. It is true that Christians are sinners; but they are redeemed sinners, and therein lies their joy. How can any of us fail to be happy when we walk the ways of life with Jesus?

(2) We are chosen for love. We are sent out into the world to love one another. Sometimes we live as if we were sent into the world to compete with one another, or to dispute with one another, or even to quarrel with one another. But Christians are to live in such a way that we show what is meant by loving our neighbours. It is here that Jesus makes another of his great claims. If we ask him: 'What right have you to demand that we love one another?' his answer is: 'No one can show greater love than to lay down his life for his friends — and I did that.' Jesus gave us a commandment which he had himself first fulfilled.

(3) Jesus called us to be his friends and the friends of God. That is a tremendous offer. It means that no longer do we need to gaze longingly at God from afar; we are not like slaves who have no right whatsoever to enter into the presence of the master; we are not like a crowd whose only glimpse of the king is in the passing on some state occasion. Jesus gave us this intimacy with God, so that he is no longer a distant stranger but our close friend.

The Spirit of Truth

John 16:12–15

To Jesus, the Holy Spirit is the Spirit of Truth, whose great work is to bring God's truth to us. We have a special name for this bringing of God's truth to us; we call it revelation, and no passage in the New Testament shows us what we might call the principles of revelation better than this one.

(1) One of the mistakes which is sometimes made is to identify God's revelation solely with the Bible. That would be to say that since about AD 120, when the latest book in the New Testament was written, God has ceased to speak. But God's Spirit is always active; he is always revealing himself. It is true that his supreme and unsurpassable revelation came in Jesus; but Jesus is not just a figure in a book, he is a living person, and in him God's revelation goes on. God is still leading us into greater realization of what Jesus means. He is not a God who spoke up to AD 120 and is now silent. He is still revealing his truth to us.

(2) God's revelation to men and women is a revelation of all truth. It is quite wrong to think of it as confined to what we might call theological truth. The theologians and the preachers are not the only people who are inspired. When a poet delivers a great message in words which defy time, that is inspiration. When H. F. Lyte wrote the words of 'Abide with Me', he had no feeling of composing them; he wrote them as to dictation. A great musician is inspired. Handel, telling of how he wrote the 'Hallelujah' chorus, said: 'I saw the heavens opened.' When a scientist discovers something which will help the world's toil and make life better for everyone, when a surgeon discovers a new technique which will save lives and ease pain, when someone discovers a new treatment which will bring life and hope to suffering humanity, that is a revelation from God. All truth is God's truth, and the revelation of all truth is the work of the Holy Spirit.

(3) That which is revealed comes from God. He is both the possessor and the giver of all truth. Truth is not a human discovery; it is God's gift. It is not something which we create; it is something already waiting to be discovered. At the back of all truth, there is God.

Eternal Life

John 17:1–5

What does it mean to know God?

(1) Undoubtedly there is an element of intellectual knowledge. It means, at least in part, to know what God is like, and to know that does make the most tremendous difference to life. Take two examples. People in primitive societies believe in a horde of gods. Every tree, brook, hill, mountain, river and stone has its gods and its spirit; all these spirits are hostile to them; and primitive people are haunted by the gods, living in perpetual fear of offending one of them. Missionaries have told us that it is almost impossible to understand the sheer wave of relief which comes to these people when they discover that there is only one God. This new knowledge makes all the difference in the world. Further, it makes a tremendous difference to know that God is not stern and cruel, but love.

We know these things; but we could never have known them unless Jesus had come to tell them. We enter into a new life, we share something of the life of God himself, when, through the work of Jesus, we discover what God is like. It is eternal life to know what God is like.

(2) But there is something else. The Old Testament regularly uses *know* for sexual knowledge. 'The man knew his wife Eve, and she conceived, and bore Cain' (Genesis 4:1). Now the knowledge of husband and wife is the most intimate there can be. Husband and wife are no longer two; they are one flesh. The sexual act itself is not the important thing; the important thing is the intimacy of heart and mind and soul which in true love precede that act. To know God is therefore not merely to have intellectual knowledge of him; it is to have an intimate personal relationship with him, which is like the nearest and dearest relationship in life. Once again, without Jesus, such intimacy with God would have been unthinkable and impossible. It is Jesus who taught us that God is not remote and unapproachable, but the Father whose name and nature are love.

To know God is to know what he is like, and to be on the most intimate terms of friendship with him; and neither of these things is possible without Jesus Christ.

April 13

The Meaning of Discipleship

John 17:6–8

This passage sheds an illuminating light on the meaning of discipleship.

(1) Discipleship is based on the realization that Jesus came forth from God. Disciples are essentially people who have realized that Jesus is God's ambassador, and that in his words we hear God's voice, and in his deeds we see God's action.

(2) Discipleship issues in obedience. Disciples are those who keep God's word as they hear it in Jesus. They have accepted the mastery of Jesus. So long as we wish to do what we like, we cannot be disciples; discipleship involves submission.

(3) Discipleship is something which is destined. The Twelve were given to Jesus by God. In God's plan, they were destined for discipleship. That does not mean that God destined some to be disciples and some to refuse discipleship. Think of it this way. Parents dream great dreams for their children; they work out a future for them; but the children can refuse that future and go their own way. A teacher thinks out a great future for a student, seeing the potential to do great work for God and for humanity; but the student can lazily or selfishly refuse the offered task. If we love someone, we are always dreaming of that person's future and planning for greatness; but the dream and the plan can be frustrated. God has his plan, his dream, his destiny for each one of us; and our tremendous responsibility is that we can accept or reject it.

When Jesus left this world, he did not seem to have great grounds for hope. He seemed to have achieved so little and to have won so few. But Jesus had that confidence which springs from God. He was not afraid of small beginnings. He was not pessimistic about the future.

Jesus had two things—belief in God and belief in humanity. It is one of the most uplifting things in the world to think that Jesus put his trust in people like ourselves. We too must never be daunted by human weakness or by the small beginning. We too must go forward with confident belief in God and in one another. Then we will never be pessimists, because with these two beliefs the possibilities of life are infinite.

April 14

Jesus' Prayer for His Disciples

John 17:9–19

The great interest of this passage is that it tells us of the things for which Jesus prayed for his disciples.

(1) The first essential is to note that Jesus did not pray that his disciples should be taken out of this world. He never prayed that they might find escape; he prayed that they might find victory. The kind of Christianity which finds its essence in prayer and meditation and in a life withdrawn from the world would have seemed to him a sadly truncated version of the faith he died to bring. He insisted that it was in the rough and tumble of life that a people must live out their Christianity.

Of course there is need of prayer and meditation and quiet times, when we shut the door upon the world to be alone with God, but all these things are not the end that we seek in life, but means to that end; and the end is to demonstrate the Christian life in the ordinary work of the world. Christianity was never meant to withdraw people from life, but to equip them better for it. It does not offer us release from problems, but a way to solve them. It does not offer us an easy peace, but a triumphant warfare. It does not offer us a life in which troubles are escaped and evaded, but a life in which troubles are faced and conquered. However much it may be true that Christians are not of the world, it remains true that it is within the world that their Christianity must be lived out. We must never desire to abandon the world, but always desire to win it.

(2) Jesus prayed for the unity of his disciples. Where there are divisions, where there is exclusiveness, where there is competition between the churches, the cause of Christianity is harmed and the prayer of Jesus frustrated. The gospel cannot truly be preached in any congregation which is not one united band of brothers and sisters. The world cannot be evangelized by competing churches. Jesus prayed that his disciples might be as fully one as he and the Father are one; and there is no prayer of his which has been so hindered from being answered by individual Christians and by the churches than this.

A Glimpse of the Future

John 17:20–21

Gradually in this section, Jesus' prayer has been going out to the ends of the earth. First, he prayed for himself as the cross faced him. Second, he prayed for his disciples, and for God's keeping power for them. Now his prayers take a sweep into the distant future, and he prays for those who in distant lands and far-off ages will also enter the Christian faith. Here we see his complete faith and his radiant certainty. At that moment his followers were few, but even with the cross facing him, his confidence was unshaken, and he was praying for those who would come to believe in his name. This passage should be specially precious to us, for it is Jesus' prayer for us.

What was his prayer for the Church which was to be? It was that all its members would be one as he and his Father are one. What was that unity for which Jesus prayed? It was not a unity of administration or organization; it was not in any sense a religious unity. It was a unity of personal relationship. It was a unity of love for which Jesus prayed, a unity in which people loved each other because they loved him, a unity based entirely on the relationship between heart and heart.

Christians will never organize their churches all in the same way. They will never worship God all in the same way. They will never even all believe precisely the same things. But Christian unity transcends all these differences and joins people together in love. The cause of Christian unity at the present time, and indeed all through history, has been injured and hindered, because people loved their own religious organizations, their own creeds, their own ritual, more than they loved each other.

If we really loved each other and really loved Christ, no church would exclude anyone who was Christ's disciple. Only love implanted in our hearts by God can tear down the barriers which we have erected between one another and between our churches.

The Gift and the Promise of Glory

John 17:22–26

First, Jesus said that he had given his disciples the glory which his Father had given him. We must fully understand what that means. What was the glory of Jesus? There were three ways in which he talked of it.

(1) The cross was his glory. Therefore, first and foremost, a Christian's glory is the cross that must be borne. It is an honour to suffer for Jesus Christ. We must never think of our cross as our penalty; we must think of it as our glory. In the Middle Ages, the harder the task a knight was given, the greater he considered its glory.

(2) Jesus' perfect obedience to the will of God was his glory. We find our glory, not in doing as we like, but in doing as God wills. When we try to do as we like—as many of us have done—we find nothing but sorrow and disaster both for ourselves and for others. We find the real glory of life in doing God's will; the greater the obedience, the greater the glory.

(3) Jesus' glory lay in the fact that, from his life, people recognized his special relationship with God. They saw that no one could live as he did unless he was uniquely near to God. As with Christ, it is our glory when others see in us the reflection of God.

Second, Jesus said that it was his will that his disciples should see his glory in the heavenly places. It is the conviction of Christians that they will share all the experiences of Christ. If they have to share Christ's cross, they will also share his glory. 'The saying is sure: If we have died with him, we will also live with him; if we endure, we will also reign with him' (2 Timothy 2:11–12).

The joy we have now is only a faint foretaste of the joy which is to come. It is Christ's promise that if we share his glory and his sufferings on earth, we shall share his glory and his triumph when life on this earth is ended. What greater promise could there be than that?

April 17

Your Will Be Done

Luke 22:39–46

The space within Jerusalem was so limited that there was no room for gardens. Many well-to-do people, therefore, had private gardens out on the Mount of Olives. Some wealthy friend had given Jesus the privilege of using such a garden, and it was there that Jesus went to fight his lonely battle. He was only thirty-three, and no one wants to die at thirty-three. He knew what crucifixion was like; he had seen it. He was in an *agony*; the Greek word is used of someone fighting a battle with sheer fear. There is no scene like this in all history. This was the very hinge and turning point in Jesus' life. He could have turned back even yet. He could have refused the cross. The salvation of the world hung in the balance as the Son of God literally sweated it out in Gethsemane; and he won.

He went into Gethsemane in the dark; he came out in the light—because he had talked with God. He went into Gethsemane in an agony; he came out with the victory won and with peace in his soul—because he had talked with God.

It makes all the difference what tone of voice is used when saying, 'Your will be done.'

(1) It may be said in a tone of helpless submission, as by one who is in the grip of a power against which it is hopeless to fight. The words may be the death-knell of hope.

(2) It may be said as by one who has been battered into submission. The words may be the admission of complete defeat.

(3) It may be said as by one who has been utterly frustrated and who sees that the dream can never come true. The words may be those of a bleak regret or even of a bitter anger.

(4) It may be said with the accent of perfect trust. That is how Jesus said it. He was speaking to one who was Father; he was speaking to a God whose everlasting arms were underneath and about him even on the cross. He was submitting, but he was submitting to the love that would never let him go. Life's hardest task is to accept what we cannot understand; but we can do even that if we are sure enough of the love of God.

The Traitor's Kiss

Luke 22:47–53

There were four different parties involved in this arrest, and their actions and reactions are very significant.

(1) There was Judas the traitor. He was the man who had abandoned God and entered into a league with Satan. It is only when people have put God out of their lives and taken Satan in that they can sink to selling Christ.

(2) There were the Jews who had come to arrest Jesus. They were the men who were blind to God. When God incarnate came to this earth, all that they could think of was how to hustle him to a cross. They had so long chosen their own way and shut their ears to the voice of God and their eyes to his guidance that in the end they could not recognize him when he came. It is a terrible thing to be blind and deaf to God.

(3) There were the disciples. They were the men who for the moment had forgotten God. Their world had fallen in and they were sure the end had come. The last thing they remembered at that moment was God; the only thing they thought of was the terrible situation into which they had come. Two things happen to those who forget God and leave him out of the situation. They become utterly terrified and completely disorganized. They lose the power to face life and to cope with it. In the time of trial, life is unlivable without God.

(4) There was Jesus. And Jesus was the one person in the whole scene who remembered God. The amazing thing about him in the last days was his absolute serenity once Gethsemane was over. In those days, even at his arrest, it was he who seemed to be in control; and even at his trial, it was he who was the judge.

When we walk with God we can cope with any situation and look any foe in the eyes, unbowed and unafraid. It is only when we have bowed to God that we can talk and act like conquerors.

April 19

Peter's Tragedy

Luke 22:31–38, 54–62

Peter was a strange paradoxical mixture. Even in spite of his denial he was fundamentally loyal. H. G. Wells once said, 'A man may be a bad musician, and yet be passionately in love with music.' No matter what Peter did, however terrible his failure, he was nonetheless passionately devoted to Jesus. There is hope for the person who even when sinning is still haunted by goodness.

Peter was overconfident. If someone says, 'That is one thing I will never do,' that is often the very thing against which he or she must most carefully guard. Throughout history fortresses have been captured because the attackers took the route which seemed unattackable and unscalable and at that very spot the defenders were off their guard. Satan is subtle. He attacks the points at which we are too sure of ourselves, for there we are most likely to be unprepared.

In all fairness it is to be noted that Peter was one of the two disciples (John 18:15) who had the courage to follow Jesus into the courtyard of the high priest's house at all. Peter fell to a temptation which could only have come to a brave man. The courageous person always runs more risks than someone who seeks a placid safety. Liability to temptation is the price paid by those who are adventurous in mind and in action. It may well be that it is better to fail in a gallant enterprise than to run away and not even to attempt it.

Jesus did not speak to Peter in anger but looked at him in sorrow. Peter could have stood it if Jesus had turned and reviled him; but that voiceless, grief-laden look went to his heart like a sword and opened a fountain of tears. The penalty of sin is to face, not the anger of Jesus, but the heartbreak in his eyes.

Jesus said a very lovely thing to Peter. 'When you have turned,' he said, 'strengthen your brothers.' It is as if Jesus said to Peter, 'You will deny me; and you will weep bitter tears; but the result will be that you will be better able to help your brothers who are going through it.' We cannot really help others until we have been in the same furnace of affliction or the same abyss of shame as they have been.

114

The Crime of Christ

Matthew 26:57, 59–68

Repeatedly Jesus warned his disciples to tell no one that he was the Messiah. How then did the high priest know to ask the question the answer to which Jesus could not escape? It may well be that when Judas passed on information against him, he also told the Jewish authorities about Jesus' revelation of his own Messiahship. It may well be that Judas had deliberately broken the bond of secrecy which Jesus had laid upon his disciples.

In any event, the high priest asked the question, and asked it upon oath: 'Are you the Messiah?' he demanded. 'Do you claim to be the Son of God?' Here was the crucial moment in the trial. We might well say that all the universe held its breath as it waited for Jesus' answer. If Jesus said 'No', the bottom fell out of the trial; there was no possible charge against him. He had only to say 'No', and walk out a free man, and escape before the Sanhedrin had time to think of another way of entrapping him. On the other hand, if he said 'Yes', he signed his own death warrant. Nothing more than a simple 'Yes' was needed to make the cross a complete and inescapable certainty.

It may be that Jesus paused for a moment once again to count the cost before he made the great decision; and then he said 'Yes'. He went further. He quoted Daniel 7:13 with its vivid account of the ultimate triumph and kingship of God's chosen one. He knew perfectly well what he was doing. Immediately there went up the cry of blasphemy. Garments were rent in a kind of synthetic and hysterical horror; and Jesus was condemned to death.

Then followed the spitting on him, the buffeting, the slapping of his face, the mockery. Even the externals of justice were forgotten, and the hostility of the Jewish authorities broke through. That meeting in the night began as a court of justice and ended in a frenzied display of hatred, in which there was no attempt to maintain even the superficialities of impartial justice.

Jesus and Pilate

John 18:28–19:16

Jesus is depicted before us with a series of masterstrokes.

(1) First and foremost, no one can read this story without seeing the sheer majesty of Jesus. There is no sense that he is upon trial. When someone faces him, it is not Jesus who is on trial; it is that person. Pilate may have treated many Jewish things with arrogant contempt, but he did not treat Jesus in that way. We cannot help feeling that it is Jesus who is in control and Pilate who is bewildered and floundering in a situation which he cannot understand. The majesty of Jesus never shone more radiantly than in the hour when he was on trial before the world.

(2) Jesus speaks with utter directness to us of his kingdom; it is not, he says, of this earth. The atmosphere in Jerusalem was always explosive; during the Passover it was sheer dynamite. If Jesus had wished to raise the standard of rebellion and to fight it out, he could have done it easily enough. But he makes it quite clear that he claims to be a king and equally clear that his kingdom is not based on force but is a kingdom in the hearts of men and women. He would never deny that he aimed at conquest; but it was the conquest of love.

(3) Jesus tells us why he came into the world. He came to witness to the truth; he came to tell people the truth about God, the truth about themselves, and the truth about life. The days of guessings and gropings and half-truths were gone. He came to tell men and women the truth. That is one of the great reasons why we must either accept or refuse Christ. There is no halfway house about the truth. We either accept it or reject it; and Christ is the truth.

In this dramatic trial scene we see the immutable majesty, the undaunted courage and the serene acceptance of the cross of Jesus. Never was he so regal as when people did their worst to humiliate him.

April 22

Silence before Herod

Luke 23:1–12

Herod was one of the very few people to whom Jesus had absolutely nothing to say. Why did he believe there was nothing to be said to Herod?

(1) Herod regarded Jesus as a sight to be gazed at. To Herod, he was simply a spectacle. But Jesus was not a sight to be stared at; he was a king to be submitted to. Epictetus, the famous Greek Stoic teacher, used to complain that people came from all over the world to his lectures to stare at him, as if he had been a famous statue, but not to accept and to obey his teaching. Jesus is not a figure to be gazed at but a master to be obeyed.

(2) Herod regarded Jesus as a joke. He jested at him; he clothed him in a king's robe as an imitation king. To put it another way—he refused to take Jesus seriously. He would show him off to his court as an amusing curiosity but there his interest stopped. The plain fact is that the vast majority of people still refuse to take Jesus seriously. If they did, they would pay more attention than they do to his words and his claims.

(3) There is another possible translation of verse 11: 'Herod with his soldiers treated him with contempt.' That could be translated, 'Herod, with his soldiers behind him, thought that Jesus was of no importance.' Herod, secure in his position as king, strong with the power of his bodyguard behind him, believed that this Galilaean carpenter did not matter.

There are still those who, consciously or unconsciously, have come to the conclusion that Jesus does not matter, that he is a factor which can well be omitted from life. They give him no room in their hearts and no influence in their lives and believe they can easily do without him. To the Christian, so far from being of no importance, Jesus is the most important person in all the universe.

April 23

Pilate's Losing Struggle

Matthew 27:1–2, 11–26

This whole passage gives the impression of a man fighting a losing battle. It is clear that Pilate did not wish to condemn Jesus.

Pilate was clearly impressed by Jesus. Plainly he did not take seriously the claim to be the King of the Jews. He knew a revolutionary when he saw one, and Jesus was no revolutionary. His dignified silence made Pilate feel that it was not Jesus but he himself who was on trial. Pilate was a man who felt the power of Jesus—and was afraid to submit to it. There are still those who are afraid to be as Christian as they know they ought to be.

Pilate sought to escape the responsibility for condemning Jesus. There is that strange and tragic picture of him washing his hands. That was a Jewish custom. There is a strange regulation in Deuteronomy 21:1–9. If a dead body was found, and it was not known who the killer was, measurements were to be taken to find what was the nearest town or village. The elders of that town or village had to sacrifice a heifer and to wash their hands to rid them of the guilt.

Pilate was warned by his sense of justice, he was warned by his conscience, he was warned by the dream of his troubled wife; but Pilate could not stand against the mob; and Pilate made the futile gesture of washing his hands. Legend has it that to this day there are times when Pilate's ghost emerges from its tomb and goes through the action of the hand-washing once again.

There is one thing of which we can never rid ourselves—and that is responsibility. It is never possible for Pilate or anyone else to say: 'I wash my hands of all responsibility,' for that is something that no one and nothing can take away. This picture of Pilate provokes in our minds pity rather than loathing; for here was a man so enmeshed in his past, and rendered helpless to such an extent by it, that he was unable to take the stand he ought to have taken. Pilate is a figure of tragedy rather than of villainy.

The Soldiers' Mockery

Matthew 27:27–31

The dreadful routine of crucifixion had now begun. The last section ended by telling us that Pilate had Jesus scourged. Roman scourging was a terrible torture. Scourging always preceded crucifixion, and 'it reduced the naked body to strips of raw flesh, and inflamed and bleeding weals'. Men died under it, and men lost their reason under it, and few remained conscious to the end of it.

We may shudder at what the soldiers did; but of all the parties involved in the crucifixion, they were least to be blamed. They were not even stationed in Jerusalem; they had no idea who Jesus was; they certainly were not Jews, for the Jews were the only nation in the Roman Empire who were exempt from military service; they were conscripts who may well have come from the four corners of the earth. They indulged in their rough horseplay; but, unlike the Jews and unlike Pilate, they acted in ignorance.

Then they prepared to lead him away to crucifixion. We are sometimes told that we should not dwell on the physical aspect of the cross; but we cannot possibly have too vivid a picture of what Jesus did and suffered for us. Joseph Klausner, the Jewish writer, says: 'Crucifixion is the most terrible and cruel death which man has ever devised for taking vengeance on his fellow-men.'

It originated in Persia; and its origin came from the fact that the earth was considered to be sacred to Ormuzd the god, and the criminal was lifted up from it that he might not defile the earth, which was the god's property. From Persia, crucifixion passed to Carthage in North Africa; and it was from Carthage that Rome learned it, although the Romans kept it exclusively for rebels, runaway slaves and the lowest type of criminal. It was indeed a punishment which it was illegal to inflict on a Roman citizen.

Klausner goes on to describe crucifixion. The criminal was fastened to his cross, already a bleeding mass from the scourging. There he hung to die of hunger and thirst and exposure, unable even to defend himself from the torture of the gnats and flies which settled on his naked body and on his bleeding wounds. It is not a pretty picture, but that is what Jesus Christ suffered — willingly — for us.

The Road to Calvary

Luke 23:26–31

Palestine was an occupied country, and any citizen could be immediately pressed into the service of the Roman government. The sign of this was a tap on the shoulder with the flat of the blade of a Roman spear. When Jesus sank beneath the weight of his cross, the Roman centurion in charge looked round for someone to carry it. Out of the country into the city there came Simon from far-off Cyrene, which is modern Tripoli. No doubt he was a Jew who all his life had scraped and saved so that he might be able to eat one Passover at Jerusalem. The flat of the Roman spear touched him on the shoulder and he found himself, suddenly without warning, carrying a criminal's cross. Try to imagine the feelings of Simon. He had come to Jerusalem to realize the cherished ambition of a lifetime, and he found himself walking to Calvary carrying a cross. His heart was filled with bitterness towards the Romans and towards this criminal who had involved him in his crime.

But if we can read between the lines the story does not end there. Mark describes Simon as the father of Alexander and Rufus (Mark 15:21). Now you do not identify a man by the names of his sons unless these sons are well-known people in the community to which you write. There is general agreement that Mark wrote his gospel to the church at Rome. Turn to Paul's letter to the church at Rome. Among the greetings at the end he writes, 'Greet Rufus, chosen in the Lord, and greet his mother—a mother to me also' (Romans 16:13). So in the Roman church there was Rufus, a Christian of such worth that he could be called one of God's chosen ones, with a mother so dear to Paul that he could call her his mother in the faith. It may well be that this was the same Rufus who was the son of Simon of Cyrene, and his mother was Simon's wife. It may well be that as he looked on Jesus, Simon's bitterness turned to wondering amazement and finally to faith; that he became a Christian; and that his family became some of the most worthy members of the Roman church.

There They Crucified Him

Luke 23:32–38

When a criminal reached the place of crucifixion, his cross was laid flat upon the ground. Usually it was a cross shaped like a T with no top piece against which the head could rest. It was quite low, so that the criminal's feet were only two or three feet above the ground. There was a company of pious women in Jerusalem who made it their practice always to go to crucifixions and to give the victim a drink of drugged wine which would deaden the terrible pain. That drink was offered to Jesus and he refused it (Matthew 27:34). He was determined to face death at its worst, with a clear mind and senses unclouded.

The victim's arms were stretched out upon the crossbar, and it was usual for the nails to be driven through the wrists. The feet were not nailed, but only loosely bound to the cross. Halfway up the cross there was a projecting piece of wood, called the saddle, which took the weight of the criminal, for otherwise the nails would have torn through his wrists. Then the cross was lifted and set upright in its socket. The terror of crucifixion was this—the pain of that process was terrible but it was not enough to kill, and the victim was left to die of hunger and thirst beneath the blazing noontide sun and the frosts of the night.

Jesus said many wonderful things, but rarely anything more wonderful than, 'Father, forgive them, for they know not what they do.' Christian forgiveness is an amazing thing. When Stephen was being stoned to death he too prayed, 'Lord, do not hold this sin against them' (Acts 7:60). There is nothing so lovely and nothing so rare as Christian forgiveness. When the unforgiving spirit is threatening to turn our hearts to bitterness, let us hear again our Lord asking forgiveness for those who crucified him, and his servant Paul saying to his friends, 'Be kind to one another, tenderhearted, forgiving one another, as God in Christ has forgiven you' (Ephesians 4:32).

Others may have in their hearts the unforgiving spirit, others may sin in ignorance; but we know better. We are Christ's men and women; and we must forgive as he forgave.

The Triumph of the End

Matthew 27:45–50

In verse 46, we have what must be the most staggering sentence in the gospel record, the cry of Jesus: 'My God, my God, why have you forsaken me?'

In human experience, as life goes on and as bitter tragedy enters into it, there come times when we feel that God has forgotten us; when we are immersed in a situation beyond our understanding and feel bereft even of God. It seems to me that that is what happened to Jesus here. In the garden Jesus knew only that he had to go on, because to go on was God's will, and he must accept what even he could not fully understand. Here we see Jesus plumbing the uttermost depths of the human situation, so that there might be no place that we might go where he has not been before.

But here is the point. It would have been a terrible thing if Jesus had died with a cry like that upon his lips — but he did not. The narrative goes on to tell us that, when he shouted with a great shout, he gave up his spirit. That great shout left its mark upon people's minds. It is in every one of the gospels (Matthew 27:50; Mark 15:37; Luke 23:46). But there is one gospel which goes further. John tells us that Jesus died with a shout: 'It is finished' (John 19:30). *It is finished* is in English three words; but in Greek it is one — *Tetelestai* — as it would also be in Aramaic. And *tetelestai* is the victor's shout; it is the cry of all those who have completed their task; it is the cry of those who have won through the struggle; it is the cry of those who have come out of the dark into the glory of the light, and who have grasped the crown. So, Jesus died a victor with a shout of triumph on his lips.

Here is the precious thing. Jesus passed through the uttermost abyss, and then the light broke. If we too cling to God, even when there seems to be no God, desperately and invincibly clutching the remnants of our faith, quite certainly the dawn will break and we will win through.

True victory comes to those who refuse to believe that God has forgotten them, even when every fibre of their being feels that they have been forsaken. Victory comes to those who have been beaten to the depths and still hold on to God, for that is what Jesus did.

April 28

Bewildered Love

John 20:1–10

To Mary belongs the glory of being the first person to see the risen Christ. The whole story is scattered with indications of her love. She had come back to the tomb; she had taken her message to Peter and John, and then must have been left behind in their race to the tomb, so that by the time she got there, they were gone. So she stood there weeping. There is no need to seek for elaborate reasons why Mary did not know Jesus. The simple and the poignant fact is that she could not see him through her tears. Her one desire was to weep her love over Jesus' dead body. As soon as she had answered the person she took to be the gardener, she must have turned again to the tomb and so turned her back on Jesus. Then came his single word, 'Mary!' and her single answer, 'Master!'

So we see there were two very simple and yet very profound reasons why Mary did not recognize Jesus.

(1) She could not recognize him because of her tears. They blinded her eyes so that she could not see. When we lose a dear one, there is always sorrow in our hearts and tears shed or unshed in our eyes. But one thing we must always remember—at such a time, our sorrow is in essence selfish. It is of our loneliness, our loss, our desolation that we are thinking. We cannot be weeping for one who has gone to be the guest of God; it is for ourselves we weep. That is natural and inevitable. At the same time, we must never allow our tears to blind us to the glory of heaven. Tears there must be, but through the tears we should glimpse the glory.

(2) She could not recognize Jesus because she insisted on facing in the wrong direction. She could not take her eyes off the tomb and so had her back to him. Again it is often so with us. At such a time, our eyes are upon the cold earth of the grave; but we must wrench our eyes away from that. That is not where our loved ones are; their worn-out bodies may be there; but the real person is in the heavenly places in the fellowship of Jesus face to face, and in the glory of God.

When sorrow comes, we must never let tears blind our eyes to glory; and we must never fasten our eyes upon the grave and forget the heavens.

123

The Sunset Road That Turned to Dawn

Luke 24:13–35

This is another of the immortal short stories of the world.

(1) It tells us of the ability of Jesus to make sense of things. The whole situation seemed to have no explanation. For these followers of Jesus all their hopes and dreams were shattered. There is all the poignant, wistful, bewildered regret in the world in their sorrowing words, 'We were hoping that he was the one who was going to rescue Israel.' They are the words of people whose hopes are dead and buried. Then Jesus came and talked with them, and the meaning of life became clear and the darkness became light.

(2) It tells how he was known to them in the breaking of bread. This always sounds a little as if it meant the sacrament; but it does not. It was at an ordinary meal in an ordinary house, when an ordinary loaf was being divided, that Jesus was recognized. It is not only at the communion table we can be with Christ; we can be with him at the dinner table too. He is not only the host in his Church; he is the guest in every home. The Christian lives always and everywhere in a Christ-filled world.

(3) It tells of two people who, when they received such great joy, hastened to share it. It was a seven-mile journey back to Jerusalem, but they could not keep the good news to themselves. The Christian message is never fully ours until we have shared it with someone else.

(4) It tells how, when they reached Jerusalem, they found others who had already shared their experience. It has been said that true friendship begins only when people share a common memory and can say to each other, 'Do you remember?' Each of us is one of a great fellowship of people who share a common experience and a common memory of their Lord.

(5) It tells that Jesus appeared to Peter. That must remain one of the great untold stories of the world. But surely it is a lovely thing that Jesus should make one of his first appearances to the man who had denied him. It is the glory of Jesus that he can restore the penitent sinner's self-respect.

April 30

The Risen Lord

John 21:1–25

There were many who said that the appearances of the risen Christ were nothing more than visions which the disciples had. Many would admit the reality
of the visions but insist that they were still only visions. Some would go further and say that they were not visions but hallucinations. The gospels go far
out of their way to insist that the risen Christ was not a vision, not a halluci-
nation, not even a spirit, but a real person. They insist that the tomb was empty
and that the risen Christ had a real body which still bore the marks of the nails
and the spear thrust in his side.

But this story goes a step further. A vision or a spirit would not be likely to
point out a shoal of fish to a party of fishermen. A vision or a spirit would not
be likely to kindle a charcoal fire on the seashore. A vision or a spirit would
not be likely to cook a meal and to share it out. And yet, as this story has it,
the risen Christ did all these things. When John tells how Jesus came back to
his disciples when the doors were shut, he says: 'He showed them his hands
and his side' (20:20). The first and simplest aim of this story is to make quite
clear the reality of the resurrection. The risen Lord was not a vision, nor the
figment of someone's excited imagination, nor the appearance of a spirit or a
ghost; it was Jesus who had conquered death and come back.

In this last chapter, the writer of the Fourth Gospel has set certain great
truths before the Church for whom he wrote. He has reminded them of the
reality of the resurrection; he has reminded them of the universality of the
Church; he has reminded them that Peter and John are not competitors in honour, but that Peter is the great shepherd and John the great witness. Now he
comes to the end; and he comes there thinking once again of the splendour of
Jesus Christ. Whatever we know of Christ, we have only grasped a fragment
of him. Whatever the wonders we have experienced, they are as nothing to
the wonders which we may yet experience.

Human categories are powerless to describe Christ, and human books are
inadequate to hold him. And so John ends with the innumerable triumphs, the
inexhaustible power and the limitless grace of Jesus Christ.

The Church Is Born

The Power to Go On

Acts 1:1–5

In two senses, Acts is the second chapter of a continued story. First, it is the second volume which Luke had sent to Theophilus. In the first volume, his gospel, Luke had told the story of the earthly life of Jesus. Now he goes on to tell the story of the Christian Church. Second, Acts is the second volume of a story which has no end. The gospel was only the story of what Jesus began to do and to teach.

The book of Acts tells of the Church that carries on the life of Christ. This passage tells us how the Church was empowered to do that by the work of the Holy Spirit. We often call the Holy Spirit the *Comforter*. That word goes back to the translation by John Wyclif, made in the fourteenth century; but in Wyclif's day it had a different meaning. It comes from the Latin *fortis*, which means *brave*; the Comforter is the one who fills people with courage and with strength. In the book of Acts, indeed all through the New Testament, it is very difficult to draw a line between the work of the Spirit and the work of the risen Christ; and we do not need to do so, for the coming of the Spirit is the fulfilment of the promise of Jesus: 'And remember, I am with you always, to the end of the age' (Matthew 28:20).

Let us note one other thing. The apostles were told to wait for the coming of the Spirit. We would gain more power and courage and peace if we learned to wait. In the business of life, we need to learn to be still. 'Those who wait for the Lord shall renew their strength' (Isaiah 40:31). Amid life's surging activity, there must be time to receive.

The Day of Pentecost

Acts 2:1–14

We may never know precisely what happened on the Day of Pentecost, but we do know that it was one of the supremely great days of the Christian Church—for, on that day, the Holy Spirit came to the Christian Church in a very special way.

It is perhaps unfortunate that we so often speak of the events at Pentecost as the coming of the Holy Spirit. The danger is that we may think that the Holy Spirit came into existence at that time. That is not so; God is eternally Father, Son and Holy Spirit. In fact, Acts makes that quite clear. The Holy Spirit was speaking in David (Acts 1:16); the Spirit spoke through Isaiah (Acts 28:25); Stephen accuses the Jews of having opposed the Spirit all through their history (Acts 7:51). In that sense, the Spirit is God in every age revealing his truth. At the same time, something special happened at Pentecost.

From that moment, the Holy Spirit became the dominant reality in the life of the early Church. For one thing, the Holy Spirit was the source of all guidance. The early Church was a Spirit-guided community. For another thing, all the leaders of the Church were men of the Spirit. And further, the Spirit was the source of day-to-day courage and power. The Christian courage to meet the dangerous situation, the Christian power to cope with life more than adequately, the Christian eloquence when eloquence is needed, and the Christian joy which is independent of circumstances are all attributed to the work of the Spirit.

Finally, Acts 5:32 speaks of the Spirit 'whom God has given to those who obey him'. This has in it the great truth that the degree to which we can possess the Spirit is conditioned by the kind of people we are. It means that anyone who is honestly trying to do the will of God will experience more and more of the wonder of the Spirit.

Save Yourselves

Acts 2:37–41

This passage shows with crystal clarity the effect of the cross. When people realized just what they had done in crucifying Jesus, their hearts were broken. 'I,' said Jesus, 'when I am lifted up from the earth, will draw all people to myself' (John 12:32). The cross, when we understand what happened there, must pierce our hearts. That experience demands a reaction. 'Repent,' said Peter, 'first and foremost.'

What does *repentance* mean? The word originally meant an *afterthought*. Often, a second thought shows that the first thought was wrong; and so the word came to mean a change of mind. But, if we are honest, a change of mind demands a change of action. Repentance must involve both change of mind and change of action. We may change our minds and come to see that our actions were wrong; but we may be so much in love with our old ways that we will not change them. We may change our ways but our minds remain the same, changing only because of fear or prudence. True repentance involves a change of mind and a change of action. When repentance comes, something happens to the past. There is God's forgiveness for what lies behind.

Let us be quite clear that the consequences of sins are not wiped out. Not even God can do that. When we sin, we may well do something to ourselves and to others which cannot be undone. Let us look at it this way. When we were young and had done something bad, there was an invisible barrier between us and our mother. But when we went and said we were sorry, the old relationship was restored, and everything was right between us again.

Forgiveness does not abolish the consequences of what we have done, but it puts us right with God. When repentance comes, something happens for the future. We receive the gift of the Holy Spirit, and in that power we can win battles we never thought to win and resist things which by ourselves we would have been powerless to resist.

May 4

The Characteristics of the Church

Acts 2:42–47

In this passage, we have a kind of lightning summary of the characteristics of
the early Church.

(1) It was a learning Church; it persisted in listening to the apostles as they
taught. We should count it a wasted day when we do not learn something new
and when we have not penetrated more deeply into the wisdom and the grace
of God.

(2) It was a Church of fellowship; it had what someone has called the great
quality of togetherness.

(3) It was a praying Church; these early Christians knew that they could
not meet life in their own strength and that they did not need to. They always
went in to God before they went out to the world; they were able to meet the
problems of life because they had first met him.

(4) It was a reverent Church. It was said of a great Greek that he moved
through this world as if it were a temple. Christians live in reverence because
they know that the whole earth is the temple of the living God.

(5) It was a Church where things happened; signs and wonders were there
(verse 43). If we expect great things from God and attempt great things for
God, things happen.

(6) It was a sharing Church (verses 44–45); these early Christians had an
intense feeling of responsibility for each other.

(7) It was a worshipping Church (verse 46); they never forgot to visit God's
house. We must remember that 'God knows nothing of solitary religion.'

(8) It was a happy Church (verse 46); gladness was there. A gloomy Christian is a contradiction in terms.

(9) It was a Church whose people others could not help liking. Real Christianity is a lovely thing. There are so many people who are good but who with
their goodness possess a streak of unlovely hardness. In the early Church,
there was a charm about God's people.

Loyalty Only to God

Acts 4:13–22

Here we see very vividly both the enemy's attack and the Christian defence. In the enemy's attack, there are two characteristics. First, there is contempt. The Authorized Version says that the Sanhedrin regarded Peter and John as unlearned and ignorant men. The word translated as *unlearned* means that they had no kind of technical education, especially in the intricate regulations of the law. The word translated as *ignorant* means that they had no special professional qualifications. The Sanhedrin, as it were, regarded them as men without a college education and with no professional status.

It is often difficult for ordinary people to deal with what might be called academic and professional snobbery. But those who have Christ in their hearts possess a real dignity which neither academic attainment nor professional status can give. Second, there are threats. But Christians know that anything the world does to them is only for a moment, whereas the things of God last forever.

Faced with this attack, Peter and John had certain defences. First, they had the defence of an unanswerable fact. That the man had been cured, it was impossible to deny. The most unanswerable defence of Christianity is the individual Christian. Second, they had the defence of an utter loyalty to God. If it was a question of choosing between obeying other people and obeying God, Peter and John were in no doubt as to what course to take. As the writer H. G. Wells said, 'The trouble with so many people is that the voice of their neighbours sounds louder in their ears than the voice of God.'

The real secret of Christianity lies in that great tribute once paid to the Scottish reformer John Knox: 'He feared God so much that he never feared the face of any man.' But the third defence was greatest of all—the defence of a personal experience of Jesus Christ. Their message was not something that they had simply heard from others. They knew at first hand that it was true, and they were so sure of it that they were willing to stake their lives upon it.

Trouble in the Church

Acts 5:1–11

This is the most vivid story in the book of Acts. There is no need to make a miracle of it. But it does show us something of the atmosphere which prevailed in the early Church. It is on record that Edward I once blazed with anger at one of his courtiers, and the man dropped dead in sheer fear. This story shows two things about the early Church—the power of suggestion on human minds and the extraordinary respect in which the apostles were held. It was in that atmosphere that the rebuke of Peter acted as it did. This is one of the stories which demonstrate the almost stubborn honesty of the Bible. It might well have been left out, because it shows that even in the early Church there were very imperfect Christians; but the Bible refuses to present an idealized picture of anything.

Once, a court painter painted the portrait of Oliver Cromwell, the Lord Protector of England. Cromwell was disfigured by warts on his face. The painter, thinking to please the great man, omitted the disfiguring warts. When Cromwell saw the picture, he said: 'Take it away, and paint me warts and all.' It is one of the great virtues of the Bible that it shows us its heroes, warts and all. There is a certain encouragement in this story, for it shows us that even in its greatest days the Church was a mixture of good and bad. Peter insists that sin is sin against God.

We do well to remember that, particularly in certain directions.

(1) Failure in care and true application is sin against God. Everything, however humble it may be, that contributes to the health, the happiness and the welfare of humanity is work done for God. Antonio Stradivari, the great maker of violins, said: 'If my hand slacked, I should rob God.' That is a motto for us all to take.

(2) Failure to use our talents is sin against God. God gave us such talents as we have; we hold them in stewardship for him; and we are responsible to him for the use we make of them.

(3) Failure in truth is sin against God. When we slip into falsehood, it is sin against the guidance of the Spirit in our hearts.

The First of the Martyrs

Acts 7:54–8:1

Stephen had a vision of a world for Christ. To the Jews, two things were especially precious—the Temple, the only place where sacrifice could be offered and God could be truly worshipped; and the law, which could never be changed. Stephen, however, said that the Temple must pass away, that the law was only a stage towards the gospel and that Christianity must go out to the whole wide world. No one could withstand his arguments, and so the Jews resorted to force and Stephen was arrested.

They flung him outside the city and began to stone him. And the witnesses placed their garments at the feet of a young man called Saul. So they stoned Stephen as he called upon God and said: 'Lord Jesus, receive my spirit.' Kneeling down he cried with a loud voice: 'Lord, set not this sin to their charge.'

There are in this scene certain notable things about Stephen.

(1) We see the secret of his courage. Beyond all that the world could do to him, he saw awaiting him the welcome of his Lord.

(2) We see Stephen following his Lord's example. As Jesus prayed for the forgiveness of his executioners (Luke 23:34), so did Stephen. Those who follow Christ the whole way will find strength to do things which it seems humanly impossible to do.

(3) The dreadful turmoil finished in a strange peace. To Stephen came the peace which comes to those who have done the right thing even if the right thing kills them.

The first half of the first verse of chapter 8 goes with this section. Paul has entered on the scene under his original name—Saul. The man who was to become the apostle to the Gentiles thoroughly agreed with the execution of Stephen. But, as St Augustine said, 'The Church owes Paul to the prayer of Stephen.' However hard he tried, Saul could never forget the way in which Stephen had died. Even at this early point, the blood of the martyrs had begun to be the seed of the Church.

Surrender

Acts 9:1–9

In this passage, we have the most famous conversion story in history. We must try as far as we can to enter into Paul's mind. When we do, we will see that this is not a sudden conversion but a sudden surrender. Something about Stephen lingered in Paul's mind and would not be banished. How could a bad man die like that? In order to put his insistent doubt to rest, Paul plunged into the most violent action possible. Paul had heard that certain of the Christians had escaped to Damascus, and he asked for letters of authority that he might go to Damascus and order them to return.

The journey only made matters worse. It was about 140 miles from Jerusalem to Damascus. The journey would be made on foot and would take about a week. Paul's only companions were the officers of the Sanhedrin, a kind of police force. Because he was a Pharisee, he could have nothing to do with them; so he walked alone; and as he walked he thought, because there was nothing else to do. The route went through Galilee, and Galilee brought Jesus even more vividly to Paul's mind.

That region had this characteristic phenomenon that when the hot air of the plain met the cold air of the mountain range, violent electrical storms resulted. Just at that moment came such a lightning storm, and out of the storm Christ spoke to Paul. In that moment, the long battle was over and Paul surrendered to Christ. So he went into Damascus a changed man. And how changed! The one who had intended to enter Damascus like an avenging fury was led by the hand, blind and helpless. There is all of Christianity in what the risen Christ said to Paul: 'Go into the city, and you will be told what to do.'

Up to this moment, Paul had been doing what he liked, what he thought best, what his will dictated. From this time forward, he would be told what to do. Christians are men and women who have ceased to do what they want to do and who have begun to do what Christ wants them to do.

The Acts of Peter

Acts 9:32–43

This passage really follows on from 8:25. It shows Peter in action. But it shows more than that. In the most definite way, it shows us the source of Peter's power. When Peter healed Aeneas, he did not say: 'I heal you'; he said: 'Jesus Christ heals you.' Before he spoke to Tabitha—Tabitha is the Hebrew for a *gazelle*, and Dorcas is the Greek for the same word—Peter prayed. It was not his own power on which Peter called; it was the power of Jesus Christ. We think too much of what we can do and too little of what Christ can do through us.

There is one very interesting word in this passage. Twice the Christians at Lydda are called saints (verses 32 and 41). The same word is used earlier in the chapter by Ananias to describe the Christians at Jerusalem (verse 13). This is the word that Paul always uses to describe the church members, for he always writes his letters to the saints who are at such and such a place.

The Greek word is *hagios*, and it has far-reaching associations. It is sometimes translated as *holy*; but the root meaning of it is *different*. Basically, Christians are men and women who are different from those who are merely people of the world. But where does that difference lie? *Hagios* was particularly used of the people of Israel. They are specifically a holy people, a different people. Their difference lay in the fact that, of all nations, God had chosen them to do his work. Israel failed in its destiny. It was disobedient, and by its actions it lost its privileges. The Church became the true Israel; and the Christians became the people who are different, their difference lying in the fact that they were chosen for the special purposes of God.

So we who are Christians are not different from others in that we are chosen for greater honour on this earth; we are different in that we are chosen for a greater service. We are saved to serve.

A Devout Soldier

Acts 10:1–8

The tenth chapter of Acts tells a story that is one of the great turning points in the history of the Church. For the first time, a Gentile is to be admitted into its fellowship. Since Cornelius is so important in Church history, let us gather together what we can learn about him.

(1) Cornelius was a Roman centurion stationed at Caesarea, the headquarters of the government of Palestine. In the Roman military set-up, there was first of all the legion. It was a force of 6,000 men and therefore was roughly equal to a division. In every legion, there were ten cohorts. A cohort therefore had 600 men. The cohort was divided into centuries, and over each century there was a centurion. One historian of the period describes the qualifications of the centurion like this: 'Centurions are desired not to be overbold and reckless so much as good leaders, of steady and prudent mind, not prone to take the offensive to start fighting wantonly, but able when overwhelmed and hard-pressed to stand fast and die at their posts.' Cornelius, therefore, was a man who first and foremost knew what courage and loyalty were.

(2) Cornelius was a God-fearer. In New Testament times, this had become almost a technical term for Gentiles who, weary of the gods and the immoralities and the frustration of their ancestral faiths, had attached themselves to the Jewish religion. They did not accept circumcision and the law, but they attended the synagogue and they believed in one God and in the pure ethic of Jewish religion. Cornelius, then, was a man who was seeking after God; and, as he sought God, God found him.

(3) Cornelius was a man given to charitable acts; he was characteristically kind. His search for God had made him love other people; and those who love others are not far from the kingdom.

(4) Cornelius was a man of prayer. Perhaps as yet he did not clearly know the God to whom he prayed; but, according to the understanding that he had, he lived close to God.

Peter Learns a Lesson

Acts 10:9–16

Before Cornelius could be welcomed into the Church, Peter had to learn a lesson. Strict Jews believed that God had no use for the Gentiles. Peter had to unlearn that before Cornelius could be allowed in. There is one point which shows that Peter was already on the way to unlearning some of the rigidness in which he had been brought up. He was staying with a man called Simon, who was a tanner (9:43; 10:5). A tanner worked with the dead bodies of animals, and therefore was permanently unclean (Numbers 19:11–13). No strict Jew would have dreamt of accepting hospitality from a tanner. It was his uncleanness that made it necessary for Simon to live on the seashore outside the city. No doubt this tanner was a Christian, and Peter had begun to see that Christianity abolished these unimportant laws and taboos.

At midday, Peter went to the roof to pray. The roofs of the houses were flat, and, since the houses were small and crowded, people often went up to the roof for privacy. There he had a vision of a great sheet being let down. Perhaps above the flat roof there stretched an awning to ward off the heat of the sun; and maybe in Peter's trance the awning became the great sheet. The word for *sheet* is the same as for a ship's sail. Maybe on the roof Peter was looking out on the blue waters of the Mediterranean and saw the ships' sails in the distance, and they wove themselves into his vision. In any event, the sheet with the animals on it appeared to him, and the voice told him to kill and eat. Now the Jews had strict food laws, recorded in Leviticus 11. Generally speaking, the Jews could eat only animals which chewed the cud and whose hooves were cloven. All others were unclean and forbidden. Peter was shocked, and protested that he had never eaten anything that was unclean. The voice told him not to call what God had cleansed unclean.

This happened three times so that there could be no possible mistake or dodging of the lesson. Once, Peter would have called a Gentile unclean; but now God had prepared him for the visitors who would come.

The Meeting of Peter and Cornelius

Acts 10:17–33

In this passage, the most surprising things are happening. Once again, let us remember that the Jews believed that other nations were quite outside the mercy of God. A really strict Jew would have no contact with a Gentile or even with a Jew who did not observe the law. In particular, strict Jews would never have as a guest nor ever be the guest of someone who did not observe the law. Remembering that, see what Peter did. When the messengers of Cornelius were at the door—and, knowing the Jewish viewpoint, they came no further than the door—Peter asked them in and gave them hospitality (verse 23).

When Peter arrived at Caesarea, Cornelius met him at the door, no doubt wondering if Peter would cross his threshold at all—and Peter came in (verse 27). In the most amazing way, the barriers are beginning to go down. That is typical of the work of Christ. A missionary tells how he once officiated at a communion service in Africa. Beside him as an elder sat an old chief of the Ngoni called Manly-heart. The old chief could remember the days when the young warriors of the Ngoni had left behind them a trail of burned and devastated towns and had come home with their spears red with blood and with the women of their enemies as booty. And what were the tribes which in those days they had ravaged? They were the Senga and the Tumbuka. And who were sitting at that communion service now? Ngoni, Senga and Tumbuka were sitting side by side, their hatred forgotten in the love of Jesus Christ.

In the first days, it was characteristic of Christianity that it broke the barriers down; and it can still do that when given the chance.

May 13

An Adventurous Journey for a Sick Man

Acts 13:1–3, 14–15

The thirteenth and fourteenth chapters of Acts tell the story of the first missionary journey. Paul and Barnabas set out from Antioch. From there they went across the sea to Cyprus, where they preached at Salamis and Paphos. From Paphos they sailed to Perga in Pamphylia. They then moved inland and came to Antioch in Pisidia.

One of the amazing things about Acts is the heroism that is passed over in a sentence. Pisidian Antioch stood on a plateau 3,600 feet above sea level. To get to it, Paul and Barnabas would have to cross the Taurus range of mountains by one of the hardest roads in Asia Minor, a road which was also notorious for robbers and brigands. But, we are bound to ask, why did they not preach in Pamphylia? Why did they leave the coast with the word unproclaimed and set out on that difficult and dangerous way? Not so very long afterwards, Paul wrote a letter to the people of Antioch in Pisidia, Iconium, Lystra and Derbe. It is the letter called the Letter to the Galatians, for all these towns were in the Roman province of Galatia. In it, he says: 'You know that it was because of a physical infirmity that I first announced the gospel to you' (Galatians 4:13).

So when he came to Galatia he was a sick man. Now Paul had what he described as a thorn in the flesh, which in spite of much prayer remained with him (2 Corinthians 12:7–8). Many guesses have been made as to what that thorn was—or stake, as it probably should be translated. The oldest tradition is that Paul suffered from debilitating headaches. And the most likely explanation is that he was the victim of a virulent recurring malarial fever which was common on the low coastal strip of Asia Minor. A traveller says that the headache characteristic of this malaria was like a red-hot bar thrust through the forehead. It is most likely that this malaria attacked Paul in low-lying Pamphylia and that he had to make for the plateau country to shake it off. Note that it never struck him to turn back.

Even when his body was aching, Paul never stopped driving himself forward as an adventurer for Christ.

A Problem Becomes Acute

Acts 15:1–5

It was almost by accident that the most epoch-making things were happening in Antioch so that the gospel was being preached both to Jews and to Gentiles and they were living together in fellowship. There were certain Jews to whom all this was quite unthinkable. They could never forget the position of the Jews as the chosen people. They were quite willing for the Gentiles to come into the Church, but on the condition that first they became Jews. If this attitude had prevailed, Christianity would have become nothing other than a sect of Judaism.

Some of these more narrow-minded Jews came down to Antioch and tried to persuade the converts that they would lose everything unless they first accepted Judaism. Paul and Barnabas argued strongly against this, and matters were at a deadlock. There was only one way out. An appeal must be made to Jerusalem, the headquarters of the Church, for a ruling.

The case which Paul and Barnabas put forward was simply the story of what had happened. They were prepared to let the facts speak for themselves. But some of the Pharisees who had become Christians insisted that all converts must be circumcised and keep the law. The principle at stake was quite simple and completely fundamental. Was the gift of God for the select few or for all the world? If we possess it ourselves, are we to look on it as a privilege or as a responsibility?

The problem may not meet us nowadays in precisely the same way; but there still exist divisions between class and class, between nation and nation, between colour and colour. We fully realize the true meaning of Christianity only when all middle walls of partition are broken down.

Peter States the Case

Acts 15:6–12

In answer to the stricter Jews, Peter reminded them how he himself had been responsible for the reception of Cornelius into the Church ten years before this. The proof that he had acted rightly was that God had granted his Holy Spirit to these very Gentiles who had been received. As far as the law's claims went, they might have been ceremonially unclean; but by his Spirit God had cleansed their hearts.

The attempt to obey the law's many different kinds of commands and so to earn salvation was a losing battle in which everyone was inadequate. There was only one way — the acceptance of the free gift of the grace of God in an act of self-surrendering faith. Peter went right to the heart of the question. In this whole dispute, the deepest of principles was involved. Can we earn the favour of God? Or must we admit our own helplessness and be ready in humble faith to accept what the grace of God gives? In effect, the Jewish party said: 'Religion means earning God's favour by keeping the law.' Peter said: 'Religion consists in casting ourselves on the grace of God.'

Underlying the debate is the difference between a religion of works and a religion of grace. Peace will never come until we realize that we can never put God in our debt, and that all we can do is take what God in his grace gives.

The paradox of Christianity is that the way to victory is through surrender; and the way to power is through admitting one's own helplessness.

May 16

Europe's First Convert

Acts 16:11-15

Neapolis—the modern Kavalla—was the seaport of Philippi. Philippi had a long history. Once it had been called Crenides, which means 'the Springs'. But Philip of Macedon, the father of Alexander, had fortified it as a barrier against the Thracians and had given it his own name. At one time it had possessed famous gold mines, but by Paul's time these had been exhausted. Later it had been the scene of one of the most famous battles in the world, when Augustus won for himself the Roman Empire.

Philippi was a Roman colony. Roman colonies were usually strategic centres. In them, Rome planted little groups of army veterans who had completed their military service. They wore the Roman form of dress, spoke the Roman language and used the Roman laws, no matter where they were. Nowhere was there greater pride in Roman citizenship than in these outposts of Rome. In Philippi, there was no synagogue from which to start. But, where the Jews were unable to have a synagogue, they had a place of prayer—and these places of prayer were usually by the riverside. On the Sabbath, Paul and his friends made their way there and talked with the women who met in that place.

The extraordinary thing about Paul's work in Philippi is the amazing cross-section of the population that was won for Christ. Lydia came from the very top end of the social scale; she was a purple-merchant. The purple dye had to be gathered drop by drop from a certain shellfish and so was extremely costly. Lydia, wealthy woman that she was, was won for Christ. Her immediate reaction was to offer the hospitality of her house to Paul and his friends.

When Paul is describing the Christian character, he says that the Christian should 'extend hospitality' (Romans 12:13). When Peter is urging Christian duty upon his converts, he tells them: 'Be hospitable to one another without complaining' (1 Peter 4:9). A Christian home is one where the door is always open.

143

The Demented Slave Girl

Acts 16:16–24

If Lydia came from the top end of the social scale, this slave girl came from the bottom. She was what was called a Pytho, that is, a person who could give oracles to guide people about the future. She was insane—and the ancient world had a strange respect for such people because, they said, the gods had taken away their wits in order to put the mind of the gods into them. She was probably also gifted with a natural aptitude for ventriloquism.

She had fallen into the hands of unscrupulous men who used her misfortune for their gain. When Paul cured her of her madness, these men felt not joy at her restoration to health but fury that their source of revenue was gone. They were astute men. They played on the natural anti-Semitism of the crowd, they appealed to the pride in things Roman which was characteristic of a Roman colony, and they succeeded in having Paul and Silas arrested. Not only were they arrested; they were put in the inner prison in the stocks. It may be that not only their feet but also their hands and their necks were held in the stocks.

The tragic thing is that Paul and Silas were arrested and ill-treated for doing good. Whenever Christianity attacks vested interests, trouble follows. It is a human characteristic that if people's pockets are affected they are up in arms. It is everyone's duty to ask: 'Is the money I am earning worth the price? Do I earn it by serving or by exploiting my neighbours?' Often, the greatest obstacle to the crusade of Christ is human selfishness.

The Philippian Jailer

Acts 16:25–40

If Lydia came from the top end of the social scale and the slave girl from the bottom, the Roman jailer was one of the sturdy middle class who made up the Roman civil service; and so in these three the whole range within society was complete. Let us look first at the scene of this passage. This was a district where earthquakes were by no means uncommon. The door was locked by a wooden bar falling into two slots, and the stocks were similarly fastened. The earthquake shook the bar free, and the prisoners were freed from their chains and the door was open. The jailer was about to kill himself because Roman law said that if a prisoner escaped the jailer must suffer the penalty the prisoner would have suffered.

Let us look at the characters. First, there is Paul. We note three things about Paul.

(1) He could sing hymns when he was confined in the stocks in the inner prison at midnight. The one thing you can never take away from a Christian is God and the presence of Jesus Christ. With God there is freedom even in a prison, and even at midnight there is light.

(2) He was quite willing to open the door of salvation to the jailer who had shut the door of the prison on him. There was never a grudge in Paul's nature. He could preach to the person who had chained him into the stocks.

(3) He could stand on his dignity. He claimed his rights as a Roman citizen. To scourge a Roman citizen was a crime punishable by death. But Paul was not standing on his dignity for his own sake but for the sake of the Christians he was leaving behind in Philippi. He wanted it to be seen that they were not without influential friends.

Second, there is the jailer. The interesting thing about the jailer is that he immediately proved his conversion by his deeds. No sooner had he turned to Christ than he washed the wounds upon the prisoners' backs and gave them food.

Unless our Christianity makes us kind, it is not real. Unless our declared change of heart is guaranteed by our change of deeds, it is superficial and false.

May 19

A Sermon to the Philosophers

Acts 17:16–31

There were many altars to unknown gods in Athens. Some 600 years before this, a terrible plague had fallen on the city which nothing could halt. A Cretan poet, Epimenides, had come forward with a plan. A flock of sheep were starved and then set loose on the Areopagus (lush with grass). It would have been unnatural for them not to eat—and those that lay down instead of eating were sacrificed on altars to an unknown god which were then constructed alongside where the sheep were lying. Many such altars were constructed, which had later fallen into disrepair. By Paul's day, one had been restored to its original condition. In the original story, the plague was lifted as a result of these sacrifices.

It is from this situation that Paul takes his starting point. There are a series of steps in his sermon.

(1) God is not the made but the maker; and the one who made all things cannot be worshipped by anything made by human hands.

(2) God has guided history. He was behind the rise and fall of nations in the days gone by; his hand is on the helm of things now.

(3) God has made human beings in such a way that instinctively they long for God and search for him in the darkness.

(4) The days of feeling our way and of ignorance are past. As long as people had to search in the shadows, they could not know God, and he excused their follies and their mistakes; but now in Christ the full blaze of the knowledge of God has come, and the day of excuses is past.

(5) The day of judgment is coming. Life is neither a progress to extinction, as it was to the Epicureans, nor a pathway to absorption to God, as it was to the Stoics; it is a journey to the judgment seat of God, where Jesus Christ is Judge.

(6) The proof of the pre-eminence of Christ is the resurrection. It is no unknown God but a risen Christ with whom we have to deal.

Incomplete Christianity

Acts 19:1–7

In Ephesus, Paul met some men whose Christianity was not yet complete. They had received the baptism of John, but they did not even know of the Holy Spirit in the Christian sense of the term. What was the difference between the baptism of John and baptism in the name of Jesus? The accounts of the preaching of John (Matthew 3:7–12; Luke 3:3–11) reveal one fundamental difference between it and the preaching of Jesus. The preaching of John was a threat; the preaching of Jesus was good news. John's preaching was a stage on the way. He himself knew that he only pointed to one still to come (Matthew 3:11; Luke 3:16).

John's preaching was a necessary stage, because there are two stages in the religious life. First, there is the stage in which we awaken to our own inadequacy and the fact that we are deserving of condemnation at the hand of God. That stage is closely linked to an endeavour to do better that inevitably fails because we try in our own strength. Second, there is the stage when we come to see that through the grace of Jesus Christ our condemnation may be taken away.

Closely linked with that stage is the time when we find that all our efforts to do better are strengthened by the work of the Holy Spirit, through whom we can do what we could never do on our own. These Christians knew the condemnation and the moral duty of being better; but the grace of Christ and the help of the Holy Spirit they did not know. Their faith was incomplete. Their religion was inevitably a matter of struggle and had not reached the stage of being an experience of peace.

The incident shows us one great truth—that without the Holy Spirit there can be no such thing as complete Christianity. Even when we see the error of our ways and repent and determine to change them, we can never make the change without the help which only the Spirit can give.

The Works of God

Acts 19:8–12

When work in the synagogue became impossible because of the embittered opposition, Paul changed his regular meeting place to the hall of a philosopher called Tyrannus. One Greek manuscript adds a touch which sounds like the additional detail an eyewitness might bring. It says that Paul taught in that hall from 11 am to 4 pm. Almost certainly, that is when Paul would teach. Until 11 am and after 4 pm, Tyrannus would need the hall himself. In the Ionian cities, all work stopped at 11 am and did not begin again until the late afternoon because of the heat. We are told that there would actually be more people sound asleep in Ephesus at 1 pm than at 1 am. What Paul must have done was to work all morning and all evening at his trade and to teach in the midday hours.

This shows us two things—the eagerness of Paul to teach and the eagerness of the Christians to learn. The only time they had was when others rested in the heat of the day—and they seized that time. It may well put many of us to shame for complaining that things are inconvenient at times. Throughout this time, wonderful deeds were being done. The sweatband was what a workman wore round his head to absorb the sweat as he worked. The apron was the girdle which a workman or servant wrapped around himself.

It is very significant that the narrative does not say that Paul did these extraordinary deeds; it says that God did them through Paul's hands. It has been said that God is everywhere looking for hands to use. We may not be able to work miracles with our hands, but without doubt we can give them to God so that he may work through them.

A Young Man Falls Asleep

Acts 20:7–12

This vivid story is clearly an eyewitness account; and it is one of the first accounts we have of what a Christian service was like. It talks twice about breaking of bread. In the early Church, there were two closely related things. One was what was called the Love Feast. All contributed to it, and it was a real meal—often the only proper meal that poor slaves got all week. Here, Christians ate in loving fellowship with each other. The other was the Lord's Supper, which was observed during or immediately after the Love Feast.

It may well be that we have lost something of great value in the happy togetherness of the common meal. It marked as nothing else could the family spirit of the Church. All this happened at night—probably because it was only at night, when the day's work was done, that slaves could come to the Christian fellowship. That also explains the case of Eutychus. It was dark. In the low-ceilinged upper room, it was hot. The many lamps made the air oppressive. Eutychus, no doubt, had already done a hard day's work, and his body was tired. He was sitting by a window to get the cool night air. The windows were not made of glass. They were either lattice or solid wood and opened like doors, coming right down almost to the floor and projecting over the courtyard below. Eutychus, overpowered by the stuffy atmosphere, succumbed to sleep and fell to the courtyard below.

We must not take it that Paul spoke on and on; there would be talk and discussion. When the crowd poured down the outside stair and found the young man lying unconscious below, they began to scream; but Paul told them to stop the fuss, for the youth was still alive. From the next verses, we learn that Paul did not go with the main company; no doubt he stayed behind to make sure that Eutychus was completely recovered from his fall.

There is something very lovely about this simple picture. The impression is that of a family meeting together rather than of a modern church service. Is it possible that we have gained in dignity in our church services at the expense of family atmosphere?

Compromise in Jerusalem

Acts 21:17–26

When Paul arrived in Jerusalem, he presented the church with a problem. The leaders accepted him and saw God's hand in his work; but rumours had been spread that he had encouraged Jews to forsake their ancestral faith. This Paul had never done. True, he had insisted that the Jewish law was irrelevant for Gentiles; but he had never sought to draw Jews away from the customs of their ancestors.

The leaders saw a way in which Paul could guarantee the orthodoxy of his own conduct. Four men were in the middle of observing the Nazirite vow. This was a vow taken in gratitude for some special blessing from the hand of God. It involved abstention from meat and wine for thirty days, during which the hair had to be allowed to grow. It seems that sometimes at least the last seven days had to be spent entirely in the Temple courts. At the end, certain offerings had to be brought—a year-old lamb for a sin offering, a ram for a peace offering, a basket of unleavened bread, cakes of fine flour mixed with oil and a meat offering and a drink offering. Finally, the hair had to be cut and burned on the altar with the sacrifice.

It is obvious that this was a costly business. Work had to be given up, and all the elements of the sacrifice had to be bought. It was quite beyond the resources of many who would have wanted to undertake it. So it was considered an act of piety for some wealthier person to cover the expenses of someone taking the vow. That was what Paul was asked to do in the case of these four men—and he agreed. By so doing, he could demonstrate for all to see that he was himself an observer of the law.

There can be no doubt that the matter was distasteful to Paul. For him, the relevance of things like that had gone. But it is the sign of all who are truly great that they can subordinate their own wishes and views for the sake of the Church. There is a time when compromise is a sign not of weakness but of strength.

The Defence of Experience

Acts 21:37–22:10

Paul's defence to the mob who are out for his blood is not to argue but to relate a personal experience; and a personal experience is the most unanswerable argument on earth.

This defence is in essence a paradox. It stresses two things.

(1) It stresses Paul's identity with the people to whom he is speaking. He was a Jew, and that was something he never forgot (cf. 2 Corinthians 11:22; Philippians 3:4–5). He was a man of Tarsus, and Tarsus was what might be called 'no mean city'. It was one of the great ports of the Mediterranean, standing at the mouth of the River Cydnus and being the terminus of a road which came all across Asia Minor from the far-off Euphrates. It was one of the greatest university cities of the ancient world. What is more, Paul was a Rabbi, trained at the feet of Gamaliel, who had been 'the glory of the law' and who had died only about five years before. He had been a persecutor in his zeal for the ancestral ways. On all these points, Paul was entirely at one with the audience to which he was speaking.

(2) It stresses the difference between Paul and his audience. The fundamental difference was that he saw Christ as the Saviour of all and God as the one who loves all people. His audience saw God as the one who loved only the Jews. They sought to keep the privileges of God to themselves and regarded anyone who would widen this circle of privilege as a blasphemer. The difference was that Paul had met Christ face to face. In one sense, Paul was identified with those to whom he spoke; in another, he was separated from them.

It is like that with every Christian. As Christians, we live in the world; but God has separated us and consecrated us to a special task.

Paul Continues His Life Story

Acts 22:11–21

Once again from the beginning, Paul is stressing his identity with his audience. When he reached Damascus, the man who instructed him was Ananias, a follower of the law, whom the Jews knew to be a good man. Paul is stressing the fact that he had come not to destroy the ancestral faith but to fulfil it. Here we have one of Luke's telescoped narratives. When we also read Acts 9 and Galatians 1, we find that it was really three years afterwards that Paul went up to Jerusalem, after his visit to Arabia and his witnessing in Damascus. In Acts 9, we were told that he left Jerusalem because he was in danger of his life from the enraged Jews; here we are told he left because of a vision.

There is no real contradiction; it is the same story told from different points of view. The point Paul makes is that he did not want to leave the Jews. When God told him to do so, Paul argued. He said that his previous record would be bound to make his change all the more impressive to the Jews; but God said that the Jews would never listen to him and he must go to the Gentiles. There is a certain sense of disappointed longing here. As with his Master, Paul's own people would not receive him (John 1:11). He is literally saying: 'I had a priceless gift for you, but you would not take it; so it was offered to the Gentiles.'

Verse 14 is a summary not only of the life of Paul but also of the Christian life. There are three items in it.

(1) To know the will of God. It is the first aim of every Christian to know God's will and to obey it.

(2) To see the Just One. It is the aim of every Christian each day to walk in the presence of the risen Lord.

(3) To hear God's voice. It was said of John Brown of Haddington that, in his preaching, he paused from time to time as if listening for a voice. Christians are always listening for the voice of God above the noise of the many voices of the world to tell them where to go and what to do.

Festus Seeks Material for His Report

Acts 25:22–27

Festus had got himself into a difficulty. It was Roman law that, if someone appealed to Caesar and was sent to Rome, there must be sent with that person a written account of the case and of the charges. Festus's problem was that, as far as he could see, there was no charge to send. That is why this meeting had been convened.

There is no more dramatic scene in all the New Testament. It was with splendour and flourish that Agrippa and Bernice had come. They would have worn their purple robes of royalty and the gold circlet of the crown on their brows. Doubtless Festus had donned the scarlet robe which a governor wore on state occasions. Close at hand there must have stood Agrippa's court, and also in attendance were the most influential figures of the Jews. Close by Festus there would stand the captains in command of the five cohorts which were stationed at Caesarea; and in the background there would be a solid formation of the tall Roman legionaries on ceremonial guard.

Into such a scene came Paul, the little Jewish tent-maker, with his hands in chains; and yet, from the moment he speaks, it is Paul who holds the stage. There are some people who have an element of power. Julian Duguid tells how he once crossed the Atlantic in the same ship as the physician and missionary Sir Wilfred Grenfell. Grenfell was not a particularly imposing figure to look at; but Duguid tells that, whenever Grenfell entered one of the ship's rooms, he could tell he was there without looking round, because a wave of power flowed from the man.

When we have Christ in our hearts and God at our right hand, we have the secret of power. Of whom then shall we be afraid?

The Defence of a Changed Man

Acts 26:1–11

One of the extraordinary things about the great characters in the New Testament story is that they were never afraid to confess what they had once been. Here in the presence of the king, Paul frankly confesses that there was a day when he had tried to eliminate the Christians.

There was a famous evangelist called Brownlow North. In his early days, he had lived a life that was anything but Christian. Once, just before he was to enter the pulpit in a church in Aberdeen, he received a letter. This letter informed him that its writer had evidence of some disgraceful thing which Brownlow North had done before he became a Christian; and it went on to say that the writer proposed to interrupt the service and to tell the whole congregation of that sin if he preached. Brownlow North took the letter into the pulpit; he read it to the congregation; he told of the thing that he had once done; and then he told them that Christ had changed him and that Christ could do the same for them. He used the very evidence of his shame to turn it to the glory of Christ.

The theologian James Denney used to say that the great function of Christianity was in the last analysis to make bad people good. The great Christians have never been afraid to point to themselves as living examples of the power of Christ. It is true that we can never change ourselves; but it is also gloriously true that what we cannot do, Jesus Christ can do for us.

In this passage, Paul insists that the centre of his whole message is the resurrection. His witness is not of someone who has lived and died but of one who is gloriously present and alive for evermore. For Paul, every day is Easter Day.

May 28

Surrender for Service

Acts 26:12–18

This passage is full of interest.

(1) The Greek word *apostolos* literally means *one who is sent forth*. For instance, an ambassador is an *apostolos* or *apostle*. The interesting thing is that a messenger of the Sanhedrin was technically known as an *apostolos* of the Sanhedrin. That means that Paul began this journey as the apostle of the Sanhedrin and ended it as the apostle of Christ.

(2) Paul was pressing on with his journey at midday. Unless travellers were in a really desperate hurry, they rested during the midday heat. So we see how Paul was driving himself on this mission of persecution. Beyond doubt, he was trying by violent action to resolve the uncertainties that were in his heart.

(3) The risen Christ told Paul that it was hard for him to kick against the spikes. When a young ox was first yoked, it tried to kick its way out. If it was yoked to a one-handed plough, the ploughman held in his hand a long stick with a sharpened end, which he held close to the ox's heels so that every time it kicked it was caught by the spike. If it was yoked to a wagon, the front of the wagon had a bar studded with wooden spikes which caught the ox if it kicked. The young ox had to learn submission the hard way — and so had Paul.

Verses 17–18 give a perfect summary of what Christ does for men and women.

(1) He opens their eyes. When Christ comes into people's lives, he enables them to see things they never saw before.

(2) He turns them from the darkness to the light. Before people meet Christ, it is as if they were facing the wrong way; after meeting Christ, they are walking towards the light, and the way ahead of them is clear.

(3) He transfers them from the power of Satan to the power of God. Once evil had control over people, but now God's triumphant power enables them to live in victorious goodness.

(4) He gives them forgiveness of sins and a share with the sanctified. For the past, the penalty of sin is broken; for the future, life is re-created and purified.

May 29

Welcome at Malta

Acts 28:1–6

It was on the island of Malta that Paul and the ship's company found themselves. The Authorized Version is a little unkind to the Maltese. It calls them the *barbarous* people. It is true that the Greek calls them *barbaroi*; but to the Greeks the barbarians were people who said *bar-bar*, that is, people who spoke an unintelligible foreign language and not the beautiful Greek language. We come nearer to the meaning when we simply call them the natives.

This passage offers vivid insights into the character of Paul. For one thing, there is the lovely and homely touch that he was a man who could not bear to be doing nothing; there was a bonfire to be kept alight, and Paul was gathering brushwood for it. Once again, we see that for all Paul's visions he was an intensely practical man; and more, that, great man though he was, he was not ashamed to be useful in the smallest thing. It is told that, in his youth, the American educationist Booker T. Washington walked hundreds of miles to one of the few universities which took in African American students. When he got there, he was told that the classes were full. He was offered a job at making beds and sweeping floors. He took it; and he swept those floors and made those beds so well that before very long they took him as a student, and he went on to become the greatest scholar and administrator of his community. It is only the small-minded individual who refuses the small task.

Further, we see Paul as someone who was cool and calm. In one of his bundles of brushwood was a sleeping viper, which was woken up by the heat and which fastened itself to his hand. It is difficult to tell whether this was a miraculous event or not. Nowadays, at least, there is no such thing as a poisonous snake in Malta; and in Paul's time a snake existed which was very like a viper but quite harmless. It is far more likely that Paul shook off the snake before it had time to pierce his skin. In any event he seems to have handled the whole affair as if it was quite insignificant. It certainly looked to the Maltese like a miracle—but clearly Paul was someone who did not fuss!

So We Came to Rome

Acts 28:11–15

After three months, Paul and the ship's company managed to get passages for Italy on another corn ship which had spent the winter in Malta. In those days, ships had figureheads. Two of the favourite gods of sailors were the Heavenly Twins, Castor and Pollux; and this ship had carved images of them as its figurehead. This time, the voyage was as prosperous as the previous one had been disastrous. Puteoli was the port of Rome. There must have been tremors in Paul's heart, for now he was on the very threshold of the capital of the world.

How would a Jewish tent-maker fare in the greatest city in the world? To the north lay the port of Misenum, where the Roman fleets were stationed; and, as he saw the warships in the distance, Paul must have thought of the power of Rome. Nearby were the beaches of Baiae, with its crowded beaches and the coloured sails of the yachts of the wealthy Romans. Puteoli, with its wharves and its storehouses and its ships, has been called the 'Liverpool of the ancient world'.

For once, there must have been a churning in Paul's stomach as he faced Rome almost alone. Then something wonderful happened. Apii Forum is forty-three miles from Rome and thirty-three miles from the Three Taverns. They were on the great Appian Way, which led from Rome to the coast. And a *deputation* of Roman Christians came to meet him. The Greek word used is that used for a city deputation going to meet a general or a king or a conqueror. They came to meet Paul as one of the great ones of the earth; and he thanked God and took courage.

What was it that so especially lifted up his heart? Surely it was the sudden realization that he was far from being alone. Christians are never alone.

(1) They have the consciousness of the unseen cloud of witnesses around and about them.

(2) They have the consciousness of belonging to a worldwide fellowship.

(3) They have the consciousness that wherever they go there is God.

(4) They have the certainty that their risen Lord is with them.

May 31

Freely and without Hindrance

Acts 28:30–31

To the end of the day, Paul is Paul. Even in prison, his own two hands supplied his needs; and he was not idle in other respects. It was there in prison that he wrote the letters to the Philippians, to the Ephesians, to the Colossians and to Philemon. Nor was he ever altogether alone. Luke and Aristarchus had come with him, and Luke remained to the end (2 Timothy 4:11). Timothy was often with him (Philippians 1:1; Colossians 1:1; Philemon 1). Sometimes Tychicus was with him (Ephesians 6:21). For a while, he had the company of Epaphroditus (Philippians 4:18). And sometimes Mark was with him (Colossians 4:10). Nor was it wasted time. He tells the Philippians that all this has happened for the furtherance of the gospel (Philippians 1:12).

We wonder why Luke never told us what happened to Paul, whether he was executed or released. The reason is that this was not Luke's purpose. At the beginning, Luke gave us his plan for Acts when he told how Jesus commanded his followers to bear witness for him in Jerusalem and all over Judaea and Samaria and away to the ends of the earth (Acts 1:8). Now the tale is finished; the story that began in Jerusalem rather more than thirty years earlier has finished in Rome. It is nothing less than a miracle of God. The Church, which at the beginning of Acts could be numbered in tens, cannot now be numbered in tens of thousands.

The story of the crucified man of Nazareth has swept across the world in its conquering course, until now without interference it is being preached in Rome, the capital of the world. The gospel has reached the centre of the world and is being freely proclaimed — and Luke's task is at an end.

Paul's Great Letter

At Home with God (1)

Romans 5:1–5

Here is one of Paul's great lyrical passages in which he almost sings the intimate joy of his confidence in God. Before Jesus came, no one could ever be really close to God. Some, indeed, have seen him as the complete stranger, the utterly untouchable. In one of H. G. Wells's books, there is the story of a businessman whose mind was so tense and strained that he was in serious danger of a complete nervous and mental breakdown. His doctor told him that the only thing that could save him was to find the peace that fellowship with God can give. 'What!' he said, 'to think of that, up there, having fellowship with me! I would as soon think of cooling my throat with the Milky Way or shaking hands with the stars!' God, to him, was the completely unfindable.

It is only when we realize that God is the Father of our Lord Jesus Christ that there comes into life that closeness to him, that new relationship, which Paul calls justification. Through Jesus, says Paul, we have an introduction to this grace in which we stand. The word he uses for *introduction* is *prosagoge*. It is a word which conjures up two great images.

(1) It is the word normally used for introducing or ushering someone into the presence of royalty. It is as if Paul was saying: 'Jesus ushers us into the very presence of God. He opens the door for us to the presence of the King of Kings; and when that door is opened what we find is grace; not condemnation, not judgment, not vengeance, but the sheer, undeserved, incredible kindness of God.'

(2) But *prosagoge* brings to mind another picture. In late Greek, it is the word for the place where ships come in, a *harbour* or a *haven*. If we take it in that sense, it means that as long as we tried to depend on our own efforts we were tempest-tossed, like sailors striving with a sea which threatened to overwhelm them completely; but, now that we have heard the word of Christ, we have reached at last the haven of God's grace, and we know the calm of depending not on what we can do for ourselves but on what God has done for us.

At Home with God (2)

Romans 5:1–5

Because of Jesus, we have entry to the presence of the King of Kings and entry to the haven of God's grace.

No sooner has Paul said this than the other side of the matter strikes him. All this is true, and it is glory; but the fact remains that, in this life, Christians are up against it. It is hard to be a Christian in Rome. Remembering that, Paul produces a great climax. 'Trouble', he said, 'produces fortitude.' The word he uses for *fortitude* is *hupomone*, which means more than endurance. It means the spirit which can overcome the world; it means the spirit which does not passively endure but which meets things head on and overcomes them.

'Fortitude', Paul goes on, 'produces character.' The word he uses for *character* is *dokime*. *Dokime* is used of metal which has been passed through the fire so that everything base has been purged out of it. When affliction is met with fortitude, out of the battle we emerge stronger, purer, better and nearer to God.

'Character', Paul goes on, 'produces hope.' Two people can meet the same situation. It can drive one of them to despair, and it can spur the other to triumphant action. To the one, it can be the end of hope; to the other, it can be a challenge to greatness. The difference corresponds to the difference between individuals. If we let ourselves become weak and flabby, if we allow circumstances to beat us, if we allow ourselves to whine and grovel under affliction, we make ourselves the kind of people who, when the challenge comes, cannot do anything but despair. If, on the other hand, we have insisted on meeting life with our heads held high, if we have always faced and, by facing, conquered things; then, when the challenge comes, we meet it with eyes alight with hope. The character that has endured the test always emerges in hope.

Then Paul makes one last great statement: 'The Christian hope never proves an illusion, for it is founded on the love of God.'

The Final Proof of Love

Romans 5:6–11

The fact that Jesus Christ died for us is the final proof of God's love. It was not good people Christ died to save but sinners, not God's friends but those who were hostile to him. Then Paul goes a step further. Through Jesus, our status with God was changed. Sinners though we were, we were put into a right relationship with God.

But that is not enough. Not only our status must be changed but also our state. The saved sinner cannot go on being a sinner, but must become good. Christ's death changed our status; his risen life changes our state. He is not dead but alive; he is with us always to help us and guide us, to fill us with his strength in order to overcome temptation, to clothe our lives with something of his radiance. Jesus begins by putting sinners into a right relationship with God even when they are still sinners; he goes on, by his grace, to enable them to quit their sin and become good. There are technical names for these things. The change of our status is justification; that is where the whole saving process begins. The change of our state is sanctification; that is where the saving process goes on, and never ends, until we see him face to face and are like him.

There is one thing to note here of quite extraordinary importance. Paul is quite clear that the whole saving process, the coming of Christ and the death of Christ, is the proof of God's love. Sometimes it is stated as if on the one side there was a gentle and loving Christ, and on the other an angry and vengeful God; and as if Christ had done something which changed God's attitude to men and women. Nothing could be further from the truth. The whole matter springs from the love of God.

Jesus did not come to change God's attitude; he came to show what it is and always was. He came to prove beyond question that God is love.

Ruin and Rescue

Romans 5:12–21

No passage of the New Testament has had such an influence on theology as this; and no passage is more difficult for us to understand today. It is difficult because Paul is thinking and speaking in terms which were familiar to Jews and perfectly understandable to them, but which are unfamiliar to us.

There are two basic Jewish ideas in the light of which this passage must be read.

(1) There is the idea of solidarity. Jews never really thought of themselves as individuals but always as part of a clan, a family or a nation, apart from which the individual had no real existence. In other societies, it happens that, when people are asked their names, they give the name of their tribe or clan. They think of themselves not as individuals but as members of a society. That is how Paul sees Adam. Adam was not an individual. He was one of all humanity; and, because of this, his sin was the sin of all.

(2) The second basic idea is intimately connected with this in Paul's argument. Death is the direct consequence of sin. It was the Jewish belief that, if Adam had not sinned, human beings would have been immortal. Sirach (Ecclesiasticus 25:24) writes: 'From a woman sin had its beginning, and because of her we all die.' The Book of Wisdom has it: 'God created us for incorruption, and made us in the image of his own eternity, but through the devil's envy death entered the world' (2:23). In Jewish thought, sin and death are integrally connected.

So, we have extracted the essence of one side of Paul's thought. Because of this idea of the complete solidarity of humanity, all men and women literally sinned in Adam; and, because it is the consequence of sin, death reigned over them all.

Into this situation comes Jesus. To God, Jesus offered perfect goodness. And, just as all human beings were involved in Adam's sin, all are involved in Jesus' perfect goodness; and, just as Adam's sin was the cause of death, so Jesus' perfect goodness conquers death and gives to men and women life eternal.

June 5

Dying to Live

Romans 6:1–11

As he has so often done in this letter, Paul is once again carrying on an argument against a kind of imaginary opponent. The argument springs from the great saying at the end of the last chapter: 'Where sin abounded, grace superabounded.' It runs something like this.

The objector: You have just said that God's grace is great enough to find forgiveness for every sin.

Paul: That is so.

The objector: Well, if that is so, let us go on sinning. The more we sin, the more grace will abound. Sin does not matter, for God will forgive anyway.

Paul's first reaction is to recoil from that argument in sheer horror. 'Do you suggest', he demands, 'that we should go on sinning in order to give grace more chance to operate? God forbid that we should pursue such an incredible course.'

In this passage lie three great permanent truths.

(1) It is a terrible thing to seek to trade on the mercy of God and to make it an excuse for sinning. Think of it in human terms. How despicable it would be for children to consider themselves free to sin because they knew that their parents would forgive. That would be taking advantage of love to break love's heart.

(2) Those who enter upon the Christian way are committed to a different kind of life. They have died to one kind of life and been born to another. In recent years, we may have tended to stress the fact that acceptance of the Christian way need not make so very much difference in a person's life. Paul would have said that it ought to make all the difference in the world.

(3) But there is more than a mere ethical change in our lives when we accept Christ. There is a real identification with Christ. We are in Christ. We cannot live our physical life unless we are in the air and the air is in us; unless we are in Christ, and Christ is in us, we cannot live the life of God.

The Practice of the Faith

Romans 6:12–14

The passage which went before was the writing of a mystic. It spoke of the way in which Christians should live so close to Christ that all their lives can be said to be lived in him. And now, after the mystical experience, comes the practical demand. Christianity is not an emotional experience; it is a way of life. Christians are not meant to wallow in an experience, however wonderful; they are meant to go out and live a certain kind of life that faces the world's attacks and problems head on.

When we go out into the world, we are confronted with an awesome situation. As Paul thinks of it, both God and sin are looking for weapons to use. God cannot work without human beings. If he wants a word spoken, he has to get someone to speak it. If he wants a deed done, he has to get someone to do it. If he wants a person encouraged, he has to get someone else to do the lifting up. It is the same with sin; everyone has to be given the first nudge in that direction. Sin is looking for people who will by their words or example seduce others into sinning. It is as if Paul was saying: 'In this world, there is an eternal battle between sin and God; choose your side.' We are faced with the tremendous alternative of making ourselves weapons in the hand of God or weapons in the hand of sin.

We might well say: 'Such a choice is too much for me. I am bound to fail.' Paul's answer is: 'Don't be discouraged and don't be despairing; sin will not have any power over you.' Why? Because we are no longer under law but under grace. Why should that make all the difference? Because we are no longer trying to satisfy the demands of law but are trying to be worthy of the gifts of love. We are no longer regarding God as the stern judge; we are regarding him as the lover of human souls. There is no inspiration in all the world like love.

The inspiration of Christians comes not from the fear of what God will do to them but from the inspiration of what God has done for them.

The Exclusive Possession

Romans 6:15–19

To a certain type of mind, the doctrine of free grace is always a temptation to say: 'If forgiveness is as easy and as inevitable as all that, if God's one desire is to forgive, and if his grace is wide enough to cover every spot and stain, why worry about sin? Why not do as we like? It will be all the same in the end.'

Paul counters this argument by using a vivid picture. He says, 'Once you gave yourselves to sin as its slave; when you did that, righteousness had no claim over you. But now you have given yourselves to God as the slaves of righteousness; and so sin has no claim over you.'

To understand this, we must understand the status of the slave. When we think of those who are employed to work for others, we think of people who give a certain agreed part of their time to their employer and who receive a certain agreed wage for doing so. Within that agreed time, they are at the disposal and under the orders of their employer. But, when that time ends, they are free to do as they like. During their working hours, they belong to their employer, but in their free time they belong to no one but themselves. But, in Paul's time, the status of slaves was quite different. Literally, they had no time which belonged to themselves; every single moment belonged to their master. They were their master's absolutely exclusive possession. That is the picture that is in Paul's mind. He says, 'At one time, you were the slave of sin. Sin had exclusive possession of you. At that time, you could not talk of anything else but sinning. But now, you have taken God as your master and he has exclusive possession of you.'

Christians are men and women who have given complete control of their lives to Christ, holding nothing back. No one who has done that can ever think of using grace as an excuse for sin.

God's Free Gift

Romans 6:20–23

The first time we do a wrong thing, we may do it with hesitation and a tremor and a shudder. The second time we do it, it is easier; and, if we go on doing it, it becomes effortless; sin loses its terror. The first time we allow ourselves some indulgence, we may be satisfied with very little of it; but the time comes when we need more and more of it to produce the same thrill. Sin leads on to sin; lawlessness produces lawlessness. To start on the path of sin is to go on to more and more.

The new life is different; it is life which is righteous. Now, the Greeks defined righteousness as giving to others and to God their due. The Christian life is one which gives God his proper place and which respects the rights of human personality. Christians will never disobey God nor ever use a human being to gratify their desire for pleasure. The Christian life leads to what the Revised Standard Version calls *sanctification*. The word in Greek is *hagiasmos*. All Greek nouns which end in -*asmos* describe not a completed state but a process. Sanctification is the road to holiness. When people give their lives to Christ, they do not then become perfect; the struggle is by no means over. But Christianity has always regarded the direction in which we are facing as more important than the particular stage we have reached. Once we are Christ's, we have started on the process of sanctification, the road to holiness.

Paul finishes with a great saying that contains a double metaphor. 'Sin's pay is death,' he says, 'but God's free gift is eternal life.' Paul uses two military words. For *pay*, he uses *opsonia*. *Opsonia* was the soldier's pay, something that he earned with the risk of his body and the sweat of his brow, something that was due to him and could not be taken from him. For *gift*, he uses *charisma*. The *charisma*, or in Latin the *donativum*, was a totally unearned gift which the army sometimes received. On special occasions, for instance on his birthday, an emperor handed out a free gift of money to the army. It had not been earned; it was a gift of the emperor's kindness and grace.

So, Paul says: 'If we got the pay we had earned, it would be death; but, out of his grace, God has given us life.'

The Law Produces Sin (1)

Romans 7:7–13

Paul deals with the torturing paradox of the law. In itself, the law is good. That is to say, it is meant to make us good. And yet the fact remains that this same law is the very thing through which sin gains entry into an individual. How does that happen? There are two ways in which the law may be said to be, in one sense, the source of sin.

(1) It defines sin. Sin without the law, as Paul said, has no existence. Until a thing is defined as sin by the law, we cannot know that it is sin. It may be legal to drive a car in either direction along a street; then that street is declared one-way; after that, a new form of lawbreaking exists—that of driving in a forbidden direction. The new regulation actually creates a new fault. The law, by making people aware of what it is, creates sin.

(2) But there is a much more serious sense in which the law produces sin. One of the strange facts of life is that forbidden things hold a fascination for us. In his *Confessions*, there is a famous passage in which St Augustine tells of the fascination of the forbidden thing:

> There was a pear tree near our vineyard, laden with fruit. One stormy night we rascally youths set out to rob it and carry our spoils away. We took off a huge load of pears—not to feast upon ourselves, but to throw them to the pigs, though we ate just enough to have the pleasure of forbidden fruit. They were nice pears, but it was not the pears that my wretched soul coveted, for I had plenty better at home. I picked them simply in order to become a thief. The only feast I got was a feast of iniquity, and that I enjoyed to the full. What was it that I loved in that theft? Was it the pleasure of acting against the law, in order that I, a prisoner under rules, might have a maimed counterfeit of freedom by doing what was forbidden? . . . The desire to steal was awakened simply by the prohibition of stealing.

Set something in the category of forbidden things or put a place out of bounds, and immediately they become fascinating. In that sense, the law produces sin.

The Law Produces Sin (2)

Romans 7:7–13

Paul has one revealing word which he uses of sin. 'Sin', he says, 'seduced me.' There is always deception in sin. C. J. Vaughan, the former headmaster of Harrow School, says that sin's delusion works in three directions.

(1) We are deluded regarding the satisfaction to be found in sin. No one ever took a forbidden thing without thinking that it would bring happiness, and no one ever found that it did.

(2) We are deluded regarding the excuse that can be made for it. Everyone thinks that doing the wrong thing can be defended; but no one's defence ever sounded anything but futile when it was made in the presence of God.

(3) We are deluded regarding the probability of escaping the consequences of it. We never commit a sin without the hope that we can get away with it. But it is true that, sooner or later, our sin will find us out.

Is the law a bad thing because it actually produces sin? Paul is certain that there is wisdom in the whole sequence.

(1) First, he is convinced that, whatever the consequence, sin had to be defined as sin.

(2) The process shows the terrible nature of sin, because sin took a thing — the law — which was holy and just and good, and twisted it into something that served the purposes of evil. The awfulness of sin is shown by the fact that it could take a fine thing and make it a weapon of evil. That is what sin does. It can take the loveliness of love and turn it into lust. It can take the honourable desire for independence and turn it into the obsession for money and for power. It can take the beauty of friendship and use it as a seduction to the wrong things. That is what Thomas Carlyle called 'the infinite damnability of sin'. The very fact that it took the law and made it a point of entry for sin shows the supreme sinfulness of sin.

The whole terrible process is not accidental; it is all designed to show us how awful a thing sin is, because it can take the loveliest things and corrupt them with a polluting touch.

The Human Situation

Romans 7:14–25

Paul is baring his very soul; and he is telling us of an experience which lies at the heart of the human situation. He knew what was right and wanted to do it; and yet, somehow, he never could. He was haunted by this feeling of frustration—his ability to see what was good and his inability to do it, his ability to recognize what was wrong and his inability to refrain from doing it. Paul's contemporaries knew this feeling well, as, indeed, we know it ourselves. Ovid, the Roman poet, had penned the famous saying: 'I see the better things, and I approve them, but I follow the worse.'

From one point of view, this passage might be called a demonstration of inadequacies.

(1) It demonstrates the inadequacy of human knowledge. If to know the right thing was to do it, life would be easy. But knowledge by itself does not make us good. It is the same in every walk of life. We may know exactly how golf should be played; but that is very far from being able to play it. We may know how poetry ought to be written; but that is very far from being able to write it. We may know how we ought to behave in any given situation; but that is very far from being able to behave in the right way.

(2) It demonstrates the inadequacy of human resolution. To resolve to do a thing is very far from doing it. There is in human nature an essential weakness of the will. The will comes up against the problems, the difficulties, the opposition—and it fails. Once, Peter made a great resolution. 'Even though I must die with you,' he said, 'I will not deny you' (Matthew 26:35); and yet he failed badly when it came to the point.

(3) It demonstrates the limitations of diagnosis. Paul knew quite clearly what was wrong; but he was unable to put it right. He was like a doctor who could accurately diagnose a disease but was powerless to prescribe a cure. Jesus is the one person who not only knows what is wrong, but who can also put right that wrong. It is not criticism he offers, but help.

The Liberation of Our Human Nature

Romans 8:1–4

Two words keep recurring again and again in this chapter—*flesh* (*sarx*) and *spirit* (*pneuma*). We will not understand the passage at all unless we understand the way in which Paul is using these words.

(1) When he is talking of the Christians, Paul is not using *flesh* simply in the sense of the body, as we say *flesh and blood*. How, then, is he using it? He really means human nature in its vulnerability to sin. To live according to the flesh is to live a life dominated by the dictates and desires of sinful human nature instead of a life dominated by the dictates and the love of God. The flesh is the lower side of human nature. It is to be carefully noted that, when Paul thinks of the kind of life lived by those dominated by the *sarx*, he is not by any means thinking exclusively of sexual and bodily sins. When he gives a list of the works of the flesh in Galatians 5:19–21, he includes the bodily and the sexual sins; but he also includes idolatry, hatred, wrath, strife, heresies, envy and murder. The flesh to him was not a physical thing but spiritual. It was human nature in all its sin and weakness; it was all that human beings are without God and without Christ.

(2) There is the word *spirit*; in this single chapter, it occurs no fewer than twenty times. Spirit, to Paul, represented a power which was divine. So, Paul says in this passage that there was a time when Christians were at the mercy of their own sinful human nature. In that state, the law simply became something that moved them to sin, and they went from bad to worse, defeated and frustrated men and women. But, when they became Christians, into their lives came the surging power of the Spirit of God, and, as a result, they entered into victorious living.

In the second part of the passage, Paul speaks of the effect of the work of Jesus on us. Because of what Jesus did, there opens out to Christians a life dominated no longer by the flesh but by that Spirit of God, which fills us with a power that is not our own. The penalty of the past is removed, and strength for our future is assured.

The Two Principles of Life

Romans 8:5–11

Paul is drawing a contrast between two kinds of life.

(1) There is the life which is dominated by sinful human nature; whose focus and centre is self; whose only law is its own desires; which takes what it likes where it likes. In different people, that life will be differently described. It may be passion-controlled, or lust-controlled, or pride-controlled, or ambition-controlled. Its characteristic is its absorption in the things that human nature without Christ sets its heart upon.

(2) There is the life that is dominated by the Spirit of God. As men and women live in the air, they live in Christ, never separated from him. As they breathe in the air and the air fills them, so Christ fills them. They have no mind of their own; Christ is their mind. They have no desires of their own; the will of Christ is their only law. They are Spirit-controlled, Christ-controlled, God-focused.

These two lives are going in diametrically opposite directions. The life that is dominated by the desires and activities of sinful human nature is on the way to death. In the most literal sense, there is no future in it—because it is getting further and further away from God. To allow the things of the world completely to dominate life is self-extinction; it is spiritual suicide. By living it, people are making themselves totally unfit ever to stand in the presence of God. They are hostile to him, resentful of his law and his control. God is not their friend but their enemy, and no one ever won the last battle against him.

The Spirit-controlled life, the Christ-centred life, the God-focused life is daily coming nearer heaven even when it is still on earth. It is a life which is such a steady progress to God that the final transition of death is only a natural and inevitable stage on the way.

June 14

Entry into the Family of God

Romans 8:12–17

Paul speaks of Christians being adopted into the family of God. It is only when we understand how serious and complicated a step Roman adoption was that we really understand the depth of meaning in this passage.

Roman adoption was always rendered more serious and more difficult by the Roman *patria potestas*. This was the father's power over his family; it was the power of absolute disposal and control, and in the early days it was actually the power of life and death. In relation to his father, a Roman son never came of age. No matter how old he was, he was still under the *patria potestas*, in the absolute possession and under the absolute control of his father. Obviously, this made adoption into another family a very difficult and serious step. In adoption, a person had to pass from one *patria potestas* to another.

But it is the consequences of adoption which are most significant for the picture that is in Paul's mind.

(1) The adopted person lost all rights in his old family and gained all the rights of a legitimate son in his new family. In the most binding legal way, he got a new father.

(2) It followed that he became heir to his new father's estate. Even if other sons were born afterwards, it did not affect his rights. He was co-heir with them, and no one could deny him that right.

(3) In law, the old life of the adopted person was completely wiped out; for instance, all debts were cancelled. He was regarded as a new person entering into a new life in which the past had no part.

So, we see that every step of Roman adoption was meaningful in the mind of Paul when he transferred the picture to our adoption into the family of God. Once, we were in the absolute control of our own sinful human nature; but God, in his mercy, has brought us into his absolute possession. The old life has no more rights over us; God has an absolute right. The past is cancelled and its debts are wiped out; we begin a new life with God and become heirs of all his riches.

The Glorious Hope (1)

Romans 8:18–25

Paul has just been speaking of the glory of adoption into the family of God; and then he comes back to the troubled state of this present world. He draws a great picture. He speaks with a poet's vision. He sees all nature waiting for the glory that shall be. At the moment, creation is in bondage to decay. The world is one where beauty fades and loveliness decays; it is a dying world; but it is waiting for its liberation from all this, and the coming of the state of glory.

The dream of the renewed world was dear to the Jews. Paul knew that; and here he, as it were, endows creation with consciousness. He thinks of nature longing for the day when sin's dominion would be broken, death and decay would be gone, and God's glory would come. With a touch of imaginative insight, he says that the state of nature was even worse than the human state. Human beings had sinned deliberately; but it was involuntarily that nature was subjected to the consequences of sin. Unwittingly, nature was involved in the consequences of human sin. 'Cursed is the ground because of you,' God said to Adam after his sin (Genesis 3:17). So here, with a poet's eye, Paul sees nature waiting for liberation from the death and decay that human sin had brought into the world.

If that is true of nature, it is even more true for us. So, Paul goes on to think of human longing. In the experience of the Holy Spirit, men and women had a foretaste, a first instalment, of the glory that shall be; now they long with all their hearts for the full realization of what adoption into the family of God means.

That final adoption will be the redemption of their bodies. In the state of glory, Paul did not think of people as disembodied spirits. In this world, every individual is a body and a spirit; and, in the world of glory, the total person will be saved. But the body will no longer be the victim of decay and the instrument of sin; it will be a spiritual body fit for the life of a spiritual person.

The Glorious Hope (2)

Romans 8:18–25

The blazing truth that lit life for Paul was that the human situation is not hopeless. Paul was no pessimist. The writer H. G. Wells once said: 'Man, who began in a cave behind a windbreak, will end in the disease-soaked ruins of a slum.' Not so Paul. He saw human sin and the state of the world; but he also saw God's redeeming power; and the end of it all for him was hope. Because of that, to Paul, life was not a state of permanent despair, waiting for an inevitable end in a world encompassed by sin, death and decay; life was an eager anticipation of a liberation, a renewal and a re-creation brought about by the glory and the power of God.

In verse 19, he uses a wonderful word for *eager expectation*. It is *apokaradokia*, and it describes the stance of someone who scans the horizon with head thrust forward, eagerly searching the distance for the first signs of the dawn breaking—the daybreak of glory. To Paul, life was not a weary, defeated waiting; it was a throbbing, vivid expectation.

Christians are involved in the human situation. Within, they must battle with their own evil human nature; without, they must live in a world of death and decay. Nonetheless, Christians do not live only in the world; they also live in Christ. They do not see only the world; they look beyond it to God. They do not see only the consequences of human sin; they see the power of God's mercy and love.

Therefore, the keynote of the Christian life is always hope and never despair. Christians wait not for death but for life.

The Interceding Spirit

Romans 8:26–27

The first two verses form one of the most important passages on prayer in the whole New Testament. Paul is saying that, because of our weakness, we do not know what to pray for, but the prayers we ought to offer are offered for us by the Holy Spirit. The New Testament scholar C. H. Dodd defines prayer in this way: 'Prayer is the divine in us appealing to the Divine above us.'

There are two very obvious reasons why we cannot pray as we ought. First, we cannot pray aright because we cannot foresee the future. We cannot see a year or even an hour ahead; and we may well pray, therefore, to be saved from things which are for our good, and we may well pray for things which would be to our ultimate harm. Second, we cannot pray aright because in any given situation we do not know what is best for us. We are often in the position of children who want something which would be bound only to hurt them; and God is often in the position of parents who have to refuse their children's requests or compel them to do something they do not want to do, because the parents know what is good for them far better than the children themselves.

Even the Greeks knew that. Pythagoras forbade his disciples to pray for themselves, because, he said, they could never in their ignorance know what was appropriate and best for them. Xenophon tells us that Socrates taught his disciples simply to pray for good things, and not to attempt to specify them, but to leave God to decide what the good things were. C. H. Dodd puts it in this way: We cannot know our own real need; we cannot with our finite minds grasp God's plan; in the last analysis, all that we can bring to God is an inarticulate sigh which the Spirit will translate to God for us.

As Paul saw it, prayer, like everything else, is of God. He knew that by no possible human effort can we justify ourselves; and he also knew that by no possible effort of the human intelligence can we know what to pray for. In the last analysis, the perfect prayer is simply: 'Father, into your hands I commend my spirit. Not my will, but yours be done.'

June 18

Intermingling All Things for Good

Romans 8:28

Paul says that those who love God, and who are called according to his purpose, know very well that God is 'intermingling all things for good' for them. It is the experience of life for Christians that all things do work together for good. We do not need to be very old to look back and see that things we thought were disasters worked out for our good; things that we thought were disappointments worked out as greater blessings. But we have to note that that experience comes only to those who love God.

The Stoics had a great idea which may well have been in Paul's mind when he wrote this passage. One of their great conceptions was the logos of God. The logos was the mind or the reason of God. The Stoics believed that this world was permeated with that logos. The logos was the reason and the mind of God in the universe, making it an order and not a chaos. The Stoics went further. They believed that the logos not only had an order for the universe, but also a plan and a purpose for the life of every individual. To put it in another way, the Stoics believed that nothing could happen to anyone which did not come from God and which was not part of God's plan for every individual. If people accepted the things that God sent them, they knew peace. If they struggled against them, they were uselessly battering their heads against the unavoidable purpose of God.

Paul has the very same thought. He says that all things work together for good, but only to those who love God. If people love, trust and accept God, if they are convinced that God is the all-wise and all-loving Father, then they can humbly accept all that he sends to them. A person may go to a physician and be prescribed a course of treatment which at the time is unpleasant or even painful; but, through trusting the doctor's wisdom and skill, the thing that is difficult to bear becomes acceptable. It is the same for us if we love God. But if people do not love and trust God, they may well resent what happens to them and may well fight against God's will.

All Is of God

Romans 8:29–30

This is a passage which has been very seriously misused. If we are ever to understand it, we must grasp the basic fact that Paul never meant it to be the expression of theology or philosophy; he meant it to be the almost lyrical expression of Christian experience. If we take it as philosophy and theology and apply the standards of cold logic to it, it must mean that God chose some and did not choose others. But that is not what it means.

Think of the Christian experience. The more Christians think of their experience, the more they become convinced that they had nothing to do with it and everything comes from God. Jesus Christ came into this world; he lived; he went to the cross; he rose again. We did nothing to bring that about; that is God's work. We heard the story of this wondrous love. We did not make the story; we only received the story. Love woke within our hearts; the conviction of sin came, and with it came the experience of forgiveness and of salvation. We did not achieve that; all is of God. That is what Paul is thinking of here.

When the Bible speaks of God knowing someone, it means that he has a purpose and a plan and a task for that person. And when we look back upon our Christian experience, all we can say is: 'I did not do this; I could never have done this; God did everything.' And we know very well that this does not take free will away. God knew Israel, but the day came when Israel refused the destiny it was meant by God to have. God's unseen guidance is in our lives, but to the end of the day we can refuse it and take our own way.

It is the deep experience of Christians that all is of God; that they did nothing and that God did everything. That is what Paul means here. He means that from the beginning of time God marked us out for salvation; that in due time his call came to us; but the pride of human hearts can wreck God's plan, and the disobedience of human will can refuse the call.

June 20

The Love from Which Nothing
Can Separate Us

Romans 8:31–39

This is one of the most lyrical passages Paul ever wrote. God has acquitted us. Who then can condemn us? The answer is that the judge of all is Jesus Christ. He is the one who has the right to condemn—but, far from condemning, he is at God's right hand interceding for us, and therefore we are safe. It may be that, in verse 34, Paul is doing a very wonderful thing. He is saying four things about Jesus. (a) He died. (b) He rose again. (c) He is at the right hand of God. (d) He makes intercession for us there.

Now, the earliest creed of the Church, which is still the essence of all Christian creeds, ran like this: 'He was crucified dead and buried; the third day he rose again from the dead; and sitteth at the right hand of God; from thence he shall come to judge the quick [living] and the dead.' Three items in Paul's statement and in the early creed are the same: that Jesus died, rose again, and is at the right hand of God. But the fourth is different. In the creed, the fourth is that Jesus will come to be the judge of the quick and the dead. In Paul, the fourth is that Jesus is at God's right hand to plead our case. It is as if Paul said: 'You think of Jesus as the judge who is there to condemn; and well he might, for he has won the right. But you are wrong; he is not there to be our prosecuting counsel but to be the advocate to plead our cause.'

With one tremendous leap of thought, Paul has seen Christ not as the judge but as the lover of human souls. Paul goes on with a poet's fervour and a lover's rapture to sing of how nothing can separate us from the love of God in our risen Lord.

Here is a vision to take away all loneliness and all fear. Paul is saying: 'You can think of every terrifying thing that this or any other world can produce. Not one of them is able to separate the Christian from the love of God which is in Jesus Christ, Lord of every terror and Master of every world.' Of what then shall we be afraid?

179

The Essential Change

Romans 12:1–2

Here, we have Paul following the pattern he always followed when he wrote to his friends. He always ends his letters with practical advice. 'Present your bodies to God,' he says. There is no more characteristically Christian demand. Christians believe that their bodies belong to God just as much as their souls, and that they can serve him just as well with their bodies as with their minds or their spirits.

The body is the temple of the Holy Spirit and the instrument through which the Holy Spirit works. After all, the great fact of the incarnation basically means that God did not grudge to take a human body upon himself, to live in it and to work through it. Take the case of a church or a cathedral. It is built for the offering of worship to God. But it has to be designed by the mind of some architect; it has to be built by the hands of craftsmen and of labourers; only then does it become a shrine where people meet to worship. It is a product of the human mind and body and of the human spirit. 'So,' Paul says, 'take your body; take all the tasks that you have to do every day; take the ordinary work of the shop, the office, the factory, the shipyard, the mine; and offer all that as an act of worship to God.'

Here, we have a most significant thing. True worship is the offering to God of one's body and all that one does every day with it. Real worship is not the offering to God of a liturgy, however noble, and a ritual, however magnificent. Real worship is the offering of everyday life to him — not something carried out in a church, but something which sees the whole world as the temple of the living God. This, Paul goes on, demands a radical change. We must be not conformed to the world but transformed from it. This must happen, Paul says, by the renewal of your mind. When Christ comes into our lives, we are new men and women; our minds are different, for the mind of Christ is in us.

When Christ becomes the centre of life, then we can present real worship, which is the offering of every moment and every action to God.

Members of One Body

Romans 12:3–8

One of Paul's favourite thoughts is of the Christian Church as a body. The members of the body neither argue with one another nor envy each other nor dispute about their relative importance. Each part of the body carries out its own function, however prominent or however humbly unseen that function may be. It was Paul's conviction that the Christian Church should be like that. Each member has a task to do; and it is only when all contribute the help of their own tasks that the body of the Church functions as it ought.

Beneath this passage lie very important rules for life.

(1) First of all, it urges us to know ourselves. One of the first basic commandments of the Greek wise men was: 'Know yourself.' We do not get very far in this world until we know what we can and what we cannot do. An honest assessment of our own capabilities, without conceit and without false modesty, is one of the first essentials of a useful life.

(2) Second, it urges us to accept ourselves and to use the gift God has given us. We are not to envy someone else's gift and regret that some other gift has not been given to us. We are to accept ourselves as we are, and use the gift we have. Even if we find that the contribution we have to offer will be unseen, without praise and without prominence, we must make it, certain that it is essential and that without it the world and the Church can never be what they are meant to be.

(3) Third, Paul is really saying that whatever gift any individual has comes from God. He calls gifts charismata. In the New Testament, a charisma is something given by God to people as individuals and which they could never have acquired or attained for themselves.

(4) Fourth, whatever gift we have, we must use it, and the motive of use must be not our personal prestige but the conviction that it is at one and the same time our duty and our privilege to make our own contribution to the common good.

The Christian Life in Everyday Action (1)

Romans 12:9–10

Paul presents his people with twelve concise rules for ordinary, everyday life. Let us look at them one by one.

(1) Love must be completely sincere. There must be no hypocrisy, no play-acting, no ulterior motive. There is such a thing as cupboard love, which gives affection with one eye on the gain which may result. There is such a thing as selfish love, whose aim is to get far more than it is to give. Christian love is cleansed of self; it is a pure outgoing of the heart to others.

(2) We must hate that which is evil and cling to that which is good. It has been said that our one security against sin lies in our being shocked by it. It was Thomas Carlyle who said that what we need is to see the infinite beauty of holiness and the infinite damnability of sin. The words Paul uses are strong. It has been said that no virtue which is not passionate is safe. No one whose life consists of a prudent avoidance of evil and a calculating adherence to that which is good is safe. We must hate evil and love good. With regard to one thing, we must be clear: what many people hate is not evil but the consequences of evil. No one is really good when that goodness simply comes from fear of the consequences of being bad. Not to fear the consequences of dishonour, but to love honour passionately, is the way to real goodness.

(3) We must be affectionate to one another in mutual love. The word Paul uses for *affectionate* is *philostorgos*, and *storge* is the Greek for *family love*. We must love each other, because we are members of one family. We are not strangers to each other within the Christian Church; much less are we isolated units; we are brothers and sisters, because we have the one father, God.

(4) We must give each other priority in honour. More than half the trouble that arises in churches concerns rights and privileges and prestige. Someone has not been given his or her place; someone has been neglected or unthanked. The mark of the truly Christian man or woman has always been humility.

The Christian Life in Everyday Action (2)

Romans 12:11

(5) There is a certain intensity in the Christian life; there is no room for lethargy in it. Christians cannot take things in an easy-going way, for the world is always a battle ground between good and evil; the time is short, and life is a preparation for eternity. Christians may burn out, but they must not rust out.

(6) We must keep our spirit at boiling point. The one whom the risen Christ could not stand was the person who was neither hot nor cold (Revelation 3:15–16). Today, people are apt to look askance upon enthusiasm; the modern battle cry is: 'I couldn't care less.' But Christians are people who are desperately in earnest; they are aflame for Christ.

(7) Paul's seventh rule may be one of two things. The ancient manuscripts vary between two readings. Some read: 'Serve the Lord,' and some read: 'Serve the time,' that is, 'Grasp your opportunities.' The reason for the double reading is this. All the ancient scribes used contractions in their writing. In particular, the more common words were always abbreviated. One of the most common ways of abbreviating was to leave out the vowels—as shorthand does—and to place a stroke along the top of the remaining letters. Now, the word for *Lord* is *kurios* and the word for *time* is *kairos*, and the abbreviation for both of these words is *krs*. In a section so filled with practical advice, it is more likely that Paul was saying to his people: 'Seize your opportunities as they come.' Life presents us with all kinds of opportunities—the opportunity to learn something new or to cut out something wrong; the opportunity to speak a word of encouragement or of warning; the opportunity to help or to comfort.

One of the tragedies of life is that we so often fail to grasp these opportunities when they come. There are three things which do not come back—the spent arrow, the spoken word and the lost opportunity.

The Christian Life in Everyday Action (3)

Romans 12:12–13

(8) Christians must be essentially optimists. Just because God is God, Christians are always certain that 'the best is yet to be'. Just because they know of the grace that is sufficient for all things and the strength that is made perfect in weakness, Christians know that no task is too much for them. There are no hopeless situations in life; there are only men and women who have grown hopeless about them. There can never be any such thing as a hopeless Christian.

(9) We are to meet tribulation with triumphant courage. Someone once said to someone who bore suffering bravely: 'Suffering colours all life, doesn't it?' 'Yes,' came the reply, 'it does, but I propose to choose the colour.' When Nebuchadnezzar cast Shadrach, Meshach and Abednego into the fiery furnace, he was amazed that they came to no harm. He asked if three men had not been cast into the flames. He was told it was so. He said: 'But I see four men unbound, walking in the middle of the fire, and they are not hurt; and the fourth has the appearance of a god' (Daniel 3:25). We can meet anything when we meet it with Christ.

(10) We are to persevere in prayer. Is it not the case that there are times in life when we let day add itself to day and week to week, and we never speak to God? When we cease to pray, we rob ourselves of the strength of Almighty God. We should not be surprised when life collapses if we insist on living it alone.

(11) We are to share with those in need. In a world intent on getting, Christians are intent on giving, because they know that 'what we keep we lose, and what we give we have'.

(12) Christians are to offer hospitality. Over and over again, the New Testament insists on this duty of the open door (Hebrews 13:2; 1 Timothy 3:2; Titus 1:8; 1 Peter 4:9). The sixteenth-century Bible translator William Tyndale used a magnificent word when he translated that the Christian should have a *harborous* disposition. A home can never be happy when it is selfish. Christianity is the religion of the open hand, the open heart and the open door.

Christians and Their Neighbours (1)

Romans 12:14–15

Paul offers a series of rules and principles which should guide our relationships with our neighbours.

(1) Christians must meet persecution with a prayer for those who persecute them. Long ago, Plato had said that the good man will choose to suffer evil rather than to do evil; and it is always evil to hate. When Christians are hurt, and insulted, and badly treated, they have the example of their Master before them, for he, upon his cross, prayed for forgiveness for those who were killing him.

(2) We are to rejoice with those who rejoice, and to weep with those who weep. There are few bonds like that of a common sorrow. A writer tells the story of a lady in Charleston who met the servant of a neighbour. 'I'm sorry to hear of your Aunt Lucy's death,' she said. 'You must miss her greatly. You were such friends.' 'Yes,' said the servant, 'I'm sorry she died. But we weren't friends.' 'Why,' said the lady, 'I thought you were. I've seen you laughing and talking together lots of times.' 'Yes. That's so,' came the reply. 'We've laughed together, and we've talked together, but we were just acquaintances. You see, Miss Ruth, we never shed any tears. Folks have got to cry together before they are friends.'

The bond of tears is the strongest of all. And yet it is much easier to weep with those who weep than it is to rejoice with those who rejoice. Long ago, in the fourth century, the Church father John Chrysostom wrote on this passage: 'It requires more of a high Christian temper to rejoice with them that do rejoice than to weep with them that weep. For this nature itself fulfils perfectly; and there is none so hard-hearted as not to weep over him that is in calamity; but the other requires a very noble soul, so as not only to keep from envying, but even to feel pleasure with the person who is in esteem.'

It is, indeed, more difficult to congratulate others on their success, especially if their success involves disappointment to us, than it is to sympathize with their sorrow and their loss. It is only when self is dead that we can take as much joy in the success of others as in our own.

Christians and Their Neighbours (2)

Romans 12:16–21

(3) We are to live in harmony with one another. When strife enters into any Christian society, the hope of doing any good work is gone.

(4) We are to avoid all pride and snobbishness. We always have to remember that the standards by which the world judges people are not necessarily the standards by which God judges them. Saintliness has nothing to do with rank, or wealth, or birth, for with God there is no respect for individual status.

(5) We are to make our conduct fair for all to see. So-called Christianity can be presented in the hardest and most unlovely way; but real Christianity is something which is fair for all to see.

(6) We are to live at peace with all. But Paul adds two qualifications.

(a) He says: if it is possible. There may come a time when the claims of courtesy have to submit to the claims of principle. Christianity is not an easy-going tolerance which will accept anything and shut its eyes to everything. There may come a time when some battle has to be fought — and, when it does, Christians will not shirk it.

(b) He says: as far as you can. Paul knew very well that it is easier for some to live at peace than for others. He knew that one person can be compelled to control as much temper in an hour as someone else in a whole lifetime. We would do well to remember that goodness is a great deal easier for some than for others; that will keep us both from criticism and from discouragement.

(7) We are to keep ourselves from all thought of taking revenge. 'If we are kind to our enemies,' says Paul, 'it will heap coals of fire on their heads.' That means not that it will store up further punishment for them but that it will move them to burning shame. To stoop to vengeance is to be ourselves conquered by evil.

Evil can never be conquered by evil. If hatred is met with more hatred, it is only increased; but, if it is met with love, an antidote for the poison is found. The only real way to destroy an enemy is to make that person a friend.

Respect for Scruples

Romans 14:1

Paul describes the ultra-scrupulous person as weak in the faith. What does he mean by that? Such people are weak in the faith for two reasons.

(1) They have not yet discovered the meaning of Christian freedom; they are at heart still legalists and see Christianity as consisting of rules and regulations.

(2) They have not yet freed themselves from a belief in the efficacy of works. In their hearts, they believe that they can gain God's favour by doing certain things and abstaining from others. Basically, they are still trying to earn a right relationship with God, and have not yet accepted the way of grace, still thinking more of what they can do for God than of what God has done for them.

Paul's sympathies are all with the broader point of view; but, at the same time, he says that any of these weaker Christians who come into the Church must be received sympathetically. When we are confronted with someone who holds the narrower view, there are three attitudes we must avoid.

(1) We must avoid irritation. An impatient annoyance with such a person gets us nowhere. However much we may disagree, we must try to see the other person's point of view and to understand it.

(2) We must avoid ridicule. People cannot remain unhurt when something that is important to them is laughed at. It is no small sin to laugh at another person's beliefs. They may seem prejudices rather than beliefs; but no one has a right to laugh at what others hold sacred. In any event, laughter will never woo other people to a wider view; it will only make them withdraw still more determinedly into their rigidity.

(3) We must avoid contempt. It is very wrong to regard narrower people as old-fashioned fools whose views may be treated with contempt. People's views are their own and must be treated with respect. Of all attitudes towards other people, the most un-Christian is contempt.

The Impossibility of Isolation

Romans 14:7–9

Paul lays down the great fact that it is impossible in the nature of things to live an isolated life. There is no such thing in this world as a completely detached individual. We can never disentangle ourselves either from other people or from God.

In three directions as individuals, we cannot disentangle ourselves from other people.

(1) We cannot isolate ourselves from the past. No one is self-made. 'I am a part', said Ulysses, 'of all that I have met.' We are receivers of a tradition. Each one of us is a mixture of all that our ancestors made us. True, we contribute something to that blend; but we do not start from nothing. For good or for ill, we start with what all the past has made us. The unseen cloud of witnesses does not only surround us; it dwells within us.

(2) We cannot isolate ourselves from the present. We live in a civilization in which people are becoming more and more closely bound together every day. Nothing we do affects only ourselves. We have the terrible power of making others happy or sad by our conduct; we have the still more terrible power of making others good or bad. Each one of us has an influence which makes it easier for others to take the high way or the low way. All our actions have consequences which affect others more or less closely.

(3) We cannot isolate ourselves from the future. As we receive life, so we hand life on. We hand on to our children a heritage of physical life and of spiritual character. We are not self-contained individual units; we are links in a chain. It is our terrible responsibility that we leave something of ourselves in the world by leaving something of ourselves in others. Sin would be a far less terrible thing if it affected only the person involved in it. The terror of every sin is that it starts a new train of evil in the world.

No human being can follow a policy of isolation. We are bound to one another and to Christ by ties that neither time nor eternity can break.

The Inclusive Church

Romans 15:7–13

Paul makes one last appeal that all people within the Church should be bound into one. The great words of the Christian faith flash out one after another.

(1) There is hope. It has long ago been said that there are no hopeless situations; there are only men and women who have grown hopeless about them. There is something in Christian hope that not all the shadows can quench—and that something is the conviction that God is alive. No individual is hopeless as long as there is the grace of Jesus Christ; and no situation is hopeless as long as there is the power of God.

(2) There is joy. There is all the difference in this world between pleasure and joy. You have longing for something, that is the pain; you get it, the longing is satisfied and there is a pause in the pain; you enjoy it and the moment is gone; and the pain comes back. Indeed, that is the way pleasure works. But Christian joy is not dependent on things outside us; its source is in our consciousness of the presence of the living Lord, the certainty that nothing can separate us from the love of God in him.

(3) There is peace. One would almost say that, today, serenity is a lost possession. Many are haunted by the chances and the changes of life. It is hard not to worry, for human beings are characteristically creatures who look forward to uncertainty and fear. The only end to that worry is the utter conviction that, whatever happens, God's hand will never cause his children a needless tear. Things will happen that we cannot understand; but, if we are sure enough of God's love, we can accept with serenity even those things which wound the heart and baffle the mind.

(4) There is power. Here is the supreme human need. It is not that we do not know the right thing; it is not that we do not recognize the fine thing; the trouble is doing it. That we can never do alone. Only when the surge of Christ's power fills our weakness can we have control of life as we ought. By ourselves, we can do nothing; but, with God, all things are possible.

More Advice from Paul

The Wisdom Which Is from God

1 Corinthians 2:6–9

In the early Church, there was a quite clear distinction between two kinds of instruction.

(1) There was what was called *kerygma*. *Kerygma* means *a herald's announcement from a king*, and this was the plain announcement of the basic facts of Christianity, the announcement of the facts of the life, death and resurrection of Jesus and his coming again.

(2) There was what was called *didache*. *Didache* means *teaching*, and this was the explanation of the meaning of the facts which had already been announced. Obviously, it is a second stage for those who have already received *kerygma*.

That is what Paul is getting at here. So far, he has been talking about Jesus Christ and about Christ crucified. That was the basic announcement of Christianity; but, he goes on to say, we do not stop there. Christian instruction goes on to teach not only the facts but also the meaning of the facts. Paul says that this is done among those who are *teleioi*. *Teleios* has a physical sense; it describes an animal or a person who has reached the height of physical development. It also has a mental sense. Pythagoras divided his disciples into those who were babes and those who were *teleioi*. That is to say, it describes a person who is a mature student. That is the sense in which Paul uses it here. He says: 'Out in the streets, and to those who have just newly come into the Church, we talk about the basic elements of Christianity; but, when people are a little more mature, we give them deeper teaching about what these basic facts mean.'

It is not that Paul is hinting at a kind of caste or class distinction between Christians; it is a difference of the stages at which they are. The tragedy so often is that people are content to remain at the elementary stage when they should be going on strenuously to think things out for themselves.

Only students who work can make themselves fit to receive the real riches of the mind of a great teacher. It is the same with us and God. The more we strive to understand, the more God can tell us; and there is no limit to this process, because the riches of God are infinite and cannot be measured.

Spiritual Things to Those Who Are Spiritual

1 Corinthians 2:10–16

There are certain very basic things in this passage.

(1) Paul lays down that the only person who can tell us about God is the Spirit of God. He uses a human analogy. There are feelings which are so personal, things which are so private, experiences which are so intimate that no one knows them except an individual's own spirit. Paul argues that the same is true of God. There are deep and intimate things in him which only his Spirit knows; and that Spirit is the only person who can lead us into really intimate knowledge of God.

(2) Even then, it is not everyone who can understand these things. Paul distinguishes two kinds of people.

(a) There are those who are *pneumatikoi*. *Pneuma* is the word for *spirit*, and the person who is *pneumatikos* is someone who is sensitive to the Spirit and whose life is guided by the Spirit.

(b) There is the person who is *psuchikos*. *Psuche* in Greek is the *principle of physical life*. Everything which is alive has *psuche*; a dog, a cat, any animal has *psuche*, but it has not got *pneuma*. *Psuche* is that physical life which human beings share with every living thing; but *pneuma* is that which makes human beings different from the rest of creation and kin to God.

So, in verse 14, Paul speaks of the person who is *psuchikos*. Such people live their lives as if there was nothing beyond physical life and there were no needs other than material needs; their values are all physical and material. People like that cannot understand spiritual things. Anyone who thinks that nothing is more important than the satisfaction of the sex urge cannot understand the meaning of chastity; anyone who ranks the amassing of material things as the supreme end of life cannot understand generosity; and anyone who never has a thought beyond this world cannot understand the things of God. To these people, the things of God appear mere foolishness.

No one needs to be like this; but, if people stifle 'the immortal longings' that are in the soul, they may make themselves like this so that the Spirit of God will speak and they will not hear.

The Supreme Importance of God

1 Corinthians 3:1–9

Paul has just been talking about the difference between the person who is spiritual (*pneumatikos*), and who therefore can understand spiritual truths, and the person who is *psuchikos*, whose interests and aims do not go beyond physical life and who is therefore unable to grasp spiritual truth. He now accuses the Corinthians of being still at the physical stage. But he uses two new words to describe them. In verse 1, he calls them *sarkinoi*. This word comes from *sarx*, which means *flesh*—a word that is so common in Paul. Now, all Greek adjectives ending in *-inos* mean *made of something or other*. So, Paul begins by saying that the Corinthians are made of flesh. That was not in itself a rebuke; human beings by their very nature are made of flesh, but they must not stay that way. The trouble was that the Corinthians were not only *sarkinoi*, they were *sarkikoi*, which means not only made of flesh but dominated by the flesh.

To Paul, the flesh is much more than merely a physical thing. It means human nature apart from God, that part of men and women, both mental and physical, which provides a point of entry for sin. So, the fault that Paul finds with the Corinthians is not that they are made of flesh—all human beings are—but that they have allowed this lower side of their nature to dominate all their outlook and all their actions.

What is it about their life and conduct that makes Paul level such a rebuke at them? It is their partisan attitude, their strife and their factions. This is extremely significant because it means that you can tell what a person's relationship with God is by looking at the way that person relates to others. If someone is at variance with others and is a quarrelsome, argumentative, troublemaking type, that person may be a diligent church-attender, even a church office-bearer, but not a child of God. But if someone is at one with others, and has relationships that are marked by love and unity and concord, then that person is on the way to being one of God's children.

The Foundation and the Builders

1 Corinthians 3:10–15

Paul was of necessity a foundation-layer and was forever on the move. Wherever he went, he laid the same foundation. That was the proclamation of the facts about and the offer of Jesus Christ. It was his tremendous function to introduce men and women to Jesus Christ because it is in him, and in him alone, that they can find three things.

(1) They find forgiveness for past sins. They find themselves in a new relationship to God and suddenly discover that they are his friends and not his enemies. They discover that God is like Jesus; where once they saw hatred they now see love, and where once they saw infinite remoteness they now see tender intimacy.

(2) They find strength for the present. Through the presence and help of Jesus, they find courage to cope with life, for they no longer feel like isolated units fighting a lonely battle with an adverse universe. They now enjoy lives in which nothing can separate them from the love of God in Christ Jesus their Lord. They walk life's ways and fight its battles with Christ.

(3) They find hope for the future. They no longer live in a world in which they are afraid to look forward but in one where God is in control and working all things together for good. They live in a world where death is no longer the end, but only the prelude to greater glory. Without the foundation of Christ, we can have none of these things. But, on this foundation of Christ, others built. Paul is thinking here not of the building up of wrong things, but of the building up of inadequate things. It is possible to present to others a version of Christianity which is weak and watered down—a one-sided view which has stressed some things too much and others too little, and in which things have got out of balance; a warped perspective in which even the greatest matters have emerged distorted.

The day that Paul refers to is the day when Christ will come again. Then will come the final test. The wrong and the inadequate will be swept away. But, in the mercy of God, even the inadequate builder will be saved, because at least that builder tried to do something for Christ.

Wisdom and Foolishness

1 Corinthians 3:16–22

To Paul, the Church was the very temple of God because it was the society in which the Spirit of God dwelt. But, if people introduce dissension and division into the fellowship of the Church, they destroy the temple of God.

Paul goes on once again to pin down the root cause of this dissension and consequent destruction of the Church. It is the worship of intellectual, worldly wisdom. It is by this very worldly wisdom that the Corinthians assess the worth of different teachers and leaders. It is this pride in the human mind which makes them evaluate and criticize the way in which the message is delivered, the correctness of the rhetoric, the weight of the oratory and the subtleties of the arguments, rather than think only of the content of the message itself.

The trouble about this intellectual pride is that it is always two things.

(1) It is always argumentative. It cannot keep silent and admire; it must talk and criticize. It cannot bear to have its opinions contradicted; it must prove that it and it alone is right. It is never humble enough to learn; it must always be laying down the law.

(2) Intellectual pride is characteristically exclusive. Its tendency is to look down on others rather than to sit down beside them. Its outlook is that all who do not agree with it are wrong. It tends to cut people off from one another rather than unite them.

Paul urges anyone who would be wise to become a fool. This is simply a vivid way of urging people to be humble enough to learn. No one can teach those who think that they know it all already. Plato said: 'He is the wisest man who knows himself to be very ill-equipped for the study of wisdom.'

The only way to become wise is to realize that we are fools; the only way to knowledge is to confess our ignorance.

The Three Judgments

1 Corinthians 4:1–5

Paul speaks of three judgments that everyone must face.

(1) We must face the judgment of others. In this case, Paul says that that is nothing to him. But there is a sense in which we cannot disregard the judgment of those around us. The odd thing is that, in spite of its occasional radical mistakes, the judgment of other people is often right. That is due to the fact that we all instinctively admire the basic qualities of honour, honesty, reliability, generosity, sacrifice and love. Antisthenes, the Cynic philosopher, used to say: 'There are only two people who can tell you the truth about yourself—an enemy who has lost his temper and a friend who loves you dearly.' It is quite true that we should never let the judgment of others deflect us from what we believe to be right; but it is also true that the judgment of others is often more accurate than we would like to think.

(2) We must face the judgment we make of ourselves. Once again, Paul disregards that. He knew very well that our judgment of ourselves can be clouded by self-satisfaction, by pride and by conceit. But, in a very real sense, we must all face our own judgment. One of the basic Greek ethical laws was: 'Man, know thyself.' The Cynics insisted that one of the first characteristics of a real man was 'the ability to get on with himself'. None of us can escape the self; and, if we lose our self-respect, life becomes an intolerable thing.

(3) We must face the judgment of God. In the last analysis, this is the only real judgment. God's is the final judgment for two reasons.

(a) Only God knows all the circumstances. He knows the struggles we have had; he knows the secrets that we can tell to no one; he knows what we might have sunk to and he also knows what we might have climbed to.

(b) Only God knows all the motives. 'Man sees the deed but God sees the intention.' Many a deed that looks noble may have been done from the most selfish and ignoble motives; and many a deed which appears despicable may have been done from the highest motives. Only he who made the human heart knows it and can judge it.

The Hymn of Love

1 Corinthians 13

Paul begins by declaring that we may possess any spiritual gift, but if it is unaccompanied by love it is useless.

(1) Some may have the gift of tongues. A characteristic of Gentile worship was the clanging of cymbals and the blaring of trumpets. Even the coveted gift of tongues was no better than the uproar of Gentile worship if love was absent.

(2) Some may have the gift of prophecy. Prophecy corresponds most closely to preaching. There are preachers whose one aim is to save souls and who woo people with the accents of love. On the other hand, there are preachers who dangle their hearers over the flames of hell and give the impression that they would rejoice in their damnation as much as in their salvation. The preaching which is all threat and no love may terrify, but it will not save.

(3) Some may have the gift of intellectual knowledge. People who have great knowledge run the grave danger of developing the spirit of contempt. Only a knowledge whose cold detachment has been set alight by the fire of love can really save men and women.

(4) Some may have a passionate faith. There was a man who visited his doctor and was informed that his heart was tired and he must rest. He telephoned his employer, a notable Christian figure, with the news, only to receive the answer: 'I have an inward strength which enables me to carry on.' These were the words of faith, but a faith which knew no love and therefore gave pain and hurt.

(5) Some may practise charity; they may distribute their goods to the poor. There is nothing more humiliating than this so-called charity without love. To give as a grim duty is not charity at all—it is pride; and pride is always cruel, for it knows no love.

(6) Some may give their bodies to be burned. Paul may have been thinking of the kind of Christian who actually courted persecution. If the motive which makes people give their lives for Christ is pride and exhibitionism, then even martyrdom becomes valueless.

The Nature of Christian Love (1)

1 Corinthians 13:4

Paul lists fifteen characteristics of Christian love.

Love is patient. The Greek word describes people who are slow to anger, and it is used of God himself in his relationship with men and women. In our dealings with others, however difficult and however unkind and hurting they are, we must exercise the same patience as God exercises with us.

Love is kind. So much Christianity is good but unkind. There was no one more religious than Philip II of Spain, and yet he founded the Spanish Inquisition and thought he was serving God by massacring those who thought differently from him. Quite apart from that persecuting spirit, there is in so many good people an attitude of criticism.

Love knows no envy. There are two kinds of envy. The one covets the possessions of other people; and such envy is very difficult to avoid, because it is a very human failing. The other is worse—it grudges the very fact that others should have what it has not; it does not so much want things for itself as wish that others had not got them. Meanness of soul can sink no further than that.

Love is not boastful. There is a self-effacing quality in love. Some people confer their love with the idea that they are conferring a favour. But people who really love cannot get over the wonder that they are loved.

Love is not inflated with its own importance. Really great people never think of their own importance. William Carey, who began life mending shoes as a cobbler, was one of the greatest missionaries and certainly one of the greatest linguists the world has ever seen. He translated some parts of the Bible into no fewer than thirty-four Indian languages. When he came to India, he was regarded with dislike and contempt. At a dinner party, a snob, with the idea of humiliating him, said in a tone that everyone could hear: 'I suppose, Mr Carey, you once worked as a shoemaker.' 'No, your lordship,' answered Carey, 'not a shoemaker, only a cobbler.' No one likes the 'important' person. It can be a sorry sight to see, as Shakespeare had it, 'man dressed in a little brief authority'.

The Nature of Christian Love (2)

1 Corinthians 13:5–6

Love does not behave gracelessly. It is a significant fact that in Greek the words for *grace* and for *charm* are the same. There is a graciousness in Christian love which never forgets that courtesy and tact and politeness are lovely things.

Love does not insist upon its rights. In the last analysis, there are in this world only two kinds of people—those who always insist upon their privileges and those who always remember their responsibilities; those who are always thinking of what life owes them and those who never forget what they owe to life. It would be the key to almost all the problems which surround us today if people would think less of their rights and more of their duties.

Love never flies into a temper. The real meaning of this is that Christian love never becomes exasperated with people. Exasperation is always a sign of defeat. When we lose our tempers, we lose everything. In his famous poem 'If', Rudyard Kipling said that it was the test of a man if he could keep his head when everyone else was losing his and blaming it on him, and if when he was hated he did not give way to hating.

Love does not store up the memory of any wrong it has received. The word translated as *store up* (*logizesthai*) is an accountant's word. It is the word used for entering up an item in a ledger so that it will not be forgotten. That is precisely what so many people do. One of the great arts in life is to learn what to forget.

Love finds no pleasure in evildoing. It is not so much delight in doing the wrong thing that is meant, as the malicious pleasure which comes to most of us when we hear something derogatory about someone else. Christian love has none of that human malice which finds pleasure in hearing unpleasant things about other people.

Love rejoices with the truth. There are times when we definitely do not want the truth to prevail, and still more times when it is the last thing we wish to hear. Christian love has no wish to conceal the truth; it has nothing to hide and so is glad when the truth wins through.

The Nature of Christian Love (3)

1 Corinthians 13:7

Love can endure anything. It is just possible that this may mean 'love can cover anything', in the sense that it will never drag into the light of day the faults and mistakes of others. It would far rather set about quietly mending things than publicly displaying and rebuking them. More likely, it means that love can bear any insult, any injury, any disappointment. It describes the kind of love that was in the heart of Jesus himself.

Love is completely trusting. It is often true that we make people what we believe them to be. If we show that we do not trust people, we may make them untrustworthy. If we show people that we trust them absolutely, we may make them trustworthy. Love can make honourable even the dishonourable by believing the best.

Love never ceases to hope. Jesus believed that no one is beyond hope. The Methodist Adam Clarke was one of the great theologians, but at school he was very slow to learn. One day, a distinguished visitor paid a visit to the school, and the teacher singled out Clarke and said: 'That is the stupidest boy in the school.' Before he left the school, the visitor came to the boy and said kindly: 'Never mind, my boy, you may be a great scholar some day. Don't be discouraged but try hard, and keep on trying.' The teacher had no hope; but the visitor was hopeful, and—who knows?—it may well have been that word of hope which made Adam Clarke what he one day became.

Love bears everything with triumphant fortitude. The verb used here is generally translated as *to bear* or *to endure*; but what it really describes is not the spirit which can passively bear things, but the spirit which, in bearing them, can conquer and change their very nature. The Scottish minister and hymn writer George Matheson, who lost his sight and who was disappointed in love, wrote in one of his prayers that he might accept God's will 'not with dumb resignation but with holy joy; not only with the absence of murmur but with a song of praise'. Love can bear things not merely with passive resignation, but with triumphant fortitude, because it knows that 'a father's hand will never cause his child a needless tear'.

The Supremacy of Love

1 Corinthians 13:8–13

In verses 8–13, Paul has three final things to say of this Christian love.

(1) He stresses its absolute permanency. When all the things in which people take pride and delight have passed away, love will still stand. In one of the most wonderfully lyrical verses of Scripture, the Song of Solomon (8:7) sings: 'Many waters cannot quench love, neither can floods drown it.' The one unconquerable thing is love. That is one of the great reasons for believing in immortality. When love is entered into, there comes into life a relationship against which the assaults of time are helpless and which transcends death.

(2) He stresses its absolute completeness. As things are, what we see are reflections in a mirror. That image presented in this statement would be even more vivid for the Corinthians than it is for us. Corinth was famous for its manufacture of mirrors. But the modern mirror as we know it, with its perfect reflection, did not emerge until the thirteenth century. The Corinthian mirror was made of highly polished metal and, even at its best, gave but an imperfect reflection.

In this life, Paul feels that we see only the reflections of God and are left with much that is mystery and riddle. We see that reflection in God's world, for the work of anyone's hands tells us something about the one who has done that work. We see it in the gospel, and we see it in Jesus Christ. Even if in Christ we have the perfect revelation, our searching and inquiring minds can grasp it only in part, for the finite can never grasp the infinite. Our knowledge is still like the knowledge of a child. But the way of love will lead us in the end to a day when the veil is drawn aside and we see face to face and know even as we are known. We cannot ever reach that day without love, because God is love, and only those who love can see him.

(3) He stresses its absolute supremacy. Great as faith and hope are, love is still greater. Faith without love is cold, and hope without love is grim. Love is the fire which gives the spark to faith, and it is the light which turns hope into certainty.

Jesus' Resurrection and Ours

1 Corinthians 15:1–11

The Greeks had an instinctive fear of death. The great dramatist Euripides wrote: 'Yet mortals, burdened with countless ills, still love life. They long for each coming day, glad to bear the thing they know, rather than face death the unknown' (Fragment 813). On the whole, the Greeks, and that part of the world influenced by Greek thought, did believe in the immortality of the soul. But, for them, the immortality of the soul involved the complete dissolution of the body. They had a proverb: 'The body is a tomb.' 'I am a poor soul,' said one of them, 'shackled to a corpse.' For the Greeks, immortality lay precisely in getting rid of the body. For them, the resurrection of the body was unthinkable. Personal immortality did not really exist, because that which gave life was absorbed again in God, the source of all life.

Paul's view was quite different. If we begin with one immense fact, the rest will become clear. The Christian belief is that, after death, individuality will survive—that you will still be you and I will still be me. Beside that, we have to set another immense fact. To the Greeks, the body could not be consecrated. It was matter, the source of all evil, the prison house of the soul. But, to Christians, the body is not evil. Jesus, the Son of God, has taken this human body upon him, and therefore it is not contemptible because it has been inhabited by God. To Christians, therefore, the life to come involves the total person, body and soul.

It is almost impossible to conceive of personality without a body, because it is through the body that the personality expresses itself. What Paul is arguing for is that, after death, the individual remains. You will still be yourself; I will survive as a person. That is what Paul means by the resurrection of the body. Everything of the body and of the soul that is necessary to make a human being a person will survive; but, at the same time, all things will be new, and both body and spirit will be very different from earthly things, for they will both be divine.

If Christ Is Not Raised

1 Corinthians 15:12–34

Why did Paul regard a belief in the resurrection of Jesus as so essential? What great values and great truths does it conserve? It proves four great facts, which can make all the difference to our view of life here and hereafter.

(1) The resurrection proves that truth is stronger than falsehood. According to the Fourth Gospel, Jesus said to his enemies: 'Now you are trying to kill me, a man who has told you the truth' (John 8:40). Jesus came with the true idea of God and of goodness; his enemies engineered his death because they did not want their own false view destroyed. If they had succeeded in finally obliterating him, falsehood would have been stronger than truth. The resurrection is the final guarantee of the indestructibility of the truth.

(2) The resurrection proves that good is stronger than evil. Again, to quote the Fourth Gospel, Jesus is represented as saying to his enemies: 'You are from your father the devil' (John 8:44). The forces of evil crucified Jesus; and, if there had been no resurrection, these forces would have been triumphant.

(3) The resurrection proves that love is stronger than hatred. Jesus was the love of God incarnate. On the other hand, the attitude of those who brought about his crucifixion was an almost virulent hatred. If there had been no resurrection, it would have meant that human hatred in the end conquered the love of God. The resurrection is the triumph of love over all that hatred could do.

(4) The resurrection proves that life is stronger than death. If Jesus had died never to rise again, it would have proved that death could take the loveliest and best life that ever lived and finally break it. The resurrection is the final proof that life is stronger than death.

Paul insisted that, if the resurrection of Jesus was not a fact, the whole Christian message was based on a lie, that many thousands had died trusting in a delusion, and that without it the greatest values in life have no guarantee. 'Take away the resurrection,' he said, 'and you destroy both the foundation and the fabric of the Christian faith.'

The Physical and the Spiritual

1 Corinthians 15:35–49

In this section, Paul is dealing with people who say: 'Granted that there is a resurrection of the body, with what kind of body do people rise again?' His answer has three basic principles in it.

(1) He takes the analogy of a seed. The seed is put in the ground and dies, but in due course it rises again; and does so with a very different kind of body from that with which it was sown. Paul is showing that, at one and the same time, there can be dissolution, difference and yet continuity. The seed is dissolved; when it rises again, there is a vast difference in its body; and yet, in spite of the dissolution and the difference, it is the same seed. So, our earthly bodies will dissolve; they will rise again in very different form—but it is the same person who rises.

(2) In the world, even as we know it, there is not one kind of body; each separate part of creation has its own. God gives to each created thing a body suitable for its part in creation. If that is so, it is only reasonable to expect that he will give us a body fitted for the resurrection life.

(3) In life, there is a development. Adam, the first man, was made from the dust of the earth (Genesis 2:7). But Jesus is far more than a man made from the dust of the earth. He is the incarnation of the very Spirit of God. Now, under the old way of life, we were one with Adam, sharing his sin, inheriting his death and having his body; but, under the new way of life, we are one with Christ and we shall therefore share his life and his being.

In the life to come, we will be such that the Spirit can truly fill us, as can never happen here, and the Spirit can truly use us, as is never possible now. Then we will be able to present the perfect worship, the perfect service, the perfect love that now can only be a vision and a dream.

July 15

The Conquest of Death

1 Corinthians 15:50–58

Paul is dealing with things which defy language and baffle expression. We must read this as we would read great poetry, rather than as we would dissect a scientific treatise. The argument follows a series of steps until it reaches its climax.

Paul insists that, as we are, we are not fit to inherit the kingdom of God. We may be well enough equipped to get on with the life of this world; but, for the life of the world to come, we will not do. A person may be able to run fast enough to catch the morning train; but the requirement would be very different for the same person to be able to qualify and run in the Olympic Games. We always need to be changed in order to enter into a higher grade of life; and Paul insists that, before we can enter the kingdom of God, we must be changed.

Paul goes on triumphantly to declare that no one need fear that change. The fear of death has always haunted people. It haunted Dr Johnson, one of the greatest and best men who ever lived. Once, his great friend James Boswell said to him that there had been times when he had not feared death. Johnson answered that 'he never had a moment in which death was not terrible to him'. He declared that the fear of death was so natural to human beings that all life was one long effort not to think about it.

Where does the fear of death come from? Partly, it comes from fear of the unknown. But still more, it comes from the sense of sin. If we felt that we could meet God easily, then to die would be only, as Peter Pan said, a great adventure.

Finally, at the end of the chapter, Paul does what he always does. Suddenly the theology becomes a challenge; suddenly the speculations become intensely practical; suddenly the sweep of the mind becomes the demand for action. He ends by saying: 'If you have all that glory to look forward to, then keep yourself unwavering in God's faith and service, for if you do, all your effort will not be in vain.' The Christian life may be difficult, but the goal is infinitely worth the struggle.

July 16

Tribulation and Triumph

2 Corinthians 4:7–15

We talk a great deal about human power and about the vast forces which we now control. But the real characteristic of human beings is not their power but their weakness.

Life has surrounded us with weakness, although Christ has surrounded us with glory, so that we may remember that the weakness is ours and the glory is God's, and recognize our own utter dependence on him. Paul goes on to describe this Christian life, in which our weakness is intermingled with God's glory, in a series of paradoxes.

(1) We are pressurized at every point but not hemmed in. There are all kinds of pressures on us, but we are never in so tight a corner that there is no way out. It is characteristic of Christians that, even if they are physically confined in some difficult environment or some restricting situation, there is always an escape route for the spirit to the spaciousness of God.

(2) We are persecuted by other people but never abandoned by God. One of the most notable things about the martyrs is that it was in their most difficult times that they had their sweetest times with Christ. As the psalmist wrote, 'If my father and mother forsake me, the Lord will take me up' (Psalm 27:10). Nothing can alter the loyalty of God.

(3) We are at our wits' end but never at our hope's end. There are times when Christians do not know what should be done, but even then they never doubt that something can be done. There are times when they cannot see clearly where life is going, but they never doubt that it is going somewhere. There are times when, as Christians, we have to learn the hardest lesson of all, the very lesson which Jesus himself had to learn in Gethsemane—how to accept what we cannot understand.

(4) We are knocked down but not knocked out. The supreme characteristic of Christians is not that they do not fall, but that every time they fall they rise again. It is not that they are never beaten, but they are never ultimately defeated. They may lose a battle, but they know that in the end they can never lose the campaign.

Joy and Judgment to Come

2 Corinthians 5:1–10

There is a very significant progression of thought in this passage, a progression which gives us the very essence of the thought of Paul.

(1) To him, it will be a day of joy when he is done with this human body. He regards it as merely a tent, a temporary dwelling place, in which we stay until the day comes when it is dissolved and we enter into the real dwelling place of our souls.

He is not looking for a Nirvana with the peace of extinction; he is not looking for absorption in the divine; he is not looking for the freedom of a disembodied spirit; he is waiting for the day when God will give him a new body, a spiritual body, in which he will still be able, even in the heavenly places, to serve and to adore God.

(2) For all his yearning for the life to come, Paul does not despise this life. He is, he says, in good heart. The reason is that, even here and now, we possess the Holy Spirit of God, and the Holy Spirit is the first instalment of the life to come. It is Paul's conviction that already Christians can enjoy the foretaste of the life everlasting. It is given to Christians to be citizens of two worlds; and the result is not that they despise this world, but that they find it wrapped round with a shining glory which is the reflection of the greater glory to come.

(3) Then comes the note of sternness. Even when Paul was thinking of the life to come, he never forgot that we are on the way not only to glory, but also to judgment. 'We must all appear before the judgment seat of Christ.' When we remember that, life becomes a tremendous and a thrilling prospect, for in it we are making or marring a destiny, winning or losing a crown. Time becomes the testing ground of eternity.

The New Creation

2 Corinthians 5:11–19

Paul is trying to persuade the Corinthians of his own sincerity. He has no doubt whatever that in the sight of God his hands are clean and his motives pure; but his enemies have cast suspicion on them, and he wishes to demonstrate his sincerity to his Corinthian friends. This is not from any selfish desire to vindicate himself. It is from the knowledge that, if his sincerity is questioned, the impact of his message will be damaged. A message will always be heard in the context of an individual's character. That is why the preacher and the teacher must be beyond suspicion. We have to avoid not only evil but the very appearance of evil, so that there can be nothing to make others think less not of us but of the message which we bring.

In verse 13, Paul insists that behind all his conduct there has been only one motive—to serve God and to help the Corinthians. More than once, Paul was thought to be out of his mind (Acts 26:24). He was suffering the same misunderstanding as Jesus suffered (Mark 3:21). The real enthusiast always runs the risk of seeming crazy to people who are indifferent.

Rudyard Kipling tells how, on a world tour, General William Booth of the Salvation Army boarded a ship at a certain port. He was bidden farewell by a horde of tambourine-beating Salvationists. The whole thing revolted Kipling's fastidious nature. Later, he got to know the general and told him how much he disapproved of this kind of thing. 'Young man,' said Booth, 'if I thought that I could win one more soul for Christ by standing on my hands and beating a tambourine with my feet, I would learn to do it.'

Real enthusiasts do not care if others think that they are fools. If people follow the Christian way of generosity, forgiveness and utter loyalty, there will always be worldly-wise people who will bluntly call them crazy. Paul knew that there was a time for calm, sensible conduct, and he knew, too, that there was a time for the behaviour which to the world appears mad. He was prepared to follow either for the sake of Christ and of others.

July 19

The Lovely Things (1)

Galatians 5:22a

Paul sets out the lovely things which are the fruit of the Spirit.

Love: the New Testament word for *love* is *agape*. This is not a word which is commonly used in classical Greek. *Agape*, the Christian word, means *unconquerable benevolence*. It means that, no matter what people may do to us by way of insult or injury or humiliation, we will never seek anything else but their highest good. It is therefore a feeling of the mind as much as of the heart; it concerns the will as much as the emotions. It describes the deliberate effort —which we can make only with the help of God—never to seek anything but the best even for those who seek the worst for us.

Joy: the Greek is *chara*, and the characteristic of this word is that it most often describes that joy which has a basis in religion (cf. Psalm 30:11; Romans 14:17, 15:13; Philippians 1:4, 1:25). It is not the joy that comes from earthly things, still less from triumphing over someone else in competition. It is a joy whose foundation is God.

Peace: in contemporary colloquial Greek, this word (*eirene*) had two interesting usages. It was used of the serenity which a country enjoyed under the just and generous government of a good emperor; and it was used of the good order of a town or village. Villages had an official who was called the superintendent of the village's *eirene*, the keeper of the public peace. Here, it means that tranquillity of heart which derives from the all-pervading consciousness that our times are in the hands of God.

Patience: the Greek word used is *makrothumia*. Generally speaking, the word is used of patience not in relation to things or events but in relation to people. The most illuminating thing about it is that it is commonly used in the New Testament of the attitude of God towards men and women (Romans 2:4, 9:22; 1 Timothy 1:16; 1 Peter 3:20). If God had been like us, he would have wiped out this world long ago; but he has that patience which puts up with all our sinning and will not reject us.

In our dealings with one another, we must reproduce this loving, forbearing, forgiving, patient attitude of God towards ourselves.

The Lovely Things (2)

Galatians 5:22b–23

Kindness and goodness are closely connected words. For *kindness*, the word is *chrestotes*. It, too, is commonly translated as *goodness*. Christ's yoke is called *chrestos* (Matthew 11:30), that is, it does not cause discomfort or irritation. The whole idea of the word is a goodness which is kind. The word Paul uses for *goodness* (*agathosune*) is a word peculiar to the Bible and does not occur in secular Greek (Romans 15:14; Ephesians 5:9; 2 Thessalonians 1:11). It is the widest word for goodness; it is defined as 'virtue equipped at every point'. What is the difference? *Agathosune* might, and could, rebuke and discipline; *chrestotes* can only help. Jesus showed *agathosune* when he cleansed the Temple and drove out those who were making it a bazaar; but he showed *chrestotes* when he was kind to the sinning woman who anointed his feet. Christians need that goodness which at one and the same time can be kind and strong.

Fidelity: this word (*pistis*) is common in secular Greek for *trustworthiness*. It is the characteristic of people who are reliable.

Gentleness: *praotes* is the most untranslatable of words. In the New Testament, it has three main meanings.

(1) It means being *submissive* to the will of God (Matthew 5:5, 11:29, 21:5).

(2) It means being *teachable*, being not too proud to learn (James 1:21).

(3) Most often of all, it means being *considerate* (1 Corinthians 4:21; 2 Corinthians 10:1; Ephesians 4:2). Aristotle defined *praotes* as the mid-point between excessive anger and excessive angerlessness, the quality of the person who is always angry at the right time and never at the wrong time.

Self-control: the word is *egkrateia*, which Plato uses of *self-mastery*. It is the spirit which has overcome and controlled its desires and its love of pleasure. It is used of the athlete's discipline of the body (1 Corinthians 9:25) and of the Christian's control of sex (1 Corinthians 7:9). It is the virtue which enables people to have such control of themselves that they are fit to be the servants of others.

The Work and the Works of Grace

Ephesians 2:4–10

Paul insists that it is by grace that we are saved. We have not earned salvation, nor could we have earned it. It is the gift of God, and our part is simply to accept it.

God is love; sin is therefore a crime, not against law, but against love. Now, it is possible to make atonement for a broken law, but it is impossible to make atonement for a broken heart; and sin is not so much breaking God's law as it is breaking God's heart. Let us take a crude and imperfect analogy. Suppose a motorist by careless driving kills a child. The driver is arrested, tried, found guilty and sentenced to a term of imprisonment and/or to a fine. After the fine has been paid and/or the term of imprisonment served, as far as the law is concerned, the whole matter is over. But it is very different in relation to the mother whose child was killed. The driver can never put things right with her by serving a term of imprisonment and paying a fine. The only thing which can restore that relationship with her is an act of free forgiveness on her part. That is the way we are to God. It is not against God's laws that we have sinned—it is against his heart. And therefore only an act of free forgiveness of the grace of God can put us back into the right relationship with him.

Paul goes on to say that we are re-created by God for good actions. Here is the Pauline paradox. All the good works in the world cannot put us right with God; but there is something radically wrong with the Christianity that does not result in good deeds.

There is nothing mysterious about this. It is simply an inevitable law of love. If some fine person loves us, we know that we do not and cannot deserve that love. At the same time, we know with utter conviction that we must spend our lives trying to be worthy of it. That is our relationship to God. We cannot earn God's love; but we can and must show how grateful we are for it, by seeking with our whole hearts to live the kind of life that will bring joy to God's heart.

True Godhead and True Humanity

Philippians 2:5–11

In many ways, this is the greatest and most moving passage Paul ever wrote about Jesus.

Being in the form of God. The word which the Authorized Version translates as *being* is from the Greek verb *huparchein*, which is not the common Greek word for *being*. It describes the very essence of every individual and that which cannot be changed. It describes that part of every one of us which, in any circumstances, remains the same. So Paul begins by saying that Jesus was essentially and unalterably God.

He made himself of no reputation. The Greek is the verb *kenoun*, which means literally *to empty*. It can be used of removing things from a container until the container is empty, of pouring something out until there is nothing left. Here, Paul uses the most vivid word possible to make clear the sacrifice of the incarnation. The glory of divinity Jesus gave up willingly in order to become human. He emptied himself of his deity to take upon himself his humanity. It is useless to ask how; we can only stand in awe at the sight of him, who is almighty God, hungry and weary and in tears.

He took upon him the form of a servant. The word used for *form* is *morphe*, which means *the essential form*. Paul means that, when Jesus became human, it was not play-acting but reality. He was not like the Greek gods, who sometimes, so the stories ran, became human beings but kept their divine privileges. Jesus truly became a man.

Verses 6–8 form a very short passage; but there is no passage in the New Testament which so movingly sets out the utter reality of the godhead and the humanity of Jesus and makes so vivid the sacrifice that he made when he laid aside his godhead and became human. How it happened, we cannot tell; but it is the mystery of a love so great that, although we can never fully understand it, we can blessedly experience it and adore it.

The Peace of Believing Prayer

Philippians 4:6–7

In this brief passage, there is a whole philosophy of prayer.

(1) Paul stresses that we can take everything to God in prayer. As it has been beautifully put, 'There is nothing too great for God's power; and nothing too small for his fatherly care.' Children may take anything, great or small, to their parents, sure that whatever happens to them is of interest there, their small triumphs and disappointments, their passing cuts and bruises. In exactly the same way, we may take anything to God, sure of his interest and concern.

(2) We can bring our prayers, our petitions and our requests to God; we can pray for ourselves. We can pray for forgiveness for the past, for the things we need in the present, and for help and guidance for the future. We can take our own past and present and future into the presence of God. We can pray for others. We can commend to God's care those near and far who are within our memories and our hearts.

(3) Paul lays it down that 'thanksgiving must be the universal accompaniment of prayer'. Christians must feel, as it has been put, that all through life they are, 'as it were, suspended between past and present blessings'. Every prayer must surely include thanks for the great privilege of prayer itself. Paul insists that we must give thanks in everything, in laughter and in tears, in sorrows and in joys alike. That implies two things. It implies gratitude and also perfect submission to the will of God. It is only when we are fully convinced that God is working all things together for good that we can really feel the perfect gratitude towards him which believing prayer demands.

The result of believing prayer is that the peace of God will stand like a sentry on guard over our hearts. The word that Paul uses (*phrourein*) is the military word for *standing on guard*. That peace of God, says Paul, as the Revised Standard Version has it, passes all understanding. That does not mean that the peace of God is such a mystery that the human mind cannot understand it, although this also is true. It means that the peace of God is so precious that the human mind, with all its skill and all its knowledge, can never produce it. It can never be of our contriving; it is only of God's giving.

True States of Mind

Philippians 4:8–9

It is a law of life that, if we think of something often enough, we will come to the stage when we cannot stop thinking about it. Our thoughts will be quite literally in a groove out of which we cannot jolt them. It is, therefore, of the first importance that we should set our thoughts upon the fine things—and here Paul makes a list of them.

There are the things which are true. Many things in this world are deceptive and illusory, promising what they can never perform, offering a false peace and happiness which they can never supply. We should always set our thoughts on the things which will not let us down.

There are the things which are honest. There are things in this world which are flippant and cheap and attractive to those who never take life seriously; but it is on the things which are serious and dignified that Christians will set their minds.

There are the things which are just. There are those who set their minds on pleasure, comfort and easy ways. The Christian's thoughts are on duty to other people and duty to God.

There are the things which are pure. This world is full of things which are sordid and shabby and soiled and smutty. The Christian's thoughts are so clean that they can stand even the scrutiny of God.

There are the things which call forth love. There are those whose minds are so set on vengeance and punishment that they cause bitterness and fear in others. There are those whose minds are so set on criticism and rebuke that they bring out resentment in others. Christians set their minds on the lovely things—kindness, sympathy, patience—so they are winsome people, whose presence inspires feelings of love.

There are the things which are of good report. It is not easy to get at the meaning of this word (*eophema*). It might not be going too far to say that it describes *the things which are fit for God to hear.* There are far too many ugly words and false words and impure words in this world. On the lips and in the minds of Christians, there should be only words which are fit for God to hear.

The Risen Life

Colossians 3:1–4

In baptism, Christians die and rise again. As the water closes over them, it is as if they were buried in death; as they emerge from the water, it is like being resurrected to a new life. Now, if that is so, Christians must rise from baptism as different men and women. Wherein is the difference? It lies in the fact that now their thoughts must be set on the things which are above. They can no longer be concerned with the trivial passing things of earth; they must be totally concerned with the eternal truths of heaven.

We must note carefully what Paul means by that. He is certainly not pleading for an other-worldliness in which Christians withdraw from all the work and activities of this world and do nothing but contemplate eternity. Immediately after this, Paul goes on to lay down a series of ethical principles which make it quite clear that he expects Christians to go on with the work of this world and to maintain all its normal relationships. But there will be this difference—from now on, Christians will view everything against the background of eternity and no longer live as if this world was all that mattered.

This will obviously provide a new set of values. Christians will no longer worry about things which the world thought important. Ambitions which dominated the world will be powerless to touch them. They will go on using the things of the world, but they will use them in a new way. They will, for instance, set giving above getting, serving above ruling, forgiving above avenging. The standard of values for Christians will be God's, not the world's.

In verse 4, Paul gives to Christ one of the great titles of devotion. He calls him Christ our life. Here is an idea which was very dear to Paul's heart. When he was writing to the Philippians, he said: 'For to me, living is Christ' (Philippians 1:21). As Paul saw it, to Christians, Christ is the most important thing in life; more, he is life. This is the kind of peak of devotion which we can only dimly understand and only haltingly and imperfectly express. Sometimes we say of people: 'Music is her life—Sport is his life—They live for their work.' Such people find life and all that it means in music, in sport, in work, as the case may be. For Christians, Christ is their life.

Everything Is from God

1 Thessalonians 3:11–13

For Paul, everything came from God.

(1) He prays to God to open a way for him whereby he may come to Thessalonica. It was to God that he turned for guidance in the ordinary day-to-day problems of life. One of the great mistakes of life is to turn to God only in the overwhelming emergencies and the shattering crises. I remember once talking to three young men who had just completed a yachting expedition up the west coast of Scotland. One said to me: 'You know, when we are at home we hardly ever listen to the weather forecasts, but when we were on that yacht we listened to them with all our ears.' It is quite possible to do without the weather forecasts when life is comfortably safe; it is essential to listen when life might depend on them.

We are apt to try to do the same with God. In ordinary things, we disregard him, thinking that we can manage well enough by ourselves; in an emergency, we clutch at him, knowing that we cannot get through without him. It was not so with Paul. Even in an ordinary routine thing like a journey from Athens to Thessalonica, it was to God that he looked for guidance. We use him to try to achieve a God-rescued life; Paul kept company with him to achieve a God-directed life.

(2) He prays to God that he will enable the Thessalonians to fulfil the law of love in their daily lives. We often wonder why the Christian life is so difficult, especially in the ordinary everyday relationships. The answer may very well be that we are trying to live it by ourselves. The person who goes out in the morning without prayer is, in effect, saying: 'I can tackle today quite well on my own.' The person who goes to bed without speaking to God is, in effect, saying: 'I can bear on my own whatever consequences today has brought.'

The writer John Buchan once described an atheist as 'a man who has no invisible means of support'. It may well be that our failure to live the Christian life well is due to our trying to live it without the help of God — which is an impossible assignment.

Lift Up Your Hearts

2 Thessalonians 1:1–4

It seems that the Thessalonians had sent a message to Paul full of self-doubtings. They had been afraid that their faith was not going to stand the test and that they were not going to make the grade. Paul's answer was to highlight their virtues and achievements in such a way that these despondent, frightened Christians might square their shoulders and say: 'Well, if Paul thinks that of us, we'll make a fight of it yet.' 'Blessed are those', said the writer Mark Rutherford, 'who heal us of our self-despisings' — and Paul did just that for the Thessalonian church. He knew that well-judged praise can often do what indiscriminate criticism cannot do, and that wise praise never makes people rest upon their laurels but fills them with the desire to do better still.

There are three things which Paul picked out as being the marks of a church that is alive.

(1) A faith which is strong. It is the mark of advancing Christians that they grow surer of Jesus Christ every day. The faith which may begin as being theoretical ends as a certainty. Christians reach that stage when to the thrill of Christian experience they add the discipline of Christian thought.

(2) A love which is increasing. People may begin serving others as a duty which their Christian faith lays upon them; they will end by doing it because in it they find their greatest joy. The life of service opens up the great discovery that unselfishness and happiness go hand in hand.

(3) A constancy which endures. The word Paul uses describes the spirit which not only endures the circumstances in which it finds itself but overcomes them. It accepts the blows of life but in accepting them transforms them into stepping-stones to new achievement.

Paul's uplifting message ends with the most inspirational vision of all. When Christ comes, he will be glorified in his saints and admired in those who have believed. Here, we have the breathtaking truth that our glory is Christ and Christ's glory is ourselves. Can any privilege or responsibility be greater than that?

The Peril of the Love of Money

1 Timothy 6:9–10

Here is one of the most misquoted sayings in the Bible. Scripture does not say that money is the root of all evil; it says that the love of money is the root of all evil.

What then are the special dangers involved in the love of money?

(1) The desire for money tends to be a thirst which cannot be satisfied. There was a Roman proverbial saying that wealth is like sea water; far from quenching thirst, it intensifies it. The more we get, the more we want.

(2) The desire for wealth is founded on an illusion. It is founded on the desire for security; but wealth cannot buy security. It cannot buy health, nor real love, and it cannot preserve from sorrow and from death. The security which is founded on material things is doomed to failure.

(3) The desire for money tends to make people selfish. If they are driven by the desire for wealth, it is nothing to them that someone has to lose in order that they may gain. The desire for wealth fixes people's thoughts upon self, and others become merely means or obstacles in the path to their own enrichment.

(4) Although the desire for wealth is based on the desire for security, it ends in nothing but anxiety. There is an old story about a peasant who performed a great service to a king, who rewarded him with a gift of much money. For a time, the man was thrilled; but the day came when he begged the king to take back his gift, for into his life had entered the hitherto unknown worry that he might lose what he had.

(5) The love of money may easily lead people into wrong ways of getting it, and therefore, in the end, into pain and remorse. That is true even physically. They may so drive their bodies in their passion to get that they ruin their health. They may discover too late what damage their desire has done to others and be saddled with remorse.

To seek to be independent and prudently to provide for the future is a Christian duty, but to make the love of money the driving force of life cannot ever be anything other than the most perilous of sins.

Trust, Human and Divine

2 Timothy 1:12–14

This passage uses a very vivid Greek word in a significant double way which is full of meaning. Paul talks of that which he has *entrusted* to God, and he urges Timothy to safeguard the *trust* God has placed in him. In both cases, the word is *paratheke*, which means *a deposit committed to someone's trust*. A man might deposit something with a friend to be kept for his children or his loved ones; or he might deposit his valuables in a temple for safekeeping, for the temples were the banks of the ancient world. In each case, the thing deposited was a *paratheke*. In the ancient world, there was no more sacred duty than the safeguarding of such a deposit and the returning of it when in due time it was claimed.

Paul says that he has made his deposit with God. He means that he has entrusted both his work and his life to him. It might seem that he had been cut off in mid-career; that he should end as a criminal in a Roman prison might seem the undoing of all his work. But he had sowed his seed and preached his gospel, and he left the result in the hands of God. Paul had entrusted his life to God; and he was sure that in life and in death he was safe. Why was he so sure? Because he knew in whom he had believed. We must always remember that Paul does not say that he knew what he had believed. His certainty did not come from the intellectual knowledge of a creed or a theology; it came from a personal knowledge of God. He knew God personally and intimately; he knew what he was like in love and in power; and to Paul it was inconceivable that he should fail him.

If we have worked honestly and done the best that we can, we can leave the result to God, however meagre that work may seem to us. With him in this or any other world, life is safe, for nothing can separate us from his love in Christ Jesus our Lord.

The Pure in Heart

Titus 1:13–16

The great characteristic of the Jewish faith was its thousands of rules and regulations. Many things were branded as unclean; many kinds of food were classified as forbidden. When Judaism and Gnosticism joined hands, even the body became unclean, and the natural instincts of the body were held to be evil. The inevitable result was that long lists of sins were constantly being created. It became a sin to touch certain things; it became a sin to eat certain foods; it even became a sin to marry and to have children. Things which were either good in themselves or quite natural were considered unclean.

So Paul declares the great principle—to the pure, all things are pure. He had already said that even more definitely in Romans 14:20 when, to those who were constantly involved in questions about clean and unclean foods, he said: 'Everything is indeed clean.' It may well be that this phrase is not only a proverb but an actual saying of Jesus. When Jesus was speaking about these numerous Jewish rules and regulations, he said: 'There is nothing outside a person that by going in can defile, but the things that come out are what defile' (Mark 7:15).

It is the heart which makes all the difference. If someone is pure in heart, all things are pure to that person. If someone is unclean in heart, then everything that person thinks about or speaks about or touches becomes unclean. This was a principle which the great classical writers had often stated. 'Unless the vessel is pure,' said Horace, 'everything you pour into it grows bitter.' Seneca said: 'Just as a diseased stomach alters the food which it receives, so the darkened mind turns everything you commit to it to its own burden and ruin.'

If we allow impurity to infect the mind, we will see all things through a mist of uncleanness. The infected mind soils every thought that enters into it; the imagination turns every picture which it forms into a source of lust. Every motive is misinterpreted. Every statement is given a double meaning. To escape that uncleanness, we must walk in the cleansing presence of Jesus Christ.

July 31

The Request of Love

Philemon

In verse 9, Paul describes himself as Paul *the aged*, and a prisoner of Christ. A good number of scholars wish to substitute another translation for *aged*. It is argued that Paul could not really be described as an old man. He certainly was not sixty years old; he was somewhere between that and fifty-five. But, on this basis, those who object to the translation *aged* are wrong. The word which Paul uses of himself is *presbutes*; and Hippocrates, the great Greek medical writer, says that a man is *presbutes* from the age of forty-nine to the age of fifty-six. Between these years, he is what we might call *senior*; only after that does he become a *geron*, the Greek for an *old man*.

But what is the other translation suggested? There are two words which are very like each other; their spelling is only one letter different, and their pronunciation exactly the same. They are *presbutes*, *old*, and *presbeutes*, *ambassador*. It is the verb of this word which Paul uses in Ephesians 6:20, when he says: 'I am an ambassador in chains.' If we think that the word ought to be *presbeutes*, Paul is saying: 'I am an ambassador, although I am an ambassador in chains.' But it is far more likely that we should retain the translation *old*, for in this letter Paul is appealing all the time, not to any office he holds or to any authority he enjoys, but only to love. It is not the ambassador who is speaking, but the man who has lived hard and is now lonely and tired.

Paul makes his request in verse 10, and it is for Onesimus. We notice how he delays using the name of Onesimus, almost as if he hesitated to do so. He does not make any excuses for him; he freely admits he was a useless character; but he makes one claim—he is useful now. Christianity, as the theologian James Denney used to say, is the power which can make bad men good. It is significant to note that Paul claims that in Christ the useless person has been made useful.

The last thing Christianity is designed to produce is vague, inefficient people; it produces people who are of use and can do a job better than they ever could if they did not know Christ.

Apostolic Wisdom

August 1

The End of Fragments

Hebrews 1:1–3

This is the most stylistically impressive piece of Greek in the whole New Testament. It is a passage that any classical Greek orator would have been proud to write. The writer begins by contrasting Jesus with the prophets who had gone before. He talks about him coming in the end of these days. The Jews divided all time into two ages—the present age and the age to come. In between, they set the day of the Lord. The day of the Lord was to be like the birth pangs of the new age. So, the writer to the Hebrews sees the world and human thought enter, as it were, into a new beginning with Christ. In Jesus, God has entered humanity, eternity has invaded time, and things can never be the same again.

God cannot reveal more than human beings can understand. His revelation comes through human minds and hearts. The revelation of the prophets was great and came in many forms, but it was fragmentary and presented by such methods as they could find to make it effective. The revelation of God in Jesus was complete and was presented in Jesus himself. In a word, the prophets were the friends of God; but Jesus was the Son. The prophets grasped part of the mind of God; but Jesus was that mind.

The writer to the Hebrews uses two great pictures to describe what Jesus was. He says that he was the *apaugasma* of God's glory. *Apaugasma* can mean one of two things in Greek. It can mean *brilliance*, the light which shines out, or it can mean *reflection*, the light which is reflected. Here, it probably means *brilliance*. Jesus is the shining of God's glory among us.

He says that he was the *character* of God's very essence. In Greek, *character* means two things—first, a *seal*, and, second, the *impression* that the seal leaves on the wax. The impression has the exact form of the seal. So, when the writer to the Hebrews said that Jesus was the *character* of the being of God, he meant that he was the exact image of God. Just as when you look at the impression, you see exactly what the seal which made it is like, so when you look at Jesus you see exactly what God is like.

August 2

The Salvation We Dare Not Neglect

Hebrews 2:1–4

In the first verse, the two key words are *prosechein* and *pararrein*. We have taken *prosechein* to mean *to pay attention to*, which is one of its most common meanings. *Pararrein* is a word of many meanings. It is used of something flowing or slipping past; it can be used of a ring that has slipped off the finger, of a point which has escaped someone in the course of an argument, of some fact that has slipped out of the mind, of something that has ebbed or leaked away. It is regularly used of something which has carelessly or thoughtlessly been allowed to become lost.

But both these words also have a nautical sense. *Prosechein* can mean *to moor a ship*; and *pararrein* can be used of a ship which has been carelessly allowed to slip past a harbour or a haven because the captain has forgotten to allow for the wind or the current or the tide. So, this first verse could be very vividly translated: 'Therefore, we must the more eagerly anchor our lives to the things that we have been taught in case the ship of life should drift past the harbour and be wrecked.' It is a vivid picture of a ship drifting to destruction because the pilot is asleep.

For most of us, the threat of life is not so much that we should plunge into disaster but that we should drift into sin. There are few people who, deliberately and in a moment, turn their backs on God; there are many who day by day drift further and further away from him. There are not many who in one moment of time commit some disastrous sin; there are many who almost imperceptibly involve themselves in some situation and suddenly awake to find that they have ruined life for themselves and broken someone else's heart. We must be continually on the alert against the peril of drifting in life.

225

The Essential Suffering

Hebrews 2:10–18

Here, the writer to the Hebrews uses one of the great titles of Jesus. He calls him *the pioneer* (*archegos*) *of glory*. An *archegos* is someone who begins something in order that others may enter into it. This is what the writer to the Hebrews means when he says that Jesus is the *archegos* of our salvation. Jesus has blazed the trail to God for us to follow.

How was Jesus enabled to take on this role? The verb translated as *make perfect* is *teleioun*, which comes from the adjective *teleios*. The basic meaning of *teleios* in the New Testament is always that the thing or person described in this way fully carries out the purpose for which he or she is designed. So, what the writer to the Hebrews is saying is that, through suffering, Jesus was made fully able to complete the task of being the pioneer of our salvation.

Why should that be?

(1) It was through his sufferings that he was really identified with us. If Jesus had come into this world in a form in which he could never have suffered, he would have been quite different from us and so no Saviour for us. It is, in fact, this identification with us which is the essence of the Christian idea of God.

(2) Through this identity, Jesus Christ sympathizes with us. He literally feels with us. It is almost impossible to understand another person's sorrows and sufferings unless we have been through them. A person without a trace of nerves has no conception of the tortures of nervousness. A person who learns easily often cannot understand why someone who is slow finds things so difficult. A person who has never known sorrow cannot understand the pain at the heart of the person into whose life grief has come. A person who has never loved can never understand either the sudden glory or the aching loneliness in the lover's heart. Before we can have sympathy, we must go through the same things that the other person has gone through — and that is precisely what Jesus did.

(3) Because he sympathizes, Jesus can really help. He has met our sorrows; he has faced our temptations. As a result, he knows exactly what help we need; and he can give it.

The Perfect High Priest

Hebrews 4:14–16

Here, we are coming to closer grips with the great characteristic conception of Hebrews—that of Jesus as the perfect high priest. The high priest at one and the same time must perfectly know what it is to be human and also know God.

No one was ever surer of Jesus' complete identity with human beings. He went through everything that an individual has to go through and is like us in all things—except that he emerged from it all completely sinless. This experience of Jesus gave him the gift of sympathy. It gave God the quality of mercy. It is easy to see why. It was because God understands. 'To know all is to forgive all'—of no one is that truer than of God. Professor John Foster of Glasgow University told how he came into his home one day in the 1930s to find his daughter, who was listening to the radio, in tears. He asked her why and found that the news bulletin had contained the sentence: 'Japanese tanks entered Canton today.' Most people would hear that with at the most a faint feeling of regret. Politicians may have heard it with grim foreboding; but to most people it did not make very much difference. Why was John Foster's daughter in tears? Because she had been born in Canton. To her, Canton meant a home, a nurse, a school, friends.

The difference was that she had been there. When you have been there, it makes all the difference. And there is no part of human experience of which God cannot say: 'I have been there.' When we have a sad and sorry tale to tell, when life has drenched us with tears, we do not go to a God who is incapable of understanding what has happened; we go to a God who has been there. That is why—if we may put it in this way—God finds it easy to forgive.

Jesus is the perfect high priest because he is perfectly God, and perfectly one with us. Because he has known our life, he can give us sympathy, mercy and power. He brought God to men and women, and he can bring them to God.

August 5

The Christian Hope

Hebrews 11:1–3

To the writer to the Hebrews, faith is a hope that is absolutely certain that what it believes is true and that what it expects will come. It is not the hope which looks forward with wistful longing; it is the hope which looks forward with utter conviction. The Christian faith is a hope that has turned to certainty. This Christian hope is such that it dictates every aspect of the way Christians conduct themselves. They live in it and they die in it; and it is the possession of it which makes them act as they do.

It is easy to argue: 'Why should I refuse the pleasure of the moment for an uncertain future?' The Christian answer is that the future is not uncertain because it belongs to God; and it is enough that God has commanded and that God has promised. The writer to the Hebrews goes on to say that it was precisely because the great heroes of the faith lived on that principle that they were approved by God. Every one of them refused what the world calls greatness and staked everything on God—and history proved them right.

The writer to the Hebrews goes further. He says that it is an act of faith to believe that God made this world, and adds that the things which are seen emerged from the things which are not seen. This was aiming a blow at the prevailing belief that God created the world out of existing matter which, being necessarily imperfect, meant that from the beginning this was an imperfect world. The writer to the Hebrews insists that God did not work with existing material but created the world from nothing. When he argued like this, he was not interested in the scientific side of the matter; he wanted to stress the fact that this is God's world.

If we can grasp the fact that this is God's world and that God is responsible for it, two things follow. First, we will use it as such. We will remember that everything in it is God's and will try to use it as God would have us use it. Second, we will remember that, even when it may not look like it, somehow God is in control.

The Discipline of God

Hebrews 12:5–11

There are many ways in which people look at the discipline which God sends.

(1) They may resign themselves to it and accept it. That is what the Stoics did. They held that nothing in this world happens outside the will of God; therefore, they argued, there is nothing to do but to accept it. That is possibly the acceptance of supreme wisdom; but nonetheless it is the acceptance not of a parent's love but of a parent's power. It is not a willing but a defeated acceptance.

(2) People may accept discipline with the grim sense of getting it over as soon as possible. To accept discipline like that is to regard it as something that is inflicted on us which is to be struggled through with defiance and certainly not with gratitude.

(3) People may accept discipline with the self-pity which leads in the end to collapse. Some people, when they are caught up in a difficult situation, give the impression that they are the only people in the world whom life ever hurt. They are lost in their self-pity.

(4) People may accept discipline as a punishment which they resent. When something happens to them or to those whom they love, their question is: 'What did I do to deserve this?' And the question is asked in such a tone as to make it clear that they regard the whole matter as an unjust punishment from God. It never dawns upon them to ask: 'What is God trying to teach me and to do with me through this experience?'

(5) So we come to the last attitude. People may accept discipline as coming from a loving father. The fourth-century biblical scholar Jerome said a paradoxical but true thing: 'The greatest anger of all is when God is no longer angry with us when we sin.' He meant that the supreme punishment is when God leaves us alone as unteachable.

We shall stop feeling self-pity and resentment and end our rebellious complaining if we remember that there is no discipline of God which does not arise out of love and is not aimed at good.

August 7

Tested and Triumphant

James 1:1–4

James never suggested to his readers that Christianity would be for them an easy way. He warns them that they will find themselves involved in what the Authorized Version calls *divers temptations*. The word translated as *temptations* is *peirasmos*, whose meaning we must understand fully if we are to see the very essence of the Christian life.

Peirasmos is not *temptation* in our sense of the term; it is *testing* (*trial* in the Revised Standard Version). *Peirasmos* is trial or testing directed towards an end, and the end is that anyone who is tested should emerge stronger and purer from the experience. The corresponding verb *peirazein*, which the Authorized Version usually translates as *to tempt*, has the same meaning. The idea is not that of enticement into sin but of strengthening and purifying. For instance, a young bird is said to test (*peirazein*) its wings. The Queen of Sheba was said to come to test (*peirazein*) the wisdom of Solomon (1 Kings 10:1). God was said to test (*peirazein*) Abraham, when he appeared to be demanding the sacrifice of Isaac (Genesis 22:1).

Here is a great and uplifting thought. F. J. A. Hort, the New Testament scholar, writes: 'The Christian must expect to be jostled by trials on the Christian way.' All kinds of experiences will come to us. There will be the test of the sorrows and the disappointments which seek to take our faith away. There will be the test of the seductions which seek to lure us from the right way. There will be the tests of the dangers, the sacrifices and the unpopularity which are so much a part of the Christian way. But they are not meant to make us fall; they are meant to make us soar. They are not meant to defeat us; they are meant to be defeated. They are not meant to make us weaker; they are meant to make us stronger. Therefore we should not complain about them; we should rejoice in them.

Christians are like athletes. The heavier the course of training they undergo, the more they are glad, because they know that it is preparing them all the better for victorious effort.

August 8

When to Be Quick and When to Be Slow

James 1:19–20

There are few among the wise who have not been impressed by the dangers of being too quick to speak and too unwilling to listen. Proverbs is full of the perils of speech which is too hasty. 'When words are many, transgression is not lacking, but the prudent are restrained in speech' (Proverbs 10:19). 'Do you see someone who is hasty in speech? There is more hope for a fool than for anyone like that' (Proverbs 29:20).

The classical writers had the same idea. When the Cynic philosopher Demonax was asked how anyone might rule best, he answered: 'Without anger, speaking little, and listening much.' One of the earliest philosophers of ancient Greece, Bias, said: 'If you hate quick speaking, you will not fall into error.' The tribute was once paid to a great linguist that he could be silent in seven different languages. Many of us would do well to listen more and to speak less.

It is James' advice that we should also be slow to anger. He is probably meeting the arguments of some that there is a place for the blazing anger of rebuke. That is undoubtedly true; the world would be a poorer place without those who blazed against the abuses and the tyrannies of sin. But too often this is made an excuse for petulant and self-centred irritation.

Teachers will be tempted to be angry with slow and backward scholars and pupils, and still more with those who are lazy. But, except on the rarest occasions, they will achieve more by encouragement than by the lash of the tongue. Preachers will be tempted to anger. But when anger gives the impression of dislike or contempt in the pulpit, it will not convert the souls of men and women. Parents will be tempted to anger. But a parent's anger is much more likely to produce a still more stubborn resistance than it is to control and direct.

The accent of love always has more power than the accent of anger; and when anger becomes constant irritability, petulant annoyance, carping nagging, it always does more harm than good. To be slow to speak, slow to anger, quick to listen is a good policy for life.

August 9

Faith and Works (1)

James 2:14–26

This passage is often used in an attempt to show that James and Paul held completely different views. It is apparently Paul's emphasis that we are saved by faith alone and that deeds do not come into the process at all: 'For we hold that a person is justified by faith apart from works prescribed by the law' (Romans 3:28). 'A person is justified not by works of the law but through faith in Jesus Christ . . . because no one will be justified by the works of the law' (Galatians 2:16). It is often argued that James is not simply differing from Paul but is flatly contradicting him. This is a matter we must investigate.

We begin by noting that James' emphasis is in fact a universal New Testament emphasis. It was the preaching of John the Baptist that men and women should prove the reality of their repentance by the excellence of their deeds (Matthew 3:8; Luke 3:8). It was Jesus' preaching that people should so live that the world might see their good works and give the glory to God (Matthew 5:16). He insisted that it was by their fruits that men and women must be known and that a faith which expressed itself in words only could never take the place of one which expressed itself in the doing of the will of God (Matthew 7:15–21).

Nor is this emphasis missing from Paul himself. However doctrinal and theological his letters may be, they never fail to end with a section in which the expression of Christianity in deeds is insisted upon. Apart from that general custom, Paul repeatedly makes clear the importance he attaches to deeds as part of the Christian life. He speaks of God who will render to all according to their works (Romans 2:6). He urges people to put off the works of darkness and put on the armour of light (Romans 13:12). We shall all receive our own reward according to our labour (1 Corinthians 3:8). We must all appear before the judgment seat of Christ so that everyone may receive good or evil, according to what he or she has done in the body (2 Corinthians 5:10). Christians have to put off the old nature and all its deeds (Colossians 3:9).

The fact that Christianity must be demonstrated ethically is an essential part of the Christian faith throughout the New Testament.

August 10

Faith and Works (2)

James 2:14–26

There are two kinds of belief. There is belief which is purely intellectual. For instance, I believe that the square on the hypotenuse of a right-angled triangle equals the sum of the squares on the other two sides; and, if I had to, I could prove it—but it makes no difference to my life and living. I accept it, but it has no effect upon me. There is another kind of belief. I believe that five and five make ten, and, therefore, I will resolutely refuse to pay more than ten pounds or ten dollars for two items marked at half that sum. I take that fact not only into my mind but also into my life and action.

What James is arguing against is the first kind of belief, the acceptance of a fact without allowing it to have any influence upon life. The devils are intellectually convinced of the existence of God; they, in fact, tremble before him, but their belief does not alter them in the slightest. What Paul held was the second kind of belief. For him, to believe in Jesus meant to take that belief into every section of life and to live by it.

The fact is that no one can be saved by works, but equally no one can be saved without producing works. By far the best analogy is that of a great human love. When we are loved, we become certain that we do not deserve to be loved; but we are also certain that we must spend our lives trying to be worthy of that love.

The difference between James and Paul is a difference of starting point. Paul starts with the great basic fact of the forgiveness of God which no one can earn or deserve; James starts with the professing Christians and insists that individuals must prove their Christianity by their deeds. We are not saved by deeds; we are saved for deeds; these are the twin truths of the Christian life. Paul's emphasis is on the first and James' is on the second. In fact, they do not contradict but complement each other, and the message of both is essential to the Christian faith in its fullest form.

The True Wisdom (1)

James 3:17a

The Jewish sages were always agreed that the true wisdom came from above. It was not the result of human attainment but the gift of God. James uses eight words to describe this wisdom, and every one has a great picture in it.

(1) The true wisdom is *pure*. The Greek is *hagnos*, and its root meaning is *pure enough to approach the gods*. On the Temple of Aesculapius at Epidaurus, there was the inscription at the entrance: 'He who would enter the divine temple must be pure [*hagnos*]; and purity is to have a mind which thinks holy thoughts.' The true wisdom is so cleansed of all ulterior motives and of self that it has become pure enough to see God. Worldly wisdom might well wish to escape God's sight; the true wisdom is able to bear his very scrutiny.

(2) The true wisdom is *eirenikos*. *Eirene* means *peace*, and when it is used in a human context its basic meaning is *right relationships between individuals, and between individuals and God*. The true wisdom produces right relationships.

(3) The true wisdom is *epieikes*. Of all Greek words in the New Testament, this is one of the most untranslatable. Aristotle defined it as that 'which is just beyond the written law' and as that 'which steps in to correct things when the law itself becomes unjust'. The person who is *epieikes* is someone who knows when it is actually wrong to apply the strict letter of the law. Such a person knows how to forgive when strict justice dictates that there is a perfect right to condemn. Such a person knows how to make allowances, when not to stand upon individual rights, and how to soften justice with mercy, and always remembers that there are greater things in the world than rules and regulations.

(4) The true wisdom is *eupeithes*. *Eupeithes* can mean *easy to persuade*, not in the sense of being pliable and weak, but in the sense of not being stubborn and of being willing to listen to reason and to appeal. The true wisdom is not rigid but is willing to listen and skilled in knowing when wisely to yield.

The True Wisdom (2)

James 3:17b–18

(5) We take the next two terms together. The true wisdom is *full of mercy* (*eleos*) *and good fruits*. *Eleos* is a word which acquired a new meaning in Christian thought. The Greeks defined it as *pity for the one who is suffering unjustly*; but Christianity means far more than that by *eleos*.

(a) In Christian thought, *eleos* means mercy for those who are in trouble, even if the trouble is their own fault. Christian pity is the reflection of God's pity, and that went out to men and women not only when they were suffering unjustly but also when they were suffering through their own fault. We are so apt to say, of someone in trouble, 'It is his own fault' or 'She brought it on herself', and therefore to feel no responsibility ourselves. Christian mercy is mercy for all who are in trouble, even if they have brought that trouble on themselves.

(b) In Christian thought, *eleos* means mercy which produces good fruits, that is, which results in practical help. Christian pity is not merely an emotion; it is action. We can never say that we have truly pitied anyone until we have given our help.

(6) The true wisdom is *adiakritos, undivided*. This means that it is not wavering and swaying; it knows its own mind, chooses its course and abides by it.

(7) The true wisdom is *anupokritos, without hypocrisy*. That is to say, it is not a pose and does not deal in deception. It is honest; it never pretends to be what it is not; and it never acts a part to gain its own ends.

(8) Finally, James says something which every Christian church and every Christian group should have written on its heart. Let us remember that peace, *eirene*, means *right relationships between individuals*. So, what James is saying is this: 'We are all trying to reap the harvest which a good life brings. But the seeds which bring the rich harvest can never flourish in any atmosphere other than one of right relationships between individuals. And the only people who can sow these seeds and reap the reward are those whose life work it has been to produce such right relationships.'

The Glory of Humility and the Tragedy of Pride

James 4:4–7

The word for *proud* is *huperephanos*, which literally means *one who shows himself above other people*. Even the Greeks hated pride. The philosopher Theophrastus described it as 'a certain contempt for all other people'. It means *haughtiness*; but those who suffer from it might well appear to be walking in downcast humility, while all the time there is in their hearts a vast contempt for other people.

This pride shuts itself off from God for three reasons.

(1) It does not know its own need. It so admires itself that it recognizes no need to be supplied.

(2) It cherishes its own independence. It will be indebted or obligated to no one and not even to God.

(3) It does not recognize its own sin. It is occupied with thinking of its own goodness and never realizes that it has any sin from which it needs to be saved. A pride like that cannot receive help, because it does not know that it needs help, and therefore it cannot ask.

The humility for which James pleads is not a cringing subservience. It has two great characteristics.

(1) It knows that if anyone takes a resolute stand against the devil, the devil will be proved to be a coward. The great example and inspiration is Jesus in his own temptations. In them, Jesus showed that the devil is not invincible; when he is confronted with the word of God, he can be put to flight. Christians have the humility that knows that they must fight their battles with the tempter, not in their own power, but in the power of God.

(2) It knows that it has the greatest privilege of all — access to God. This is a tremendous thing, for the right of approach to God under the old order of things belonged only to the priests (Exodus 19:22). But, through the work of Jesus Christ, anyone can come boldly before the throne of God, certain of finding mercy and grace to help in time of need (Hebrews 4:16).

Christians must have humility, but it is a humility which gives them unfailing courage and which knows that the way to God is open to the most fearful saint.

The Social Passion of the Bible

James 5:1–3

Not even the most cursory reader of the Bible can fail to be impressed with the social passion which blazes through its pages. No book condemns dishonest and selfish wealth with such searing passion as it does.

The book of the prophet Amos was called 'The Cry for Social Justice' by the Old Testament scholar J. E. McFadyen. Amos condemns those who store up violence and robbery in their palaces (Amos 3:10). He condemns those who tread on the poor and themselves have houses of hewn stone and pleasant vineyards—which in the wrath of God they will never enjoy (Amos 5:11). He lets loose his wrath on those who give short weight and short measure, who buy the poor for silver and the needy for a pair of shoes, and who palm off on the poor the refuse of their wheat. 'I will never forget any of their deeds', says God (Amos 8:4–7).

Isaiah warns those who build up great estates by adding house to house and field to field (Isaiah 5:8). The sage insists that those who trust in riches shall fall (Proverbs 11:28). Luke quotes Jesus as saying: 'Woe to you that are rich!' (Luke 6:24). It is only with difficulty that those who have riches enter into the kingdom of God (Luke 18:24). Riches are a temptation and a snare; the rich are liable to foolish and hurtful desires which end in ruin, for the love of money is the root of all evils (1 Timothy 6:9–10).

One of the mysteries of social history is how the Christian religion ever came to be regarded as 'the opium of the people' or to seem an otherworldly affair. There is no book in any literature which speaks so explosively of social injustice as the Bible, nor any book which has proved so powerful a social dynamic. It does not condemn wealth as such; but there is no book which more strenuously insists on wealth's responsibility and on the perils which surround those who are abundantly blessed with this world's goods.

The Rebirth of Christians

1 Peter 1:1–5

Christians are men and women who have been given new birth by God to a new kind of life. This idea of rebirth runs all through the New Testament. Let us try to collect what it says about it.

(1) Christian rebirth happens by the will and by the act of God (John 1:13; James 1:18). It is not something which we achieve any more than we achieve our physical birth.

(2) Another way to put that is to say that this rebirth is the work of the Spirit (John 3:1–15). It happens to people, not by their own effort, but when they give themselves up to be possessed and re-created by the Spirit within them.

(3) It happens by the word of truth (James 1:18; 1 Peter 1:23). In the beginning, it was the word of God which created heaven and earth. It is the creative word of God in Jesus Christ which brings about this rebirth in our lives.

(4) The result of this rebirth is that those who are reborn become the first fruits of a new creation (James 1:18). It lifts them out of this world of change and decay, of sin and defeat, and brings them here and now into touch with eternity.

(5) When we are reborn, it is to a living hope (1 Peter 1:3). That hope came from the resurrection of Jesus Christ (1 Peter 1:3). Christians had always beside them—even more, were one with—this Jesus Christ who had conquered even death, and therefore there was nothing of which they needed to be afraid.

(6) The rebirth of Christians is a rebirth to righteousness (1 John 2:29, 3:9, 5:18). That is not to say that those who are reborn will never sin, but it is to say that every time they fall, they will be given the power and the grace to rise again.

(7) The rebirth of Christians is a rebirth to love (1 John 4:7). Because the life of God is in them, there is in them something of the forgiving and sacrificial love of God.

(8) Finally, the rebirth of Christians is rebirth to victory (1 John 5:4). Life ceases to be defeat and begins to be victory, over self and sin and circumstances. Because the life of God is in them, Christians have learned the secret of victorious living.

What to Lose and What to Yearn For

1 Peter 2:1–3

Peter urges his people to be done with evil things and to set their hearts on that which alone can nourish life. There are things which must be *stripped off*. *Apothesthai* is the word for *stripping off* one's clothes. There are things of which Christians must divest themselves as they would strip off a soiled garment. They are all faults of character which hurt the great Christian virtue of mutual love.

There is *deceitfulness* (*dolos*). *Dolos* is the trickery of those who are out to deceive others to achieve their own ends, the vice of people whose motives are never pure.

There is *hypocrisy* (*hupokrisis*). *Hupokrites* (*hypocrite*) is a word with a curious history. It is the noun from the verb *hupokrinesthai*, which means *to answer*; a *hupokrites* begins by being an *answerer*. Then, it comes to mean an *actor*, the one who takes part in the question-and-answer of the stage. Next, it comes to mean a *hypocrite*, someone who all the time is acting a part and whose real motives are concealed. Hypocrites are people whose professed allegiance to Christianity is for their own profit and prestige and not for the service and glory of Christ.

There is *envy* (*phthonos*). It may well be said that envy is the last sin to die. As long as self remains active within someone's heart, there will be envy in that person's life. If we look at the commentaries, E. G. Selwyn calls envy 'the constant plague of all voluntary organisations, not least religious organisations'.

There is *gossiping disparagement* (*katalalia*). *Katalalia* is a word with a definite flavour. It means *evil-speaking*; it is almost always the fruit of envy in the heart; and it usually takes place when its victim is not there to offer a defence. Disparaging gossip is something which everyone admits to be wrong and which at the same time almost everyone enjoys; and yet there is nothing more likely to produce heartbreak, and nothing is so destructive of mutual love and Christian unity.

These, then, are the things which those who are reborn must strip off—for, if they continue to allow them to have a grip upon their lives, the unity of the church community will inevitably be injured.

The Greatness of Jesus Christ for Us

2 Peter 1:1–7

In verses 3 and 4, there is a tremendous and comprehensive picture of Jesus Christ.

(1) He is the Christ of power. In him, there is the divine power which cannot be ultimately defeated or frustrated. In this world, one of the tragedies of life is that love is so often frustrated because it cannot give what it wants to give, cannot do what it wants to do and must so often stand helpless while the loved one meets disaster. But Christ's love is always backed by his power and is, therefore, a victorious love.

(2) He is the Christ of generosity. He bestows on us all things necessary for true life and true religion. The word Peter uses for religion is *eusebeia*, the usual meaning of which is *practical religion*. Peter is saying that Jesus Christ tells us what life is and then enables us to live it as it ought to be lived.

(3) He is the Christ of the precious and great promises. That does not so much mean that he brings us the great and precious promises as that in him these promises come true.

(4) He is the Christ by whom we escape the world's corruption. As long as we live in this world, sin will never completely lose its fascination for us; but in the presence of Christ we have our defence against that fascination.

(5) He is the Christ who makes us sharers in the divine nature. Here again, Peter is using an expression which was well known in the world outside the Church, where the major thinkers spoke much about sharing in the divine nature. But there was this difference—they believed that human beings had a share in the divine nature by virtue of being human. All that people had to do was to live in accordance with the divine nature already in them. The trouble about that is that life flatly contradicts it. On every side we see bitterness, hatred, lust, crime; on every side we see moral failure, helplessness and frustration.

Christianity says that men and women are capable of becoming sharers in the divine nature. It realistically faces the actuality of human existence but at the same time sets no limit to the potentiality. 'I came', said Jesus, 'that they may have life, and have it abundantly' (John 10:10).

August 18

God Is Light

1 John 1:1–5

It is certainly the case that our individual characters will be determined by the character of the god whom we worship; and, therefore, John begins by laying down the nature of the God and Father of Jesus Christ whom Christians worship. God, he says, is light, and there is no darkness in him. What does this statement tell us about God?

(1) It tells us that he is splendour and glory. There is nothing so glorious as a blaze of light piercing the darkness. To say that God is light tells us of his sheer splendour.

(2) It tells us that God is self-revealing. Above all things, light is seen; and it lights up the darkness round about it. To say that God is light is to say that there is nothing secretive or furtive about him. He wishes to be seen and to be known.

(3) It tells us of God's purity and holiness. In God, there is none of the darkness which cloaks hidden evil. That he is light speaks to us of his white purity and stainless holiness.

(4) It tells us of the guidance of God. It is one of the great functions of light to show the way. The road that is lit is the road that can be seen clearly. To say that God is light is to say that he offers his guidance for the path we must tread.

(5) It tells us of the revealing quality in the presence of God. Light is the great revealer. Flaws and stains which are hidden in the shade are obvious in the light. Light reveals the imperfections in any piece of work or material.

We can never know either the depth to which life has fallen or the height to which it may rise until we see it in the revealing light of God.

The Necessity of Walking in the Light

1 John 1:6–7

Here, John is writing to counteract one heretical way of thought. There were those who claimed to be specially intellectually and spiritually advanced, but whose lives showed no sign of it. They claimed to have advanced so far along the road of knowledge and of spirituality that, for them, sin had ceased to matter and the laws had ceased to exist. In answer, John insists on certain things.

(1) He insists that, to have fellowship with the God who is light, we must walk in the light, and that, if we are still walking in the moral and ethical darkness of the Christless life, we cannot have that fellowship. This is precisely what the Old Testament had said centuries before. God said: 'You shall be holy, for I the Lord your God am holy' (Leviticus 19:2; cf. 20:7, 20:26). Those who would find fellowship with God are committed to a life of goodness which reflects God's goodness.

This does not mean that we must be perfect before we can have fellowship with God; if that were the case, all of us would be shut out. But it does mean that we must spend our whole lives in the awareness of our obligations, in the effort to fulfil them and in penitence when we fail. It will mean that we must never think that sin does not matter; it will mean that the nearer we come to God, the more terrible sin will be to us.

(2) He insists that these mistaken thinkers have the wrong idea of truth. He says that, if people who claim to be specially advanced still walk in darkness, they are not doing the truth. This means that, for Christians, truth is never only intellectual; it is always moral. It is not something which exercises only the mind; it is something which exercises the whole personality. It is possible to look on Christianity as a series of intellectual problems to be solved, and on the Bible as a book about which illuminating information is to be gathered. But Christianity is something to be followed, and the Bible is a book to be obeyed. It is possible for intellectual superiority and moral failure to go hand in hand. For Christians, the truth is something first to be discovered and then to be obeyed.

Jesus Christ the Atoning Sacrifice

1 John 2:1–2

John goes on to say that Jesus is, as the Authorized Version has it, the *propitiation for our sins*. The Greek word for *propitiation* is *hilasmos*; and the corresponding verb is *hilaskesthai*. This verb has three meanings.

(1) When it is used with a person as the subject, it means to placate or to pacify someone who has been injured or offended, and especially to placate a god. It is to bring a sacrifice or to perform a ritual whereby a god, offended by sin, is pacified.

(2) If the subject is God, the verb means to forgive, for then the meaning is that God himself provides the means whereby the lost relationship between him and the people concerned is restored.

(3) The third meaning is allied with the first. The verb often means to perform some deed by which the taint of guilt is removed. People sin; at once they become tainted by sin; something is needed which, to use the scholar C. H. Dodd's metaphor, will disinfect them from that contamination and enable them once again to enter into the presence of God. In that sense, *hilaskesthai* means not to propitiate but to *expiate*—not so much to pacify God as to disinfect from the taint of sin and by that means make people once again fit to enter into fellowship with God.

When John says that Jesus is the *hilasmos* for our sins, he is, we think, bringing all these different meanings together into one. Jesus is the person through whom guilt for past sin and defilement from present sin are removed. The great basic truth behind this word is that it is through Jesus Christ that our fellowship with God is first restored and then maintained. We note one other thing. As John sees it, this work of Jesus was carried out not only for us but for the whole world.

There is in the New Testament a strong line of thought in which the universality of the salvation of God is stressed. God so loved the world that he sent his Son (John 3:16). Jesus is confident that, if he is lifted up, he will draw all people to him (John 12:32). God desires everyone to be saved (1 Timothy 2:4).

It would indeed be a bold person who would set limits to the grace and love of God or to the effectiveness of the work and sacrifice of Jesus Christ.

Rivals for the Human Heart

1 John 2:15–17

We must be careful to understand what John meant by the *world*, the *kosmos*. Christians did not hate the world as such. It was God's creation; and God made all things well. Jesus had loved the beauty of the world; not even Solomon in all his glory was clothed like one of the scarlet anemones which bloomed for a day and died. Jesus again and again took his illustrations from the world. In that sense, Christians did not hate the world. The earth was not the devil's; the earth and all its fullness was the Lord's. But *kosmos* acquired a moral sense. It began to mean *the world apart from God*. C. H. Dodd defines this meaning of *kosmos*: 'Our author means human society in so far as it is organized on wrong principles, and characterized by base desires, false values, and egoism.' In other words, to John the world was nothing other than the society of the Roman Empire with its false values and its false gods.

The world in this passage does not mean the world in general, for God loved the world which he had made; it means the world which, in fact, had forsaken the God who made it. It so happened that there was a factor in the situation of John's people which made the circumstances even more perilous. It is clear that, although they might be unpopular, they were not undergoing persecution. They were, therefore, under the great and dangerous temptation to compromise with the world. It is always difficult to be different, and it was particularly difficult for them.

To this day, Christians cannot escape the obligation to be different from the world. In this passage, John sees things as he always sees them—in terms of black and white. As B. F. Westcott has it, 'There cannot be a vacuum in the soul.' This is a matter in which there is no neutrality; a person loves either the world or God. Jesus himself said: 'No one can serve two masters' (Matthew 6:24). The ultimate choice remains the same. Are we to accept the world's standards or the standards of God?

God Is Love

1 John 4:7–21

In this passage, there occurs what is probably the greatest single statement about God in the whole Bible, that God is love. It is amazing how many doors that single statement unlocks and how many questions it answers.

(1) It is the explanation of creation. Sometimes we are bound to wonder why God created this world. The disobedience and the lack of response in human beings is a continual grief to him. Why should he create a world which was to bring him nothing but trouble? The answer is that creation was essential to his very nature. If God is love, he cannot exist in lonely isolation. Love must have someone to love and someone to love it.

(2) It is the explanation of free will. Had God been only law, he could have created a world in which people moved like robots, having no more choice than a machine. But, if God had made people like that, there would have been no possibility of a personal relationship between him and them. Love is of necessity the free response of the heart; and, therefore, God, by a deliberate act of self-limitation, had to endow men and women with free will.

(3) It is the explanation of providence. Had God been simply mind and order and law, he might, so to speak, have created the universe, wound it up, set it going and left it. But, because God is love, his creating act is followed by his constant care.

(4) It is the explanation of redemption. If God had been only law and justice, he would simply have left men and women to the consequences of their sin. The moral law would operate; the soul that sinned would die; and the eternal justice would inexorably hand out its punishments. But the very fact that God is love meant that he had to seek out and to save the lost.

(5) It is the explanation of the life beyond. If God were simply creator, human beings might live their brief span and die forever. The life which ended early would be only another flower which the frost of death had withered too soon. But the fact that God is love makes it certain that the chances and changes of life do not have the last word and that his love will readjust the balance of this life.

The Necessary Obedience

1 John 5:3–4a

John quite suddenly says a most surprising thing. God's commandments, he says, are not heavy. How is this to be explained? How can it be said that the tremendous demands of Jesus are not a heavy burden?

(1) It is the way of God never to lay a commandment on anyone without also giving strength to carry it out. With the vision comes the power; with the need for it comes the strength. God does not give us his commandments and then go away and leave us to ourselves. He is there by our side to enable us to carry out what he has commanded. What is impossible for us becomes possible with God.

(2) But there is another great truth here. Our response to God must be the response of love; and, for love, no duty is too hard and no task too great. Things that we would never do for a stranger we will willingly attempt for a loved one. Something that would be an impossible sacrifice, if a stranger demanded it, becomes a willing gift when love needs it. There is an old story which is a kind of parable of this. Someone once met a young boy going to school long before the days when transport was available. The boy was carrying on his back a smaller boy who was clearly lame and unable to walk. The stranger said to the boy: 'Do you carry him to school every day?' 'Yes,' said the boy. 'That's a heavy burden for you to carry,' said the stranger. 'He's not a burden', said the boy. 'He's my brother.'

Love turned the burden into no burden at all. It must be so with us and Christ. His commandments are not a burden but a privilege and an opportunity to show our love. The commandments of Christ are indeed difficult; but burdensome they are not, for Christ never laid a commandment on anyone without giving strength to carry it; and every commandment laid upon us provides another chance to show our love.

August 26

The Conquest of the World

1 John 5:4b–5

There is something in Christians which makes them able to conquer the world. The *kosmos* is the world apart from God and in opposition to him. The thing that enables us to conquer the *kosmos* is faith. John defines this conquering faith as the belief that Jesus is the Son of God. It is belief in the incarnation. Why should that be able to give us power to overcome? If we believe in the incarnation, it means that we believe that, in Jesus, God entered the world and took our human life upon himself. If he did that, it means that he cared enough for us to take upon himself the limitations of humanity, which is the act of a love that is beyond human understanding. Faith in the incarnation is the conviction that God shares and God cares. Once we possess that faith, certain things follow.

(1) We have a defence to resist the infections of the world. From within and from outside come the temptations which are part of the human situation in a world and a society not interested in and sometimes hostile to God. But, once we are aware of the constant presence of God in Jesus Christ with us, we have a strong protection against the infections of the world.

(2) We have a strength to stand up to the attacks of the world. The human situation is full of things which seek to take our faith away. There are the sorrows and the perplexities of life; there are the disappointments and the frustrations of life; there are, for most of us, the failures and discouragements of life. But, if we believe in the incarnation, we believe in a God who himself went through all this, even to the cross, and who can, therefore, help others who are going through it.

(3) We have the indestructible hope of final victory. The world did its worst to Jesus. It relentlessly pursued him and slandered him. It branded him a heretic and a friend of sinners. It judged him and crucified him and buried him. It did everything humanly possible to eliminate him — and it failed. After the cross came the resurrection; after the shame came the glory. That is the Jesus who is with us, one who saw life at its grimmest, to whom life did its worst — who died, who conquered death, and who offers us a share in that victory which was his.

The Essence of the Faith

1 John 5:11–13

The essence of the Christian life is eternal life. The word for *eternal* is *aionios*. It means far more than simply *lasting forever*. A life which lasted forever might well be a curse and not a blessing, an intolerable burden and not a shining gift. There is only one person to whom *aionios* may properly be applied, and that is God. In the real sense of the term, it is God alone who possesses and inhabits eternity. Eternal life is, therefore, nothing other than the life of God himself. What we are promised is that, here and now, there can be given to each one of us a share in the very life of God.

In God, there is peace; and, therefore, eternal life means serenity. It means a life liberated from the fears which haunt the human situation. In God, there is power; and, therefore, eternal life means the defeat of frustration. It means a life filled with the power of God and, therefore, victorious over circumstance. In God, there is holiness; and, therefore, eternal life means the defeat of sin. It means a life clothed with the purity of God and armed against contamination from a wicked world. In God, there is love; and, therefore, eternal life means the end of bitterness and hatred. It means a life which has the love of God in its heart and the undefeatable love of men and women in all its feelings and in all its actions. In God, there is life; and, therefore, eternal life means the defeat of death. It means a life which is indestructible because it has in it the indestructibility of God himself.

It is John's conviction that such a life comes through Jesus Christ and in no other way. Why should that be? If eternal life is the life of God, it means that we can possess that life only when we know God and are enabled to approach him and rest in him. We can do these two things only in Jesus Christ. The Son alone fully knows the Father; and, therefore, only he can fully reveal to us what God is like. As John had it in his gospel, 'No one has ever seen God. It is God the only Son, who is close to the Father's heart, who has made him known' (John 1:18).

The Basis and the Principle of Prayer

1 John 5:14–15

Here are set down both the basis and the principle of prayer.

(1) The basis of prayer is the simple fact that God listens to our prayers. The word which John uses for *confidence* is interesting. It is *parresia*. Originally, *parresia* meant *freedom of speech*, that freedom to speak boldly which exists in a true democracy. Later, it came to mean any kind of confidence. With God, we have freedom of speech. He is always listening, more ready to hear than we are to pray. We never need to force our way into his presence or compel him to pay attention. He is waiting for us to come.

(2) The principle of prayer is that, to be answered, it must be in accordance with the will of God. Three times in his writings, John lays down what might be called the conditions of prayer.

(a) He says that obedience is a condition of prayer. We receive whatever we ask because we keep his commandments (1 John 3:22).

(b) He says that remaining in Christ is a condition of prayer. If we abide in him and his words abide in us, we will ask for anything and it will be done for us (John 15:7).

(c) He says that to pray in his name is a condition of prayer. If we ask anything in his name, he will do it (John 14:14). The ultimate test of any request is whether we can say to Jesus: 'Give me this for your sake and in your name.'

Prayer must be in accordance with the will of God. Jesus himself, in the moment of his greatest agony and crisis, prayed: 'Not what I want but what you want. . . . Your will be done' (Matthew 26:39, 42). Here is the very essence of prayer. A. E. Brooke suggests that John thought of prayer as 'including only requests for knowledge of, and acquiescence in, the will of God'.

Here is something on which to ponder. We are so apt to think that prayer is asking God for what we want, whereas true prayer is asking God for what he wants. Prayer is not only talking to God; even more, it is listening to him.

Love and Truth

2 John 1–3

It is of great interest to note how in this passage love and truth are insepara-
bly connected. It is because of the truth that he loves and writes to the church.
In Christianity, we learn two things about love.

(1) Christian truth tells us the way in which we ought to love. *Agape* is the
word for Christian love. *Agape* is not passion with its ebb and flow, its flicker
and its flame; nor is it an easy-going and indulgent sentimentalism. And it is
not an easy thing to acquire or a light thing to put into practice. *Agape* is undefeatable goodwill; it is the attitude towards others which, no matter what they
do, will never feel bitterness and will always seek their highest good. There
is a love which seeks to possess; there is a love which softens and weakens;
there is a love which makes people draw back from a challenge; there is a love
which shuts its eyes to faults and to ways which end in ruin. But Christian
love will always seek the highest good of others and will accept all the difficulties, all the problems and all the toil which that search involves. It is of significance that John writes in love to warn.

(2) Christian truth tells us the reason for the obligation of love. In his first
letter, John clearly sets it down. He has talked of the suffering, sacrificing,
incredibly generous love of God; and then he says: 'Beloved, since God loved
us so much, we also ought to love one another' (1 John 4:11). Christians must
love because they are loved. They cannot accept the love of God without
showing love to other men and women whom God loves. Because God loves
us, we must love others with the same generous and sacrificial love.

Christian Hospitality

3 John 1–8

A group of travelling missionaries is on its way to the church of which Gaius is a member, and John urges him to receive them, to give them every support and to send them on their way in a truly Christian manner.

In the ancient world, hospitality was a sacred duty. Strangers were under the protection of Zeus Xenios, Zeus the god of strangers (*xenos* is the Greek for a *stranger*). In the ancient world, inns were notoriously unsatisfactory. The Greeks had an instinctive dislike of taking money in return for hospitality; and, therefore, the profession of innkeeper was looked down upon. Inns were often dirty and flea-infested. Innkeepers had a reputation for being greedy, so that Plato compared them to pirates who hold their guests to ransom before they allow them to escape. The ancient world had a system of guest-friendships whereby families in different parts of the country undertook to give each other's members hospitality when the occasion arose. This connection between families lasted throughout the generations; and, when it was claimed, the claimants brought with them a *sumbolon*, or *token*, which identified them to their hosts. Some cities kept an official called the *Proxenos* in other larger cities to whom their citizens, when travelling, might appeal for shelter and for help.

If the Gentile world accepted the obligation of hospitality, it was only to be expected that the Christians would take it even more seriously. It is Peter's instruction: 'Be hospitable to one another without complaining' (1 Peter 4:9). 'Do not neglect to show hospitality to strangers', says the writer to the Hebrews, and adds: 'for by doing that some have entertained angels without knowing it' (Hebrews 13:2). In the Pastoral Epistles, a widow is to be honoured if she has 'shown hospitality' (1 Timothy 5:10). Paul requests the Romans to 'extend hospitality' (Romans 12:13).

In the early Church, the Christian home was the place of the open door and the loving welcome. There can be few nobler actions than to give a stranger the right of entry to a Christian home. The Christian family circle should always be wide enough to have a place for strangers, wherever they come from.

The Final Ascription of Praise

Jude 24–25

Three times in the New Testament, praise is given to the God who is able. In Romans 16:25, Paul gives praise to the God who is able to strengthen us. In Ephesians 3:20, Paul gives praise to the God who is able to do far more than we can ever ask or even dream of. Here, Jude offers his praise to the God who is able.

(1) God is able to keep us from slipping. The word is *aptaistos*. It is used both of a sure-footed horse which does not stumble and of a person who does not fall into error. To walk with God is to walk in safety even on the most dangerous and the most slippery path. In mountaineering, climbers are roped together so that, even if the inexperienced climber should slip, the skilled mountaineer can take the weight and save the other person. In the same way, when we bind ourselves to God, he keeps us safe.

(2) He can make us stand blameless in the presence of his glory. The word for *blameless* is *amomos*. This is characteristically a sacrificial word; and it is commonly and technically used of an animal which is without spot or blemish and is therefore fit to be offered to God. The amazing thing is that, when we submit ourselves to God, his grace can make our lives nothing less than a sacrifice fit to offer to him.

(3) He can bring us into his presence exultant. Surely the natural way to think of entry into the presence of God is in fear and in shame. But, by the work of Jesus Christ and in the grace of God, we know that we can go to God with joy and with all fear banished. Through Jesus Christ, God the stern Judge has become known to us as God the loving Father. We note one last thing. Usually we associate the word *Saviour* with Jesus Christ; but here Jude attaches it to God. He is not alone in this, for God is often called Saviour in the New Testament (Luke 1:47; 1 Timothy 1:1, 2:3, 4:10; Titus 1:3, 2:10, 3:4). So, we end with the great and comforting certainty that at the back of everything there is a God whose name is Saviour.

Christians have the joyous certainty that in this world they live in the love of God and that in the next world they go to that love. The love of God is both the atmosphere and the goal of all their living.

The Law of Love

The Supreme Blessedness

Matthew 5:1–3

The beatitudes are not pious hopes of what shall be; they are not glowing but vague prophecies of some future bliss; they are congratulations on what is. The blessedness which belongs to Christians is not a blessedness which is postponed to some future world of glory; it is a blessedness which exists here and now. It is not something into which Christians will enter; it is something into which they have entered. True, it will find its fullness and its consummation in the presence of God; but, for all that, it is a present reality to be enjoyed here and now. The very form of the beatitudes is the statement of the joyous thrill and the radiant gladness of the Christian life. In the light of the beatitudes, a gloom-encompassed Christianity is unthinkable.

The word *blessed* which is used in each of the beatitudes is a very special word. It is the Greek word *makarios*. *Makarios* describes that joy which has its secret within itself, that joy which is serene and untouchable, and self-contained, that joy which is completely independent of all the chances and the changes of life. The English word *happiness* gives its own case away. It contains the root *hap*, which means *chance*. Human happiness is something which is dependent on the chances and the changes of life, something which life may give and which life may also destroy. The Christian blessedness is completely untouchable and unassailable. 'No one', said Jesus, 'will take your joy from you' (John 16:22). The beatitudes speak of that joy which seeks us through our pain, that joy which sorrow and loss, and pain and grief, are powerless to touch, that joy which shines through tears, and which nothing in life or death can take away.

The world can win its joys, and the world can equally well lose its joys. A change in fortune, a collapse in health, the failure of a plan, the disappointment of an ambition, even a change in the weather, can take away the fickle joy the world can give. But the Christian has the serene and untouchable joy which comes from walking forever in the company and in the presence of Jesus Christ.

The Salt of the Earth

Matthew 5:13

In the time of Jesus, salt was connected in people's minds with three special qualities.

(1) Salt was connected with purity. No doubt its glistening whiteness made the connection easy. The Romans said that salt was the purest of all things, because it came from the purest of all things — the sun and the sea. Salt was indeed the most primitive of all offerings to the gods, and to the end of the day the Jewish sacrifices were offered with salt. So, if the Christians are to be the salt of the earth, they must be examples of purity.

(2) In the ancient world, salt was the commonest of all preservatives. It was used to keep things from going bad, and to hold putrefaction at bay. If Christians are to be the salt of the earth, they must have a certain antiseptic influence on life; they must be the ones who by their presence defeat corruption and make it easier for others to be good.

(3) But the greatest and the most obvious quality of salt is that salt lends flavour to things. Food without salt is a sadly insipid and even a sickening thing. Christianity is to life what salt is to food. Christianity lends flavour to life.

The tragedy is that, so often, people have connected Christianity with precisely the opposite. They have connected Christianity with that which takes the flavour out of life. The American judge Oliver Wendell Holmes once said: 'I might have entered the ministry if certain clergymen I knew had not looked and acted so much like undertakers.' Robert Louis Stevenson once entered in his diary, as if he was recording an extraordinary phenomenon: 'I have been to Church today, and am not depressed.'

We need to discover the lost radiance of the Christian faith. There should be a sheer sparkle about Christians, but too often they dress like mourners at a funeral, and talk like spectres at a feast. Wherever they are, if they are to be the salt of the earth, Christians must be diffusers of joy.

The Light of the World

Matthew 5:14–15

A light is first and foremost something which is meant to be seen. The houses in Palestine were very dark, with only one little circular window perhaps not more than eighteen inches across. The primary duty of the light of the lamp was to be seen. So, Christianity is something which is meant to be seen. Jesus did not say: 'You are the light of the Church'; he said: 'You are the light of the world'—and in our lives in the world our Christianity should be evident to all.

A light is a guide. On the estuary of any river, we may see the line of lights which marks the channel for the ships to sail in safety. We know how difficult even the city streets are when there are no lights. A light is something to make clear the way. So, Christians must make the way clear to others. That is to say, Christians must of necessity be examples. One of the things which this world needs more than anything else is people who are prepared to be channels for goodness. There are many people in this world who do not have the moral strength and courage to take a stand by themselves, but if someone gives them a lead, they will follow.

A light can often be a warning light. It is sometimes the duty of Christians to bring to others the necessary warning. That is often difficult, and it is often hard to do it in a way which will not do more harm than good. It was said of Florence Allshorn, the famous teacher and principal, that if she ever had occasion to rebuke her students, she did it 'with her arm round about them'. If our warnings are given not in anger, not in irritation, not in criticism, not in condemnation, not in the desire to hurt, but in love, they will be effective.

The light which can be seen, the light which warns, the light which guides—these are the lights which Christians must be.

The Essence of the Law

Matthew 5:17–20

What then did Jesus mean by the law? He said that he had come not to destroy the law, but to fulfil the law. That is to say, he came really to bring out the real meaning of the law. What then is the real principle behind the whole law, that principle which Jesus came to fulfil, the true meaning of which he came to show?

When we look at the Ten Commandments, which are the essence and the foundation of all law, we can see that their whole meaning can be summed up in one word—*respect*, or even better, *reverence*. Reverence for God and for the name of God, reverence for God's day, respect for parents, respect for life, respect for property, respect for personality, respect for the truth and for another person's good name, respect for oneself so that wrong desires may never overpower us—these are the fundamental principles behind the Ten Commandments, principles of reverence for God, and respect for our neighbours and for ourselves. Without them there can be no such thing as law. On them all law is based.

That reverence and that respect Jesus came to fulfil. He came to show men and women in actual life what reverence for God and respect for one another are like. Justice, said the Greeks, consists in giving to God and to others that which is their due. Jesus came to show in actual life what it means to give to God the reverence and to other people the respect which are their due.

That reverence and that respect did not consist in obeying a multitude of petty rules and regulations. They consisted not in sacrifice but in mercy; not in legalism but in love; not in prohibitions which demanded that men and women should not do things, but in the instruction to mould their lives on the positive commandment to love.

The reverence and the respect which are the basis of the Ten Commandments can never pass away; they are the permanent stuff of our relationship to God and to one another.

September 5

The Forbidden Anger

Matthew 5:21–22

In Greek, there are two words for *anger*. There is *thumos*, which was described as being like the flame which comes from dried straw. It is the anger which quickly blazes up and which just as quickly dies down. It is an anger which rises speedily and which just as speedily passes.

Then there is *orge*, which was described as anger that has become deep-rooted. It is the long-lived anger; it is the anger of those who nurse their wrath to keep it warm; it is the anger over which people brood, and which they will not allow to die.

That anger is liable to the judgment court. The judgment court is the local village council which dispensed justice. That court was composed of the local village elders, and varied in number from three in villages of fewer than 150 inhabitants, to seven in larger towns and twenty-three in still bigger cities.

So, then, Jesus condemns all selfish anger. The Bible is clear that anger is forbidden. 'Your anger', said James, 'does not produce God's righteousness' (James 1:20). Paul orders his people to put off all 'anger, wrath, malice, slander' (Colossians 3:8). Even the highest pagan thought saw the folly of anger. Cicero said that when anger entered into the scene, 'nothing could be done rightly and nothing sensibly'. In a vivid phrase, Seneca called anger 'a brief insanity'.

So, Jesus forbids forever the anger which broods, the anger which will not forget, the anger which refuses to be pacified, the anger which seeks revenge. If we are to obey Jesus, all anger must be banished from life, and especially that anger which lingers too long. It is a warning thing to remember that we cannot call ourselves Christians and lose our temper because of any personal wrong which we have suffered.

September 6

The Insurmountable Barrier

Matthew 5:23–24

The idea behind sacrifice was quite simple. If someone did a wrong thing, that action disturbed the relationship between that person and God, and the sacrifice was meant to be the cure which restored that relationship. But two most important things have to be noted. First, it was never held that sacrifice could atone for deliberate sin, for what the Jews called 'the sin of a high hand'. If someone committed a sin unawares, or was swept into sin in a moment of passion when self-control broke, then sacrifice was effective; but if a person deliberately, defiantly, callously and with open eyes committed sin, then sacrifice was powerless to atone.

Second, to be effective, sacrifice had to include confession of sin and true penitence; and true penitence involved the attempt to rectify any consequences sin might have had. The picture which Jesus is painting is very vivid. The worshipper, of course, did not make his own sacrifice; he brought it to the priest, who offered it on his behalf. The worshipper has entered the Temple; he is standing at the rail, ready to hand over his victim to the priest; his hands are on it to confess; and then he remembers his breach with his friend, the wrong done to his neighbour. If his sacrifice is to avail, he must go back and mend that breach and undo that wrong, or nothing can happen.

Jesus is quite clear about this basic fact — we cannot be right with God until we are right with one another; we cannot hope for forgiveness until we have confessed our sin, not only to God, but also to others, and until we have done our best to remove the practical consequences of it.

We sometimes wonder why there is a barrier between us and God; we sometimes wonder why our prayers seem unavailing. The reason may well be that we ourselves have erected that barrier, through being at variance with our neighbours, or because we have wronged someone and have done nothing to put things right.

261

Make Peace in Time

Matthew 5:25–26

Here, Jesus is giving the most practical advice; he is telling people to get trouble sorted out in time, before it piles up still worse trouble for the future. Again and again, it is the experience of life that if a quarrel, or a difference, or a dispute is not healed immediately, it can go on breeding worse and worse trouble as time goes on. Bitterness breeds bitterness.

It has often happened that a quarrel between two people has descended to their families, and has been inherited by future generations, and has in the end succeeded in splitting a church or a society in two. If at the very beginning one of the parties had had the grace to apologize or to admit fault, a grievous situation need never have arisen. If ever we are at variance with someone else, we must get the situation put right straightaway. It may mean that we must be humble enough to confess that we were wrong and to make apology; it may mean that, even if we were in the right, we have to take the first step towards healing the breach. When personal relations go wrong, in nine cases out of ten immediate action will mend them; but if that immediate action is not taken, they will continue to deteriorate, and the bitterness will spread in an ever-widening circle.

It may be that in Jesus' mind there was something even more fundamental than this. It may be that he is saying: 'Put things right with your neighbours while life lasts, for some day—you know not when—life will finish, and you will go to stand before God, the final Judge of all.' The greatest of all Jewish days was the Day of Atonement. Its sacrifices were held to atone for sin known and unknown; but even this day had its limitations. The Talmud clearly lays it down: 'The Day of Atonement does atone for the offences between man and God. The Day of Atonement does not atone for the offences between a man and his neighbour, unless the man has first put things right with his neighbour.'

Here again we have the basic fact—we cannot be right with God unless we are right with one another. We must so live that the end will find us at peace with all people.

September 8

The Forbidden Desire

Matthew 5:27–28

Here is Jesus' second example of the new standard. The law laid it down: 'You shall not commit adultery' (Exodus 20:14). So serious a view did the Jewish teachers take of adultery that the guilty parties could be punished by nothing less than death (Leviticus 20:10); but once again, Jesus lays it down that not only the forbidden action but also the forbidden thought is guilty in the sight of God.

It is necessary that we should understand what Jesus is saying here. He is not speaking of the natural, normal desire, which is part of human instinct and human nature. According to the literal meaning of the Greek, the man who is condemned is the man who looks at a woman with the deliberate intention of lusting after her. The man who is condemned is the man who deliberately uses his eyes to awaken his lust, the man who looks in such a way that passion is awakened and desire deliberately stimulated.

The Jewish Rabbis knew well the way in which the eyes can be used to stimulate the wrong desire. They had their sayings: 'The eyes and the hand are the two brokers of sin.' 'Eye and heart are the two handmaids of sin.' 'Passions lodge only in him who sees.' 'Woe to him who goes after his eyes, for they are adulterous!' As someone has said, 'There is an internal desire of which adultery is only the fruit.' In a tempting world, there are many things which are deliberately designed to excite desire—books, pictures, plays, even advertisements.

The man whom Jesus here condemns is the man who deliberately uses his eyes to stimulate his desires, or who finds a strange delight in things which waken the desire for what is forbidden. To the pure, all things are pure. But the man whose heart is corrupted can look at any scene and find something in it to titillate and excite the wrong desire.

September 9

The Surgical Cure

Matthew 5:29–30

Here Jesus makes a great demand, and it is literally a surgical demand. He insists that anything which is a cause of, or a seduction to, sin should be completely cut out of life. Of course, the words of Jesus are not to be taken with a crude literalism. What they mean is that anything which helps to seduce us to sin is to be ruthlessly rooted out of life. If there is a habit which can be seduction to evil, if there is an association which can be the cause of wrongdoing, if there is a pleasure which could turn out to be our ruin, then that thing must be surgically excised from our life.

Coming as it does immediately after the passage which deals with forbidden thoughts and desires, this passage compels us to ask: how shall we free ourselves from these unclean desires and corrupting thoughts? It is the inevitable law of human nature that the more we say we will not think of something, the more that something will present itself to our thoughts.

There are only two ways to defeat the forbidden thoughts. The first way is by Christian action. The best way to defeat such thoughts is to do something, to fill life so full with Christian labour and Christian service that there is no time for these thoughts to enter in; to think so much of others that in the end we entirely forget ourselves; to rid ourselves of a diseased and morbid introspection by concentrating not on ourselves but on other people. The real cure for evil thoughts is good action.

The second way is to fill the mind with good thoughts. The only way to defeat evil thoughts is to begin to think of something else. If people are harassed by thoughts of the forbidden and unclean things, they will certainly never defeat the evil things by withdrawing from life and saying, I will not think of these things. They can do so only by plunging into Christian action and Christian thought. They will never do it by trying to save their own lives; they can do it only by flinging their lives away for others.

The Bond Which Must Not Be Broken

Matthew 5:31–32

Theoretically, no nation ever had a higher ideal of marriage than the Jews had. Marriage was a sacred duty which a man was bound to undertake. He might delay or abstain from marriage for only one reason—to devote his whole time to the study of the law. If a man refused to marry and have children, he was said to have broken the positive commandment which instructed men to be fruitful and to multiply, and he was said to have 'lessened the image of God in the world' and to have 'slain his posterity'.

Ideally, the Jews abhorred divorce. The voice of God had said: 'I hate divorce' (Malachi 2:16). The Rabbis had the loveliest sayings: 'We find that God is long-suffering to every sin except the sin of unchastity.' 'Unchastity causes the glory of God to depart.' 'Every Jew must surrender his life rather than commit idolatry, murder or adultery.' 'The very altar sheds tears when a man divorces the wife of his youth.' The tragedy was that practice fell so far short of the ideal.

One thing detracted from the whole marriage relationship. The woman in the eyes of the law was a thing. She was at the absolute disposal of her father or of her husband. She had virtually no legal rights at all. To all intents and purposes, a woman could not divorce her husband for any reason, and a man could divorce his wife for any cause at all. In the time of Jesus, divorce had grown easier and easier, so that a situation had arisen in which girls were actually unwilling to marry, because marriage was so insecure.

When Jesus said this, he was not speaking as some theoretical idealist; he was speaking as a practical reformer. He was seeking to deal with a situation in which the structure of family life was collapsing, and in which national morals were becoming ever more lax.

A Word Is a Pledge

Matthew 5:33–37

In the time of Jesus the Jews divided oaths into two classes: those which were absolutely binding and those which were not. Any oath which contained the name of God was absolutely binding; any oath which succeeded in evading the name of God was held not to be binding. The result was that if a man swore by the name of God in any form, he would rigidly keep that oath; but if he swore by heaven, or by earth, or by Jerusalem, or by his head, he felt quite free to break that oath. The result was that evasion had been brought to a fine art.

The idea behind this was that if God's name was used, God became a partner in the transaction; whereas if God's name was not used, God had nothing to do with the transaction. The principle which Jesus lays down is quite clear. In effect, Jesus is saying that, far from having to make God a partner in any transaction, no one can keep God out of any transaction. God is already there. Heaven is the throne of God; the earth is the footstool of God; Jerusalem is the city of God; our own heads do not belong to us; we cannot even make a hair white or black; our lives are God's; there is nothing in the world which does not belong to God; and therefore it does not matter whether God is actually named in so many words or not. God is there already.

Here is a great eternal truth. Life cannot be divided into compartments in some of which God is involved and in others of which he is not involved. He is everywhere, all through life and every activity of life. He hears not only the words which are spoken in his name; he hears all words; and there cannot be any such thing as a form of words which evades bringing God into a transaction. We will regard all promises as sacred, if we remember that all promises are made in the presence of God.

September 12

The End of Resentment and of Retaliation

Matthew 5:38–42

For the Christian, Jesus abolishes the old law of limited vengeance and introduces the new spirit of non-resentment and of non-retaliation.

He says that if anyone smites us on the right cheek, we must turn to him the other cheek also. There is far more here than meets the eye, far more than a mere matter of blows on the face. Suppose a right-handed man is standing in front of another man, and suppose he wants to slap the other man on the right cheek, how must he do it? Unless he goes through the most complicated contortions, and unless he empties the blow of all force, he can hit the other man's cheek only in one way—with the back of his hand. Now according to Jewish Rabbinic law, to hit a man with the back of the hand was twice as insulting as to hit him with the flat of the hand. So, what Jesus is saying is this: 'Even if someone should direct at you the most deadly and calculated insult, you must on no account retaliate, and you must on no account resent it.'

Jesus goes on to say that if anyone tries to take away our tunic in a lawsuit, we must not only let that go, but must offer our cloak also. Again there is much more than meets the eye. The tunic, *chiton*, was the long, sack-like inner garment made of cotton or of linen. Even the poorest man would have a change of tunics. The cloak was the great, blanket-like outer garment which a man wore as a robe by day and used as a blanket at night. Of such garments, a Jew would have only one. Now it was actually the Jewish law that a man's tunic might be taken as a pledge, but not his cloak. The point is that by right a man's cloak could not be taken permanently from him.

What Jesus is saying is this: Christians will never think of their right to do as they like, but always of their duty to be of help. The question is: how do we measure up to that?

267

Christian Love

Matthew 5:43–48

Greek is a language which is rich in synonyms; its words often have shades of meaning which English does not possess. In Greek, there are four different words for *love*.

(1) There is the noun *storge* with its accompanying verb *stergein*. These words are the characteristic words of *family love*.

(2) There is the noun *eros* and the accompanying verb *eran*. These words describe the love between the sexes; there is always passion there.

(3) There is *philia* with its accompanying verb *philein*. These are the warmest and the best Greek words for love. They describe real love, real affection. *Ho philountes*, the present participle, is the word which describes a person's closest and nearest and truest friends.

(4) There is *agape* with its accompanying verb *agapan*. These words indicate *unconquerable benevolence, invincible goodwill*. (*Agape* is the word which is used here.) If we regard people with *agape*, it means that no matter what they do to us, no matter how they treat us, no matter if they insult us or injure us or grieve us, we will never allow any bitterness against them to invade our hearts, but will regard them with that unconquerable benevolence and goodwill which will seek nothing but their highest good. From this, certain things emerge.

Jesus never asked us to love our enemies in the same way as we love our nearest and dearest. The very word is different; to love our enemies in the same way as we love our nearest and dearest would be neither possible nor right. This is a different kind of love. In the case of our nearest and dearest, we cannot help loving them; we speak of falling in love; it is something which comes to us quite unsought; it is something which is born of the emotions of the heart. But in the case of our enemies, love is not only something of the heart; it is also something of the will. It is not something which we cannot help; it is something which we have to will ourselves into doing. It is in fact a victory over that which comes instinctively to us by our very nature.

September 14

Right Things from the Wrong Motive

Matthew 6:1

To the Jews, there were above all three great works of the religious life, three great pillars on which the good life was based—almsgiving, prayer and fasting. Jesus would not for a moment have disputed that; what troubled him was that so often in human life the finest things were done from the wrong motives. It is a strange fact that these three principal good works readily lend themselves to wrong motives. It was Jesus' warning that when these things were done with the sole intention of bringing glory to the doer, they lost by far the most important part of their value.

As Jesus saw it, there is no doubt at all that that kind of thing does receive a certain kind of reward. Three times Jesus uses the phrase, as the Revised Standard Version has it: 'Truly I say to you, they have their reward' (Matthew 6:2, 5, 16). It would be better to translate it: 'They have received payment in full.' The word that is used in the Greek is the verb *apechein*, which was the technical business and commercial word for receiving payment in full. It was the word which was used on receipted accounts. For instance, one man signs a receipt given to another man: 'I have received [*apecho*] from you the rent of the olive press which you have on hire.'

What Jesus is saying is this: 'If you make charitable gifts to demonstrate your own generosity, you will get the admiration of the world—but that is all you will ever get. That is your payment in full. If you pray in such a way as to flaunt your piety in the face of others, you will gain the reputation of being an extremely devout person—but that is all you will ever get. That is your payment in full. If you fast in such a way that everyone knows that you are fasting, you will become known as an extremely abstemious and ascetic person—but that is all you will ever get. That is your payment in full.'

Jesus is saying: 'If your one aim is to get yourself the world's rewards, no doubt you will get them—but you must not look for the rewards which God alone can give.' And we would be sadly short-sighted creatures if we grasped the rewards of time and let the rewards of eternity go.

September 15

The Motives of Giving

Matthew 6:2–4

Let us now look at some of the motives which lie behind the act of giving.

(1) People may give from a sense of duty. They may give not because they wish to give, but because they feel that giving is a duty which they cannot easily escape. It was said of a great but superior man: 'With all his giving he never gives himself.' When someone gives, as it were, from a sense of superiority, when the giving is done always with a certain calculation, when it comes from a sense of duty, even a sense of Christian duty, that person may give generously of things, but it is not enough. The one thing such people never give is themselves, and therefore the giving is incomplete.

(2) People may give from motives of prestige. They may give to take for themselves the glory of giving. The chances are that, if no one is to know about it, or if there is no publicity attached to it, they would not give at all. Unless they are duly thanked and praised and honoured, they are sadly disgruntled and discontented. They give, not to the glory of God, but to the glory of themselves. They give, not primarily to help those in need, but to gratify their own vanity and their own sense of power.

(3) People may give simply because they have to. They may give simply because the overflowing love and kindliness in their hearts will not allow them to do anything else. They may give because, try as they may, they cannot rid themselves of a sense of responsibility for those in need.

We have the pattern of this perfect giving in Jesus Christ himself. Paul wrote to his friends at Corinth: 'For you know the generous act of our Lord Jesus Christ, that though he was rich, yet for your sakes he became poor, so that by his poverty you might become rich' (2 Corinthians 8:9).

Our giving must never be the grim and self-righteous outcome of a sense of duty. Still less must it be done to enhance our own glory and prestige in society; it must be the instinctive outflow of the loving heart; we must give to others as Jesus Christ gave himself to us.

How Not to Pray

Matthew 6:5–8

No nation ever had a higher ideal of prayer than the Jews had; and no religion ever ranked prayer higher in the scale of priorities than the Jews did. 'Great is prayer,' said the Rabbis, 'greater than all good works.' One of the loveliest things that was ever said about family worship is the Rabbinic saying: 'He who prays within his house surrounds it with a wall that is stronger than iron.' The only regret of the Rabbis was that it was not possible to pray all day long.

But certain faults had crept into the Jewish habits of prayer. It is to be noted that these faults are by no means peculiar to Jewish ideas of prayer; they can and do occur anywhere. And it is to be noted that they could only occur in a community where prayer was taken with the greatest seriousness. They are not the faults of neglect; they are the faults of misguided devotion.

In effect, Jesus lays down two great rules for prayer.

(1) He insists that all true prayer must be offered to God. The real fault of the people whom Jesus was criticizing was that they were praying to others and not to God. A certain great preacher once described an ornate and elaborate prayer offered in a Boston church as 'the most eloquent prayer ever offered to a Boston audience'. The preacher was much more concerned with impressing the congregation than with making contact with God. Whether in public or in private prayer, we should have no thought in our minds and no desire in our hearts but God.

(2) He insists that we must always remember that the God to whom we pray is a God of love who is more ready to answer than we are to pray. His gifts and his grace have not to be unwillingly extracted from him. We do not come to a God who has to be coaxed, or pestered, or battered into answering our prayers. We come to one whose one wish is to give.

When we remember that, it is surely sufficient to go to God with the sigh of desire in our hearts, and on our lips the words 'Your will be done.'

September 17

The Disciple's Prayer

Matthew 6:9–15

We must note the order of the petitions in the Lord's Prayer. The first three petitions have to do with God and with the glory of God; the second three petitions have to do with our needs and our necessities. That is to say, God is first given his supreme place—and then, and only then, do we turn to ourselves and our needs and desires. It is only when God is given his proper place that all other things fall into their proper places.

The second part of the prayer deals with the three essential human needs and the three spheres of time within which we all move. First, it asks for bread, for that which is necessary for the maintenance of life, and thereby brings the needs of the present to the throne of God. Second, it asks for forgiveness and thereby brings the past into the presence of God. Third, it asks for help in temptation and thereby commits all the future into the hands of God. In these three brief petitions, we are taught to lay the present, the past and the future before the footstool of the grace of God.

But not only is this a prayer which brings the whole of life to the presence of God; it is also a prayer which brings the whole of God to our lives. When we ask for bread to sustain our earthly lives, that request immediately directs our thoughts to God the Father, the Creator and the Sustainer of all life. When we ask for forgiveness, that request immediately directs our thoughts to God the Son, Jesus Christ our Saviour and Redeemer. When we ask for help for future temptation, that request immediately directs our thoughts to God the Holy Spirit, the Comforter, the Strengthener, the Illuminator, the Guide and the Guardian of our way.

In the most amazing way, this brief second part of the Lord's Prayer takes the present, the past and the future, the whole of human life, and presents them to God the Father, God the Son and God the Holy Spirit, to God in all his fullness.

In the Lord's Prayer, Jesus teaches us to bring the whole of life to the whole of God, and to bring the whole of God to the whole of life.

Forgiveness, Human and Divine

Matthew 6:12, 14–15

Human forgiveness and divine forgiveness are inextricably intertwined. Our forgiveness of one another and God's forgiveness of us cannot be separated; they are interlinked and interdependent.

If we are to have Christian forgiveness in our lives, three things are necessary.

(1) We must learn to understand. There is always a reason why people do things. If they are boorish and impolite and bad-tempered, maybe they are worried or in pain. If they treat us with suspicion and dislike, maybe they have misunderstood, or have been misinformed about something we have said or done. Maybe they are victims of their own environment or their own heredity. Maybe they find life difficult, and human relations are a problem for them. Forgiveness would be very much easier for us if we tried to understand before we allowed ourselves to condemn.

(2) We must learn to forget. As long as we brood upon a snub or an insult, there is no hope that we will forgive. We so often say: 'I can't forget what so-and-so did to me,' or: 'I will never forget how I was treated by such-and-such a person or in such-and-such a place.' These are dangerous sayings, because we can in the end make it humanly impossible for us to forget. We can print the memory indelibly upon our minds. Nothing but the cleansing spirit of Christ can take from these memories of ours the old bitterness that we must forget.

(3) We must learn to love. We have already seen that Christian love, *agape*, is that unconquerable benevolence, that undefeatable goodwill, which will never seek anything but the highest good of others, no matter what they do to us, and no matter how they treat us. That love can come to us only when Christ, who is that love, comes to dwell within our hearts—and he cannot come unless we invite him.

To be forgiven we must forgive, and that is a condition of forgiveness which only the power of Christ can enable us to fulfil.

September 19

The True Fasting

Matthew 6:16–18

Although Jesus condemned the wrong kind of fasting, his words imply that there is a wise fasting, in which he expected that the Christian would take part. There are many reasons why a wise fasting is an excellent thing.

(1) Fasting is good for health. Many of us live a life in which it is easy to get soft and flabby. It is even possible for people to reach the stage when they live to eat instead of eating to live.

(2) Fasting preserves us from becoming the slaves of a habit. There are not a few of us who indulge in certain habits because we find it impossible to stop them. We develop such a craving for certain things that what ought to be a pleasure has become a necessity. If we practised a wise fasting, no pleasure would become a chain, and no habit would come to rule our lives.

(3) Fasting preserves the ability to do without things. One of the great tests in life is the number of things which we have come to regard as essential. Clearly, the fewer things we regard as essentials, the more independent we will be. When all kinds of things become essentials, we are at the mercy of the luxuries of life.

(4) Fasting makes us appreciate things all the more. It may be that there was a time in life when some pleasure came so seldom that we really enjoyed it when it did come. It may be that nowadays what was once a sharp pleasure has become simply a drug which we cannot do without. Fasting keeps the thrill in pleasure by keeping pleasure always fresh and new.

Jesus condemned the wrong kind of fasting, but he never meant that fasting should be completely eliminated from life and living. We would do well to practise it in our own way and according to our own need.

Treasure in Heaven

Matthew 6:19–21

The Jews were very familiar with the phrase *treasure in heaven*. They identified such treasure with two things in particular.

(1) They said that the deeds of kindness which people did upon earth became their treasure in heaven. That was also the principle of the Christian Church in the days to come. The early Church always lovingly cared for the poor, the sick, the distressed, the helpless and those for whom no one else cared.

(2) The Jews always connected the phrase *treasure in heaven* with character. When Rabbi Yose ben Kisma was asked if he would dwell in a pagan city on condition of receiving very high pay for his services, he replied that he would not dwell anywhere except in a home of the law, 'for', he said, 'in the hour of a man's departure neither silver, nor gold, nor precious stones accompany him, but only his knowledge of the law, and his good works'. As the grim Spanish proverb has it, 'There are no pockets in a shroud.'

(3) Jesus ends this section by stating that where a person's treasure is, that person's heart is there also. If everything that people value and set their hearts upon is on earth, then they will have no interest in any world beyond this world; if all through their lives their eyes are on eternity, then they will evaluate lightly the things of this world.

This world is not the end of life, it is a stage on the way; and therefore we should never lose our hearts to this world and to the things of this world. Our eyes ought to be forever fixed on the goal beyond.

September 21

The Necessity of the Generous Eye

Matthew 6:22–23

Here, Jesus speaks of one special virtue which fills the eye with light, and one special fault which fills the eye with darkness. The Authorized Version speaks here about the eye being single and the eye being evil. The word for *single* is *haplous*, and its corresponding noun is *haplotes*. Regularly in the Greek of the Bible, these words mean *generous* and *generosity*.

The word which is translated in the Authorized Version as *evil* is *poneros*. Certainly that is the normal meaning of the word; but both in the New Testament and in the Septuagint, *poneros* regularly means *niggardly* or *grudging*.

So Jesus is saying: 'There is nothing like generosity for giving you a clear and undistorted view of life and of people; and there is nothing like the grudging and ungenerous spirit for distorting your view of life and of people.'

There are three great evils of the ungenerous spirit, of the eye that is grudging.

(1) It makes it impossible to live with ourselves. If people are forever envying others their success, grudging others their happiness and shutting their hearts against the needs of others, they become the most pitiable of creatures—people who bear a grudge. There grows within them a bitterness and a resentment which robs them of their happiness, steals away their peace and destroys their contentment.

(2) It makes it impossible to live with other people. Mean people are abhorred by all; the people whom everyone despises are those who are miserly of heart. Charity covers a multitude of sins, but the grudging spirit makes useless a multitude of virtues.

(3) It makes it impossible to live with God. There is no one so generous as God; and, in the last analysis, there can be no fellowship between two people who guide their lives by diametrically opposite principles. There can be no fellowship between the God whose heart is afire with love, and the man or woman whose heart is frozen with meanness.

The grudging eye distorts our vision; the generous eye alone sees clearly, for it alone sees as God sees.

276

September 22

The Place of Material Possessions

Matthew 6:24

At the basis of Jesus' teaching about possessions, there are three great principles.

(1) In the last analysis, all things belong to God. Scripture makes that abundantly clear. 'The earth is the Lord's and all that is in it, the world and those who live in it' (Psalm 24:1). There is nothing in this world of which we can say: 'This is mine.' Of all things, we can only say: 'This belongs to God, and God has given me the use of it.' There is nothing in this world of which anyone can say: 'This is mine, and I will therefore do what I like with it.' Of everything, we must say: 'This is God's, and I must use it as its owner would have it to be used.'

(2) The second basic principle is that people are always more important than things. If possessions have to be acquired, if money has to be amassed, if wealth has to be accumulated at the expense of treating people as things, then all such riches are wrong. Whenever and wherever that principle is forgotten, or neglected, or defied, far-reaching disaster is certain to follow.

(3) The third principle is that wealth is always a subordinate good. The Bible does not say that 'money is the root of all evil'; it says that 'the love of money is a root of all kinds of evil' (1 Timothy 6:10). If people desire material things for an honourable independence, to help their families and to do something for others, that is good; but if they desire it simply to heap pleasure upon pleasure, and to add luxury, if wealth has become the thing they live for and live by, then wealth has ceased to be a subordinate good, and has usurped the place in life which only God should occupy.

One thing emerges from all this—the possession of wealth, money and material things is not a sin, but it is a grave responsibility. If people own many material things, it is not so much a matter for congratulation as it is a matter for prayer, that they may use them as God would want them to.

The Folly of Worry

Matthew 6:25–34

Let us see if we can gather up Jesus' arguments against worry.

(1) Worry is needless, useless and even actively injurious. Worry cannot affect the past, for the past is past. It is not that we can or ought to dissociate ourselves from our past; but we ought to use our past as a spur and a guide for better action in the future, and not as something about which we brood until we have worried ourselves into a paralysis of action. Equally, worry about the future is useless, and the future of reality is seldom as bad as the future of our fears.

But worry is worse than useless; it is often actively injurious. The two typical diseases of modern life are the stomach ulcer and the coronary thrombosis, and in many cases both are the result of worry. It is a medical fact that those who laugh most live longest. The worry which wears out the mind wears out the body along with it. Worry affects our judgment, lessens our powers of decision and renders us progressively incapable of dealing with life. Let each of us give our best to every situation—we cannot give more—and let us leave the rest to God.

(2) Worry is blind. Worry refuses to learn the lesson of nature. Jesus bids men and women look at the birds, and see the bounty which is behind nature, and trust the love that lies behind that bounty.

(3) Worry is essentially irreligious. Worry is not caused by external circumstances. In the same circumstances, one person can be absolutely serene and another can be worried to death. Both worry and serenity come not from circumstances but from the heart. Isaiah said it long ago: 'Those of steadfast mind you keep in peace—in peace because they trust in you' (Isaiah 26:3).

There may be greater sins than worry, but very certainly there is no more disabling sin. 'Take no anxious thought for the morrow'—that is the commandment of Jesus, and it is the way not only to peace but also to power.

September 24

The Error of Judgment

Matthew 7:1–5

There is hardly anyone who has not been guilty of some grave misjudgment; there is hardly anyone who has not suffered from someone else's misjudgment. And yet the strange fact is that there is hardly any commandment of Jesus which is more consistently broken and neglected.

No one knows the strength of another person's temptations. People who have a placid and equable temperament know nothing of the temptations of hot-blooded people whose emotions are quickly aroused. People brought up in good homes and in Christian surroundings know nothing of the temptation of those brought up in a slum, or in a place pervaded by evil. Those of us who are blessed with fine parents know nothing of the temptations of people who bear the burden of a difficult upbringing. The fact is that if we realized what some people have to go through, so far from condemning them, we would be amazed that they have succeeded in being as good as they are.

No more do we know the whole person. In one set of circumstances, a person may be unlovely and graceless; in another, that same person may be a tower of strength and beauty. There is a kind of crystal called Labrador spar. At first sight it is dull and without lustre; but if it is turned round and round, and here and there, it will suddenly come into a position where the light strikes it in a certain way and it will sparkle with flashing beauty. People are like that. They may seem unlovely simply because we do not know the whole person. Everyone has something good in him or her. Our task is not to condemn, and to judge by, the superficial unloveliness, but to look for the underlying beauty. That is what we would have others do to us, and that is what we must do to them.

We have quite enough to do to rectify our own lives without seeking censoriously to rectify the lives of others. We would do well to concentrate on our own faults, and to leave the faults of others to God.

The Charter of Prayer

Matthew 7:7–11

God will never refuse our prayers; and God will never mock our prayers. The Greeks had their stories about the gods who answered people's prayers, but the answer was an answer with a barb in it, a double-edged gift. Aurora, the goddess of the dawn, fell in love with Tithonus, a mortal youth, so the Greek story ran. Zeus, the king of the gods, offered her any gift that she might choose for her mortal lover. Aurora very naturally chose that Tithonus might live forever, but she had forgotten to ask that Tithonus might remain forever young; and so Tithonus grew older and older and older, and could never die, and the gift became a curse.

There is a lesson here: God will always answer our prayers; but he will answer them in his way, and his way will be the way of perfect wisdom and of perfect love. Often, if he answered our prayers as we at the moment desired, it would be the worst thing possible for us, for in our ignorance we often ask for gifts which would be our ruin. This saying of Jesus tells us not only that God will answer, but also that God will answer in wisdom and in love.

Although this is the charter of prayer, it lays certain obligations upon us. In Greek, there are two kinds of imperative: there is the aorist imperative, which issues one definite command. 'Shut the door behind you' would be an aorist imperative. There is the present imperative, which issues a command that a person should always do something or should go on doing something. 'Always shut doors behind you' would be a present imperative. The imperatives here are present imperatives; therefore Jesus is saying: 'Go on asking; go on seeking; go on knocking.' He is telling us to persist in prayer; he is telling us never to be discouraged in prayer.

Clearly, therein lies the test of our sincerity. Do we really want a thing? Is a thing such that we can bring it repeatedly into the presence of God, for the biggest test of any desire is: can I pray about it?

September 26

The Everest of Ethics

Matthew 7:12

This is probably the most universally famous thing that Jesus ever said. With this commandment, the Sermon on the Mount reaches its summit. This saying of Jesus has been called 'the capstone of the whole discourse'. It is the topmost peak of social ethics, and the Everest of all ethical teaching.

It is not difficult to find this rule in Jewish teaching in its negative form, but there is no parallel to the positive form in which Jesus put it. The same is true of the teaching of other religions. In its negative form, this rule is in fact the basis of all ethical teaching; but no one but Jesus ever put it in its positive form. Many voices had said: 'Do not do to others what you would not have them do to you,' but no voice had ever said: 'Do to others what you would have them do to you.'

It is perfectly possible for people to observe the negative form of the Golden Rule. They could without very serious difficulty so discipline their lives that they would not do to others what they did not wish others to do to them; but the only people who can even begin to satisfy the positive form of the rule are those men and women who have the love of Christ within their hearts. They will try to forgive as they would wish to be forgiven, to help as they would wish to be helped, to praise as they would wish to be praised, to understand as they would wish to be understood. They will never seek to avoid doing things; they will always look for things to do.

Clearly this will make life much more complicated; clearly they will have much less time to spend on their own desires and their own activities, for time and time again they will have to stop what they are doing to help someone else. It will be a principle which will dominate their lives at home, in the factory, on the bus, in the office, in the street, on the train, in their leisure activities—everywhere. They can never do it until self withers and dies within their hearts.

To obey this commandment, we must become new men and women with a new centre to our lives; and if the world was composed of people who sought to obey this rule, it would be a new world.

Life at the Crossroads

Matthew 7:13–14

In every action of life, we are confronted with a choice. We must always take one way or the other. Let us examine the difference between the two ways.

(1) It is the difference between the hard and the easy way. There is never any easy way to greatness; greatness is always the product of toil. Even when a thing is done with an appearance of ease, that ease is the product of unremitting toil. The skill of the concert pianist or the champion golfer did not come without sweat. There has never been any other way to greatness than the way of toil, and anything else which promises such a way is a delusion and a snare.

(2) It is the difference between the long and the short way. Very rarely, something may emerge complete and perfect in a flash, but far oftener greatness is the result of long labour and constant attention to detail. No one ever arrived at a masterpiece by a short cut. In this world, we are constantly faced with the short way, which promises immediate results, and the long way, of which the results are in the far distance. But the lasting things never come quickly; the long way is the best way in the end.

(3) It is the difference between the disciplined and the undisciplined way. Nothing was ever achieved without discipline; and many athletes and many men and women in other fields have been ruined because they abandoned discipline and let themselves go.

(4) It is the difference between the thoughtful and the thoughtless way. Here we come to the heart of the matter. None of us would ever take the easy, the short, the undisciplined way, if we only thought. Everything in this world has two aspects—how it looks at the moment, and how it will look in the time to come. The easy way may look very inviting at the moment, and the hard way may look very daunting.

The only way to get our values right is to see not the beginning but the end of the way, to see things not in the light of time but in the light of eternity.

The Fruits of Falseness

Matthew 7:15–20

What are the false effects, the evil fruits, which a false prophet may produce?

(1) Teaching is false if it produces a religion which consists solely or mainly in the observance of externals. It is easy to confuse religion with religious practices. It is possible — and indeed not uncommon — to teach that religion consists in going to church, observing the Lord's Day, fulfilling one's financial obligations to the church and reading one's Bible. A person might do all these things and be far from being a Christian, for Christianity is an attitude of the heart to God and to one another.

(2) Teaching is false if it produces a religion which consists in prohibitions. Any religion which is based on a series of 'you shall nots' is a false religion. If we could become Christians simply by abstaining from doing things, Christianity would be a much easier religion than it is. But the whole essence of Christianity is that it does not consist in not doing things; it consists in doing things. A negative Christianity on our part can never answer the positive love of God.

(3) Teaching is false if it produces an easy religion. Any teaching which takes the iron out of religion, any teaching which takes the cross out of Christianity, any teaching which eliminates the threat from the voice of Christ, any teaching which pushes judgment into the background and makes people think lightly of sin, is false teaching.

(4) Teaching is false if it divorces religion and life. Any teaching which removes the Christian from the life and activity of the world is false. Christians are not spectators from the balcony; they are involved in the warfare of life.

(5) Teaching is false if it produces a religion which is arrogant and separatist. Religion is meant to bring people closer together, not to drive them apart. Religion is meant to gather people into one family, not to split them up into hostile groups. The teaching which declares that any church or any sect has a monopoly of the grace of God is false teaching, for Christ is not the Christ who divides, he is the Christ who unites.

On False Pretences

Matthew 7:21–23

There is an apparently surprising feature about this passage. Jesus is quite ready to concede that many of the false prophets will do and say wonderful and impressive things. There was many an impostor who rendered lip service to Jesus Christ and who used his name to produce wonderful effects on demon-possessed people. What Jesus is saying is that if anyone uses his name under false pretences, the day of reckoning will come. The real motives will be exposed, and that person will be banished from the presence of God.

There are two great permanent truths within this passage. There is only one way in which people's sincerity can be proved, and that is by their practice. Fine words can never be a substitute for fine deeds. There is only one proof of love, and that proof is obedience. There is no point in saying that we love a person and then doing things which break that person's heart. When we were young, maybe we used sometimes to say to our mothers: 'Mother, I love you.' And maybe our mothers sometimes smiled a little wistfully and said: 'I wish you would show it a little more in the way you behave.' So often we confess God with our lips and deny him with our lives. It is not difficult to recite a creed, but it is difficult to live the Christian life. Faith without practice is a contradiction in terms, and love without obedience is an impossibility.

At the back of this passage is the idea of judgment. All through it there runs the certainty that the day of reckoning comes. Some people may succeed over a period in maintaining the pretences and the disguises, but there comes a day when the pretences are shown for what they are, and the disguises are stripped away.

We may deceive others with our words, but we cannot deceive God. 'You discern my thoughts from far away,' said the psalmist (Psalm 139:2). No one can ultimately deceive the God who sees the heart.

The Only True Foundation

Matthew 7:24–27

Jesus was in a double sense an expert. He was an expert in Scripture. The writer of Proverbs gave him the hint for his picture: 'When the tempest passes, the wicked are no more, but the righteous are established for ever' (Proverbs 10:25). Here is the germ of the picture which Jesus drew of the two houses and the two builders. But Jesus was also an expert in life. He was the crafts-man who knew all about the building of houses, and when he spoke about the foundations of a house he knew what he was talking about.

In Palestine, the builder must think ahead. There were many gullies which in summer were pleasant sandy hollows, but in winter became raging torrents of rushing water. A man might be looking for a house; he might find a pleas-antly sheltered sandy hollow; and he might think this a very suitable place. But, if he was a shortsighted man, he might well have built his house in the dried-up bed of a river, and when the winter came, his house would disinte-grate. Only a house whose foundations are firm can withstand the storm; and only a life whose foundations are sure can stand the test.

Jesus demanded two things.

(1) He demanded that men and women should listen. One of the great dif-ficulties which face us today is the simple fact that people often do not know what Jesus said or what the Church teaches. The first step to the Christian life is simply to give Jesus Christ a chance to be heard.

(2) He demanded that men and women should do. Knowledge only becomes relevant when it is translated into action. It would be perfectly pos-sible to pass an examination in Christian ethics with the highest distinction, and yet not to be a Christian. Knowledge must become action; theory must become practice; theology must become life.

Is there any word in which hearing and doing are summed up? There is such a word, and that word is *obedience*. It is Jesus' claim that obedience to him is the only sure foundation for life; and it is his promise that the life which is founded on obedience to him is safe, no matter what storms may come.

Signs and Wonders

October 1

A Mother's Faith

John 2:1–11

This story shows us very beautifully two things about Mary's faith in Jesus.

(1) Instinctively Mary turned to Jesus whenever something went wrong. She knew her son. It was not till he was thirty years old that Jesus left home; and all these years Mary lived with him. There is an old legend which tells of the days when Jesus was a little baby in the home in Nazareth. It tells how in those days, when people felt tired and worried and hot and bothered and upset, they would say: 'Let us go and look at Mary's child,' and they would go and look at Jesus, and somehow all their troubles rolled away. It is still true that those who know Jesus intimately turn instinctively to him when things go wrong—and they never find him wanting.

(2) Even when Mary did not understand what Jesus was going to do, even when it seemed that he had refused her request, Mary still believed in him so much that she turned to the serving folk and told them to do whatever Jesus told them to do. Mary had the faith which could trust even when it did not understand. She did not know what Jesus was going to do, but she was quite sure that he would do the right thing. In every life come periods of darkness when we do not see the way. In every life come things which are such that we do not see why they came or any meaning in them. Happy are those who in such a case still trust even when they cannot understand.

Still further, this story tells us something about Jesus. In answer to Mary, he said: 'My hour has not yet come.' All through the gospel story, Jesus talks about his hour. All through his life, Jesus knew that he had come into this world for a definite purpose and a definite task. He saw his life not in terms of his wishes, but in terms of God's purpose for himself. He saw his life not against the shifting background of time, but against the steady background of eternity.

It is not only Jesus who came into this world to fulfil the purpose of God. It has been said that each one of us is 'a dream and an idea of God'. We, too, must think not of our own wishes and our own desires, but of the purpose for which God sent us into his world.

The Spirit of an Unclean Devil

Luke 4:31–37

The ancient world believed that the air was thickly populated with evil spirits which sought entry into people. Often they entered through food or drink. All illness was caused by them. There were spirits of deafness, of dumbness, of fever; spirits which took a person's sanity and wits away; spirits of lying and of deceit and of uncleanness. It was such a spirit that Jesus exorcised here. To many people this is a problem. On the whole, we regard belief in spirits as something primitive and superstitious which we have outgrown. Yet Jesus seemed to believe in them. There are three possibilities.

(1) Jesus actually did believe in them. If that is so, as far as scientific knowledge went he was not in advance of his own age but under all the limitations of contemporary medical thought. There is no need to refuse such a conclusion for, if Jesus was really human, in scientific things he must have had the knowledge available at that time.

(2) Jesus did not believe in them. But the sufferer did believe intensely and Jesus could cure people only by assuming their beliefs about themselves to be true. Saying to someone who is ill, 'There's nothing wrong with you', is no help. The reality of the pain has to be admitted before a cure can follow.

(3) Increasingly people are prepared to admit that perhaps there is something in demons after all. There are certain troubles which have no bodily cause as far as can be discovered. Since there is no physical explanation, some people now think there must be a spiritual one and that demons may not be so unreal after all.

The people were astonished at Jesus' power—and no wonder. It was his sheer authority which staggered them. Jesus' authority was something quite new. When the Rabbis taught they supported every statement with quotations. They always said, 'There is a saying that . . .' 'Rabbi so and so said that . . .' When the prophets spoke, they said, 'Thus saith the Lord.' When Jesus spoke, he said, 'I say to you.' He needed no authorities to buttress him; his was not a delegated authority; he was authority incarnate. He speaks and we know that this is beyond human argument—this is God.

A Miracle in a Cottage

Luke 4:38–39

Here Luke the doctor writes. The Greek medical writers divided fevers into two classes—major and minor. Luke knew just how to describe this illness. There are three great truths in this short incident.

(1) Jesus was always ready to serve. He had just left the synagogue. Preachers know what it is like after a service. They have given of themselves and need rest. The last thing they want is a crowd of people and a fresh call upon their energy. But no sooner had Jesus left the synagogue and entered Peter's house than the insistent cry of human need was at him. He did not claim that he was tired and must rest. He answered it without complaint.

Members of the Salvation Army tell of a Mrs Berwick in the days of the London blitzes of the Second World War. She had been in charge of the Army's social work in Liverpool and had retired to London. People had strange ideas during the blitzes and they had the idea that somehow Mrs Berwick's house was safe; and so they gathered there. Though she had retired, the instinct to help was still with her. She got together a simple first-aid box and then put a notice in her window, 'If you need help, knock here.' Always Jesus was ready to help; his followers must be the same.

(2) Jesus did not need a crowd to work a miracle. So often we will make an effort in company that we will not make among our own private circle. So often we are at our best in society and at our worst at home. But Jesus was prepared to put out all his power in a village cottage in Capernaum when the crowds were gone.

(3) When Peter's mother-in-law was cured, immediately she began to serve them. She realized that she had been given back her health to spend it in the service of others. She wanted no fussing and no petting; she wanted to get on with cooking and serving her family and Jesus. Mothers are like that. We would do well to remember that if God gave us the priceless gift of health and strength, he gave it that we might use it always in the service of others.

Human Helplessness and Christ's Power

John 5:1–9

In this story, we see very clearly the conditions under which the power of Jesus operated. He gave his orders to people, and, in proportion as they tried to obey, power came to them.

(1) Jesus began by asking the man if he wanted to be cured. It was not so foolish a question as it may sound. The man had waited for thirty-eight years, and it might well have been that hope had died and left behind a passive and dull despair. In his heart of hearts, the man might be well content to remain an invalid for, if he was cured, he would have all the burden of making a living. He might have grown accustomed to his disability, being able to leave the working and the worrying to someone else.

The first essential towards receiving the power of Jesus is to have intense desire for it. Jesus says: 'Do you really want to be changed?' If in our inmost hearts we are well content to stay as we are, there can be no change for us.

(2) Jesus went on to tell the man to get up. It is as if he said to him: 'Man, bend your will to it and you and I will do this thing together!' The power of God never dispenses with human effort. Nothing is truer than that we must realize our own helplessness; but in a very real sense it is true that miracles happen when our will and God's power co-operate to make them possible.

(3) In effect, Jesus was commanding the man to attempt the impossible. 'Get up!' he said. His bed would simply be a light stretcher-like frame—the Greek is *krabbatos*, a colloquial word which really means a *pallet*—and Jesus told him to pick it up and carry it away. The man might well have said with a kind of injured resentment that for thirty-eight years his bed had been carrying him and there was not much sense in telling him to carry it. But he made the effort along with Christ—and the thing was done.

(4) Here is the road to achievement. There are so many things in this world which defeat us. When we have intensity of desire and determination to make the effort, hopeless though it may seem, the power of Christ gets its opportunity, and with him we can conquer the things that for a long time have conquered us.

The Conditions of a Miracle

Luke 5:1–11

We are here confronted with a turning point in the career of Jesus. He would go anywhere where people would listen to him. When the synagogue was shut Jesus took to the open road. There is in this story what we might call a list of the conditions of a miracle.

(1) There is the eye that sees. There is no need to think that Jesus created a shoal of fishes for the occasion. In the Sea of Galilee there were phenomenal shoals which covered the sea as if it was solid for as much as an acre. Most likely Jesus' discerning eye saw just such a shoal and his keen sight made it look like a miracle. We need the eye that really sees. Many people saw steam raise the lid of a kettle; only James Watt went on to think of a steam engine. Many people saw an apple fall; only Isaac Newton went on to think out the law of gravity. The earth is full of miracles for the eye that sees.

(2) There is the spirit that will make an effort. If Jesus said it, tired as he was Peter was prepared to try again. For most people the disaster of life is that they give up just one effort too soon.

(3) There is the spirit which will attempt what seems hopeless. The night was past and that was the time for fishing. All the circumstances were unfavourable, but Peter said, 'Let circumstances be what they may, if you say so, we will try again.' Too often we wait because the time is not opportune. If we wait for a perfect set of circumstances, we will never begin at all. If we want a miracle, we must take Jesus at his word when he bids us attempt the impossible.

October 6

Touching the Untouchable

Luke 5:12–15

Dr A. B. MacDonald, in an article on the leper colony in Itu, of which he was in charge, wrote, 'The leper is sick in mind as well as body. For some reason there is an attitude to leprosy different from the attitude to any other disfiguring disease. It is associated with shame and horror, and carries, in some mysterious way, a sense of guilt, although innocently acquired like most contagious troubles. Shunned and despised, frequently do lepers consider taking their own lives and some do.'

Lepers were hated by others until they came to hate themselves. The leper came to Jesus; he was unclean; and Jesus touched him.

(1) Jesus touched the untouchable. His hand went out to the man from whom everyone else would have shrunk away. Two things emerge. First, when we despise ourselves, when our hearts are filled with bitter shame, let us remember that, in spite of all, Christ's hand is still stretched out. The writer Mark Rutherford wished to add a new beatitude: 'Blessed are those who heal us of our self-despisings.' That is what Jesus did and does. Second, it is of the very essence of Christianity to touch the untouchable, to love the unlovable, to forgive the unforgivable. Jesus did—and so must we.

(2) Jesus sent the man to carry out the normal, prescribed routine for cleansing. The regulations are described in Leviticus 14. That is to say a miracle did not dispense with what medical science of the time could do. It did not absolve the man from carrying out the prescribed rules. We will never get miracles by neglecting the gifts and the wisdom God has given us. It is when human skill combines with God's grace that wonder happens.

(3) Verse 15 tells us of the popularity Jesus enjoyed. But it was only because people wanted something out of him. Many desire the gifts of God but repudiate the demands of God—and there can be nothing more dishonourable.

October 7

Forgiven and Healed

Luke 5:18–26

What does the passage about forgiving sins mean? We must remember that sin and suffering were in Palestine inextricably connected. It was implicitly believed that suffering was the consequence of sin. And therefore the sufferer very often had an even morbid sense of sin. That is why Jesus began by telling the man that his sins were forgiven. Without that the man would never believe that he could be cured.

This shows how in debate the scribes and Pharisees were completely routed. They objected to Jesus claiming to extend forgiveness to the man. But on their own arguments and assumptions the man was ill because he had sinned; and if he was cured that was proof that his sins were forgiven. The complaint of the Pharisees recoiled on them and left them speechless. The wonderful thing is that here is a man who was saved by the faith of his friends. Jesus saw their faith; the eager faith of those who stopped at nothing to bring their friend to Jesus won his cure. It still happens.

(1) There are those who are saved by the faith of their parents. Thomas Carlyle used to say that still across the years there came his mother's voice to him, 'Trust in God and do the right.' When Augustine was living a reckless and immoral life his devout mother came to ask the help of a Christian bishop. 'It is impossible', he said, 'that the child of such prayers and tears should perish.' Many of us would gladly witness that we owe all that we are and ever will be to the faith of godly parents.

(2) There are those who are daily saved by the faith of those who love them. When H. G. Wells was newly married and success was bringing new temptations to him, he said, 'It was as well for me that behind the folding doors at 12 Mornington Road there slept one so sweet and clean that it was unthinkable that I should appear before her squalid or drunken or base.' Many of us would do the shameful thing but for the fact that we could not meet the pain and sorrow in someone's eyes.

In the very structure of life and love—blessed be God—there are precious influences which save human souls.

The Defiance of Jesus

Luke 6:6–11

In this incident Jesus openly broke the law. To heal was to work and work was prohibited on the Sabbath day. But Jesus laid down the great principle that, whatever the rules and regulations may say, it is always right to do a good thing on the Sabbath day. He asked the piercing questions, 'Is it legal to save life or to destroy it on the Sabbath?' That must have struck home, for while he was seeking to help the life of the man, they were doing all they could to destroy him.

In this story there are three characters.

(1) There is the man with the withered hand. He was a man who was prepared to attempt the impossible. He did not argue when Jesus told him to stretch out his useless hand; he tried and, in the strength Jesus gave him, he succeeded. Impossible is a word which should be banished from the vocabulary of the Christian. As a famous scientist said, 'The difference between the difficult and the impossible is only that the impossible takes a little longer to do.'

(2) There is Jesus. There is in this story a glorious atmosphere of defiance. Jesus knew that he was being watched but without hesitation he healed. He asked the man to stand out in front of everybody. This thing was not going to be done in a corner. There is a story of one of John Wesley's preachers who proposed to preach in a hostile town. He hired the town crier to announce the meeting and the town crier announced it in a terrified whisper. The preacher took the bell from him and rang it and thundered out, 'Mr So and So will preach in such and such a place and at such and such a time tonight—and I am the man.' Real Christians display with pride the banner of their faith and bid the opposition do its worst.

(3) There are the Pharisees. Here were men who took the quite extraordinary course of hating a man who had just cured a sufferer. They are the outstanding example of men who loved their rules and regulations more than they loved God. We see this happen in churches over and over again. There is an ever-present danger of setting loyalty to a system above loyalty to God.

October 9

A Soldier's Faith

Luke 7:1–10

The central character is a Roman centurion; and he was no ordinary man.

(1) He had a completely unusual attitude to his slave. He loved this slave and would go to any trouble to save him. In Roman law a slave was defined as a living tool; he had no rights; a master could ill-treat him and even kill him if he chose. Normally when a slave was past his work he was thrown out to die. The attitude of this centurion to his slave was quite unusual.

(2) He was clearly a deeply religious man. A man would need to be more than superficially interested before he would go to the lengths of building a synagogue. It is true that the Romans encouraged religion from the cynical motive that it kept people in order. But this centurion was no administrative cynic; he was a sincerely religious man.

(3) He had an extremely unusual attitude to the Jews. If the Jews despised the Gentiles, the Gentiles hated the Jews. Anti-Semitism is not a new thing. The Romans called the Jews a filthy race; they spoke of Judaism as a barbarous superstition; they spoke of the Jewish hatred of humankind; they accused the Jews of worshipping an ass's head and annually sacrificing a Gentile stranger to their God. But the whole atmosphere of this story implies a close bond of friendship between this centurion and the Jews.

(4) He was a humble man. He knew quite well that a strict Jew was forbidden by the law to enter the house of a Gentile (Acts 10:28), just as he was forbidden to allow a Gentile into his house or have any communication with him. The centurion would not even come to Jesus himself. He persuaded his Jewish friends to approach him. This man who was accustomed to command had an amazing humility in the presence of true greatness.

(5) He was a man of faith. His faith is based on the soundest argument. He argued from his own experience to an understanding of God. If his authority produced the results it did, how much more must that of Jesus? He came with that perfect confidence which looks up and says, 'Lord, I know you can do this.' If only we had a faith like that, for us too the miracle would happen and life become new.

October 10

The Compassion of Christ

Luke 7:11–17

In many ways this is the loveliest story in all the gospels.

(1) It tells of the pathos and the poignancy of human life. The funeral procession would be headed by the band of professional mourners with their flutes and their cymbals, uttering in a kind of frenzy their shrill cries of grief. There is all the ageless sorrow of the world in the austere and simple sentence, 'He was his mother's only son, and she was a widow.' In the nature of things we live in a world of broken hearts.

(2) To the pathos of human life, Luke adds the compassion of Christ. Jesus was moved to the depths of his heart. There is no stronger word in the Greek language for sympathy and again and again in the gospel story it is used of Jesus (Matthew 14:14, 15:32, 20:34; Mark 1:41, 8:2).

To the ancient world this must have been a staggering thing. The noblest faith in antiquity was Stoicism. The Stoics believed that the primary characteristic of God was apathy, incapability of feeling. Here we are presented with the amazing conception of one who was the Son of God being moved to the depths of his being. For many that is the most precious thing about the God and Father of our Lord Jesus Christ.

(3) To the compassion of Jesus, Luke adds the power of Jesus. He went up and touched the bier. It was not a coffin, for coffins were not used in the Middle East. Very often long wickerwork baskets were used for carrying the body to the grave. It was a dramatic moment. In the words of one great commentator, 'Jesus claimed as his own what death had seized as his prey.'

It may well be that here we have a miracle of diagnosis; that Jesus with those keen eyes of his saw that the young man was in a cataleptic trance and saved him from being buried alive, as so many were in Palestine. It does not matter; the fact remains that Jesus claimed for life a young man who had been marked for death. Jesus is not only the Lord of life; he is the Lord of death who himself triumphed over the grave and who has promised that, because he lives, we shall live also (John 14:19).

Faith's Test and Faith's Reward

Matthew 9:27–31

The name by which these two blind men addressed Jesus was Son of David. For centuries, the Jews had awaited the promised deliverer of David's line, the leader who would not only restore their freedom, but who would lead them to power and glory and greatness. It was in that way that these blind men thought of Jesus; they saw in him the wonder-worker who would lead the people to freedom and to conquest.

The way in which Jesus dealt with them is illuminating.

(1) Clearly, he did not answer their shouts at once. Jesus wished to be quite sure that they were sincere and earnest in their desire for what he could give them. It might well have been that they had taken up a popular cry just because everyone else was shouting, and that, as soon as Jesus had passed by, they would simply forget. He wanted first of all to be sure that their request was genuine and that their sense of need was real.

(2) It is interesting to note that Jesus in effect compelled these people to see him alone. Because he did not answer them in the streets, they had to come to him in the house. It is the law of the spiritual life that sooner or later every individual must confront Jesus alone. It is all very well to take a decision for Jesus on the flood tide of emotion at some great gathering, or in some little group which is charged with spiritual power. But after the crowd, people have to go home and be alone; after the fellowship, they must go back to the essential isolation of every human soul; and what really matters is not what people do in the crowd, but what they do when they are alone with Christ. Jesus compelled these men to face him alone.

(3) Jesus asked these men only one question: 'Do you believe that I am able to do this?' The one essential for a miracle is faith. There is nothing mysterious or theological about this. No doctor can cure a sick person who goes to him in a completely hopeless frame of mind. No medicine will do any good if those taking it think they might as well be drinking water. The way to a miracle is to place one's life in the hands of Jesus Christ and say: 'I know that you can make me what I ought to be.'

October 12

The Two Reactions

Matthew 9:32–34

It must always remain true that what the eye sees depends upon what the heart feels. The crowds looked on Jesus with wonder, because they were simple people with a crying sense of need; and they saw that in Jesus their need could be supplied in the most astonishing way. Jesus will always appear wonderful to those with a sense of need; and the deeper the sense of need, the more wonderful Jesus will appear to be.

The Pharisees saw Jesus as one who was in league with all the powers of evil. They did not deny his wondrous powers; but they attributed them to his complicity with the prince of the devils. This verdict of the Pharisees was due to certain attitudes of mind.

(1) They were too set in their ways to change. As far as they were concerned not one word could be added to or subtracted from the law. To them, all the great things belonged to the past. To them, to change a tradition or a convention was a deadly sin. Anything that was new was wrong. And when Jesus came with a new interpretation of what real religion was, they hated him, as they had hated the prophets long ago.

(2) They were too proud in their self-satisfaction to submit. If Jesus was right, they were wrong. The Pharisees were so well satisfied with themselves that they saw no need to change; and they hated anyone who wished to change them. Repentance is the gate whereby we all must enter the kingdom; and repentance means the recognition of the error of our ways, the realization that in Christ alone there is life, and the surrender to him and to his will and power, whereby alone we can be changed.

(3) They were too prejudiced to see. Their eyes were so blinded by their own ideas that they could not see in Jesus Christ the truth and the power of God.

Those who have a sense of need will always see wonders in Jesus Christ. People who are so set in their ways that they will not change, people who are so proud in their self-righteousness that they cannot submit, people who are so blinded by their prejudices that they cannot see, will always resent and hate and seek to eliminate him.

October 13

Calm amid the Storm

Luke 8:22–25

Luke tells this story with an extraordinary economy of words, and yet with extraordinary vividness. It was no doubt for much needed rest and quiet that Jesus decided to cross the lake. As they sailed, he fell asleep.

It is a lovely thing to think of the sleeping Jesus. He was tired, just as we become tired. He, too, could reach the point of exhaustion when the claim of sleep is imperative. He trusted his disciples; they were the fishermen of the lake and he was content to leave things to their skill and seamanship, and to relax. He trusted God; he knew that he was as near to God by sea as ever he was by land.

Then the storm came down. Everything that Jesus did had more than a merely temporal significance. And the real meaning of this incident is that, wherever Jesus is, the storm becomes a calm.

(1) Jesus calms the storms of temptation. Sometimes temptation comes with almost overwhelming force. As Robert Louis Stevenson once said, 'You know the Caledonian Railway Station in Edinburgh? One cold bleak morning I met Satan there.' It comes to us all to meet Satan. If we meet the tempest of temptation alone we will perish; but Christ brings the calm in which temptations lose their power.

(2) Jesus calms the storms of passion. Life is doubly difficult for the hot-headed person who has a blazing temper. A friend met someone just like that. 'I see', he said, 'that you have succeeded in conquering your temper.' 'No,' said the man, 'I didn't conquer it. Jesus conquered it for me.' It is a losing battle unless Jesus gives us the calm of victory.

(3) Jesus calms the storms of sorrow. Into every life some day the tempest of sorrow must come, for sorrow is so often the penalty of love and if we love we will also know sorrow. When the nineteenth-century theologian E. B. Pusey's wife died, he said, 'It was as if there was a hand beneath my chin to hold me up.' In that day, in the presence of Jesus, the tears are wiped away and the wounded heart is soothed.

October 14

The Defeat of the Demons

Luke 8:26–39

This man was a case of violent insanity. He was too dangerous to live in the community and he lived amid the tombs, which were believed to be the home and the haunt of demons. When Jesus asked the man his name, he answered, 'Legion.' A Roman legion was a regiment of 6,000 soldiers. Doubtless this man had seen a Roman legion on the march, and his poor, afflicted mind felt that there was not one demon but a whole regiment inside him. It may well be that the word haunted him because he had seen atrocities carried out by a Roman legion when he was a child. It is possible that it was the sight of such atrocities which left a scar upon his mind and ultimately caused his mental illness.

We must look at the reaction of two sets of people.

(1) There were the Gerasenes. They asked Jesus to go away. They hated having the routine of life disturbed. Life went peacefully on till there arrived this disturbing Jesus; and they hated him. More people hate Jesus because he disturbs them than for any other reason. If he says to someone, 'You must give up this habit, you must change your life'; if he says to an employer, 'You can't be a Christian and make people work under conditions like that'; if he says to a landlord, 'You can't take money for slums like that'—one and all are liable to say to him, 'Go away and let me be in peace.' They loved their swine more than they valued a human soul. One of life's supreme dangers is to value things more than persons. That is what created slums and vicious working conditions. Nearer home, that is what makes us selfishly demand our ease and comfort even if it means that someone who is tired has to slave for us. No thing in this world can ever be as important as a person.

(2) There was the man who was cured. Very naturally he wanted to come with Jesus but Jesus sent him home. Christian witness, like Christian charity, begins at home. It would be so much easier to live and speak for Christ among people who do not know us. But it is our duty, where Christ has set us, there to witness for him.

An Only Child Is Healed

Luke 8:40–42, 49–56

Here is the pathos of life suddenly turned to gladness. Jairus was the president of the synagogue. That is to say, he was the man who was responsible for the administration of the synagogue and the ordering of public worship. He had reached the highest post that life could give him in the respect of his community. No doubt he was well to do; no doubt he had climbed the ladder of earthly ambition and prestige. It seemed as if life—as it sometimes does—had given lavishly of many things but was about to take the most precious thing away.

We must note one very practical touch. Jesus ordered that the girl should be given something to eat. Is it possible that he was thinking just as much of the mother as of the girl? The mother, with the pain of grief and the sudden shock of joy, must have been almost on the point of collapse. At such a time to do some practical thing with one's hands is a lifesaver. And it may well be that Jesus, in his kindly wisdom, was giving the over-wrought mother a job to do to calm her nerves.

But by far the most interesting character in this story is Jairus.

(1) He was clearly a man who could swallow his pride. He was the president of the synagogue. By this time the synagogue doors were rapidly closing on Jesus, if indeed they had not already closed. He could have had no love for Jesus and he must have regarded Jesus as a breaker of the law. But in his hour of need, he swallowed his pride and asked for help. It is easy to think that we can handle life ourselves. But the way to find the miracles of the grace of God is to swallow our pride and humbly to confess our need and ask.

(2) Jairus was clearly a man of a stubborn faith. Whatever he felt, he did not wholly accept the verdict of the wailing women; for with his wife he went into the room where the girl lay. He hoped against hope. No doubt in his heart there was the feeling, 'You never know what this Jesus can do.' And none of us knows all that Jesus can do. In the darkest day we can still hope in the unsearchable riches and the all-sufficient grace and the unconquerable power of God.

October 16

Not Lost in the Crowd

Luke 8:43–48

This story laid hold on the heart and the imagination of the early Church. It was believed that the woman was a Gentile from Caesarea Philippi. Eusebius, the great church historian, relates how it was said that the woman had at her own cost erected a statue commemorating her cure in her native city. It was said that that statue remained there until Julian, the Roman emperor who tried to bring back the pagan gods, destroyed it, and erected his own in place of it, only to see his own statue blasted by a thunderbolt from God. The shame of the woman was that ceremonially she was unclean (Leviticus 15:19–33). Her issue of blood had cut her off from life. That was why she did not come openly to Jesus but crept up in the crowd; and that was why at first she was so embarrassed when Jesus asked who touched him.

All devout Jews wore robes with fringes on them (Numbers 15:37–41; Deuteronomy 22:12). The fringes ended in four tassels of white thread with a blue thread woven through them. They were to remind a Jew every time he dressed that he was a man of God and committed to the keeping of God's laws. Later, when it was dangerous to be a Jew, these tassels were worn on the undergarments. Nowadays they still exist on the *talith* or shawl that Jews wear round their heads and shoulders when they are at prayer. But in the time of Jesus they were worn on the outer garment, and it was one of these the woman touched.

The lovely thing about this story is that from the moment Jesus was face to face with the woman, there seemed to be nobody there but the two of them. It happened in the middle of a crowd, but the crowd was forgotten and Jesus spoke to that woman as if she was the only person in the world. She was a poor, unimportant sufferer, with a trouble that made her unclean, and yet to that one unimportant person Jesus gave all of himself.

We are very apt to attach labels to people and to treat them according to their relative importance. To Jesus a person had none of these labels. He or she was simply a human soul in need.

Food for the Hungry

Luke 9:10–17

This is the only miracle of Jesus related in all the four gospels (cf. Matthew 14:13; Mark 6:30; John 6:1). It begins with a lovely thing. The Twelve had come back from their tour. Never was there a time when Jesus needed more to be alone with them, so he took them to the neighbourhood of Bethsaida, a village on the far side of the Jordan to the north of the Sea of Galilee. When the people discovered where he had gone they followed him in hordes—and he welcomed them. There is all the divine compassion here. Most people would have resented the invasion of their hard-won privacy. How would we feel if we had sought out some lonely place to be with our most intimate friends and suddenly a clamorous throng of people turned up with their insistent demands?

This is a story which tells us many things.

(1) Jesus was concerned that people were hungry. It would be most interesting to work out how much time Jesus spent, not talking, but easing human pain and satisfying hunger. He still needs the service of human hands. The mother who has spent a lifetime cooking meals for a hungry family; the nurse, the doctor, the friend, relation or parent who has sacrificed life and time to ease another's pain; social reformers who have burned themselves out to seek better conditions for men and women—they have all preached far more effective sermons than the eloquent orator.

(2) Jesus' help was generous. There was enough, and more than enough. In love there is no nice calculation of the less and more. God is like that. When we sow a packet of seeds we usually have to thin the plants out and throw away far more than we can keep. God has created a world where there is more than enough for all if we will share it.

(3) As always there is permanent truth in an action in time. In Jesus all our needs are supplied. There is a hunger of the soul; there is in each of us, sometimes at least, a longing to find something in which we may invest our lives. Our hearts are restless until they rest in him. 'My God will fully satisfy every need of yours,' said Paul (Philippians 4:19)—even in the desert places of this life.

October 18

A Very Present Help in Time of Trouble

John 6:16–21

Here is just the kind of story that a fisherman like John would have loved and remembered. Every time he thought of it, he would feel that night again — the grey silver of the moonlight, the rough oar against his hand, the flapping sail, the shriek of the wind, the sound of the surging water, the astonishingly unexpected appearance of Jesus, the sound of his voice across the waves and the crunch of the boat as it reached the Galilaean side.

As he remembered, John saw wonders which are still there for us.

(1) He saw that Jesus watches. Up on the hill, Jesus had been watching them. He had not forgotten. He was not too busy with God to think of them. John suddenly realized that all the time they had pulled at the oars, Jesus' loving look was on them. When we are up against it, Jesus watches. He does not make things easy for us. He lets us fight our own battles. Like a parent watching a son or daughter put up a splendid effort in some athletic contest, he is proud of us; or, like a parent watching a son or daughter let the side down, he is sad. Life is lived with the loving eye of Jesus upon us.

(2) He saw that Jesus helps. He watches, and he helps. It is the wonder of the Christian life that there is nothing that we are left to do alone. A teacher in a little country school told this story to her children, and she must have told it well. Some short time afterwards, there was a blizzard of wind and snow. When school finished, the teacher was helping the children home. Sometimes she had practically to drag them through the drifts. When they were all very nearly exhausted with the struggle, she overheard a little boy say, half to himself: 'We could be doing with that chap Jesus here now.' We could always be doing with Jesus, and we never need to do without him.

(3) He saw that Jesus brings us to the haven. It seemed to John, as he remembered it, that, as soon as Jesus arrived, the keel of the boat grated on the shingle — and they were there. As the psalmist had it: 'Then they were glad because they had quiet, and he brought them to their desired haven' (Psalm 107:30). Somehow in the presence of Jesus the longest journey is shorter and the hardest battle easier.

Faith Tested and Faith Answered

Matthew 15:21–28

There are certain things about this woman which we must note.

(1) First and foremost, she had love. Pagan she might be, but in her heart there was that love for her child which is always the reflection of God's love for his children. It was love which made her approach this stranger; it was love which made her accept his silence and yet still appeal; it was love which made her suffer the apparent rebuffs; it was love which made her able to see the compassion beyond and behind the words of Jesus. The driving force of this woman's heart was love; and there is nothing stronger and nothing nearer God than that very thing.

(2) This woman had faith.

(a) It was a faith which grew in contact with Jesus. She began by calling him Son of David; that was a popular title, a political title. It was a title which looked on Jesus as a great and powerful wonder-worker, but which looked on him in terms of earthly power and glory. She came asking a favour of one whom she took to be a great and powerful man. She came with a kind of superstition as she might have come to any magician. She ended by calling Jesus Lord. Jesus, as it were, compelled her to look at himself, and in him she saw something that was not expressible in earthly terms at all, but was nothing less than divine. That is precisely what Jesus wanted to awaken in her before he granted her request. He wanted her to see that a request to a great man must be turned into a prayer to the living God. We can see this woman's faith growing as she is confronted with Christ, until she glimpsed him, however distantly, for what he was.

(b) It was a faith which worshipped. She began by following; she ended upon her knees. She began with a request; she ended in prayer. Whenever we come to Jesus, we must come first with adoration of his majesty, and only then with the statement of our own need.

(3) This woman had the gift of cheerfulness. She was in the midst of trouble; she was passionately in earnest; and yet she could smile. She had a certain sunny-heartedness about her. God loves the cheerful faith, the faith in whose eyes there is always the light of hope, the faith with a smile which can light the gloom.

Doing All Things Well

Mark 7:31–37

When Jesus arrived back in the regions of Galilee, he came into the district of the Decapolis, and there they brought to him a man who was deaf and who had an impediment in his speech. There is no miracle which so beautifully shows Jesus' way of treating people.

(1) He took the man aside from the crowd, all by himself. Here is the most tender considerateness. Deaf people are always a little embarrassed. In some ways, it is more embarrassing to be deaf than it is to be blind. Deaf people know they cannot hear; and when someone in a crowd shouts at them and tries to make them hear, in their excitement they can become all the more helpless. Jesus showed the most tender consideration for the feelings of a man for whom life was very difficult.

(2) Throughout the whole miracle, Jesus acted what he was going to do in dumb show. He put his hands in the man's ears and touched his tongue with spittle. In those days, people believed that spittle had a curative quality. Jesus looked up to heaven to show that it was from God that help was to come. Then he spoke the word and the man was healed.

The whole story shows us most vividly that Jesus did not consider the man merely a case; he considered him as an individual. The man had a special need and a special problem, and with the most tender considerateness Jesus dealt with him in a way that spared his feelings and in a way that he could understand.

When it was completed, the people declared that he had done all things well. That is none other than the verdict of God upon his own creation in the very beginning (Genesis 1:31). When Jesus came, bringing healing to broken bodies and salvation to human souls, he had begun the work of creation all over again.

In the beginning, everything had been good; human sin had spoiled it all; and now Jesus was bringing back the beauty of God to the world which human sin had rendered ugly.

October 21

A Blind Man Learns to See

Mark 8:22–26

Only Mark tells us this story, and yet there are certain extremely interesting things in it.

(1) Again we see the unique considerateness of Jesus. He took the blind man out of the crowd and out of the village that he might be alone with him. Why? Think about it. This man was blind and apparently had been born blind. If he had been suddenly given back his sight in the middle of a crowd, there would have flashed upon his newly seeing eyes hundreds of people and things, and dazzling colours, so that he would have been completely bewildered. Jesus knew it would be far better if he could be taken to a place where the thrill of seeing would break less suddenly upon him.

All great doctors and great teachers have one outstanding characteristic. Great doctors are able to enter into the very minds and hearts of their patients; they understand their fears and their hopes; they literally sympathize—suffer—with them. Great teachers enter into the very minds of their pupils. They see their problems, their difficulties, their stumbling blocks. That is why Jesus was so supremely great. He could enter into the minds and hearts of the people whom he sought to help. He had the gift of considerateness, because he could think with their thoughts and feel with their feelings. God grant to us this Christ-like gift.

(2) Jesus used methods that the man could understand. The ancient world believed in the healing power of spittle. The belief is not so strange when we remember that it is a first instinct to put a cut or burned finger into our mouth to ease the pain. Of course the blind man knew of this, and Jesus used a method of curing him which he could understand. Jesus was wise. He did not begin with words and methods which were far above the heads of ordinary people. He spoke to them and acted on them in a way that their minds could grasp and understand.

There have been times when unintelligibility has been accounted a virtue and a sign of greatness. Jesus had the still greater greatness—the greatness which could be easily grasped.

October 22

Coming down from the Mount

Luke 9:37–45

A man had come to the disciples seeking their help, for his only son was an epileptic. Of course his epilepsy was attributed to the malign activity of a demon. The word used in verse 42 is very vivid. As he was coming to Jesus, the demon *dashed him down*. It is the word used of a boxer dealing a knock-out blow to his opponent or of a wrestler throwing someone. It must have been a pitiful sight to see the boy convulsed; and the disciples were quite helpless to cure him.

Two things stand out.

(1) The moment on the mount was absolutely necessary, but it could not be prolonged beyond its own time. Peter, not really knowing what he was saying, would have liked to linger on the mountaintop. He wished to build three tabernacles so that they might stay there in all the glory; but they had to descend again. Often there come to us moments that we would like to prolong indefinitely. But after the time on the mountaintop we must come back to the battle and the routine of life; that time is meant to give us strength for life's everyday struggles.

(2) In no incident is the sheer competence of Jesus so clearly shown. When he came down from the mountain the situation was out of hand. The whole impression is that of people running about not knowing what to do. The disciples were helplessly baffled; the boy's father was bitterly disappointed and upset. Into this scene of disorder came Jesus. He gripped the situation in a flash and in his mastery the disorder became a calm. So often we feel that life is out of control; that we have lost our grip on things. Only the Master of life can deal with life with the calm competence that brings everything under control.

(3) Once again the incident finished with Jesus pointing at the cross. Here was triumph; here Jesus had mastered the demons and astonished the people. And in that very moment when they were ready to acclaim him, Jesus told them he was on the way to die. It would have been so easy to take the way of popular success; it was Jesus' greatness that he rejected it and chose the cross.

The Temple Tax

Matthew 17:24–27

In this passage, we see Jesus paying this Temple tax. The tax authorities came to Peter and asked him if his Master paid his taxes. There is little doubt that the question was asked with malicious intent and that the hope was that Jesus would refuse to pay; for, if he refused, the orthodox would have grounds for making an accusation against him. Peter's immediate answer was that Jesus did pay. Then he went and told Jesus of the situation, and Jesus used a kind of parable in verses 25 and 26.

The tax in question was for the Temple, which was the house of God. Jesus was the Son of God. Did he not say when his parents sought him in Jerusalem: 'Did you not know that I must be in my Father's house?' (Luke 2:49). How could the Son be under obligation to pay the tax which was for his own Father's house? Nonetheless, Jesus said that they must pay, not because of the compulsion of the law, but because of a higher duty. He said they must pay 'lest we should offend them'.

The New Testament always uses the verb *to offend* (*skandalizein*) and the noun *offence* (*skandalon*) in a special way. The verb never means to insult or to annoy or to injure the pride of. It always means *to put a stumbling block in someone's way*, to cause someone to trip up and to fall. Therefore Jesus is saying: 'We must pay so as not to set a bad example to others. We must not only do our duty, we must go beyond duty, in order that we may show others what they ought to do.' Jesus would allow himself nothing which might make someone else think less of the ordinary obligations of life. In life, there may sometimes be exemptions we could claim; there may be things we could quite safely allow ourselves to do. But we must claim nothing and allow ourselves nothing which might possibly be a bad example to someone else.

We may well ask: why is it that this story was ever transmitted at all? For reasons of space, the gospel writers had to select their material. Why select this story? This story was put into the gospels to tell the Christians, especially the Jewish Christians, that, however unpleasant the duties of a citizen might be, they must be shouldered.

Mercy More than Law

Luke 13:10–17

This is the last time we ever hear of Jesus being in a synagogue. It is clear that by this time the authorities were watching his every action and waiting to pounce upon him whenever they got the chance. Jesus healed a woman who for eighteen years had not been able to straighten her bent body; and then the president of the synagogue intervened. He had not even the courage to speak directly to Jesus. He addressed his protest to the waiting people, although it was meant for Jesus.

Jesus had healed on the Sabbath; technically healing was work; and, therefore he had broken the Sabbath. But he answered his opponents out of their own law. The Rabbis abhorred cruelty to animals and, even on the Sabbath, it was perfectly legal to loose animals from their stalls and water them. Jesus demanded, 'If you can loose an animal from a stall and water it on the Sabbath day, surely it is right in the sight of God to loose this poor woman from her infirmity.'

The president of the synagogue and those like him were people who loved systems more than people. They were more concerned that their own petty little laws should be observed than that a woman should be helped.

One of the great problems of a developed civilization is the relationship of the individual to the system. In times of war the individual vanishes. Men and women cease to be individuals and become members of such and such an age group or the like. They are lumped together, not as individuals, but as living ammunition that is, in that terrible word, expendable.

Strangely enough, this worship of systems commonly invades the Church. There are many church people—it would be a mistake to call them Christian people—who are more concerned with the method of church government than they are with the worship of God and the service of others. It is all too tragically true that more trouble and strife arise in churches over legalistic details of procedure than over any other thing.

In the world and in the Church we are constantly in peril of loving systems more than we love God and more than we love one another.

October 25

Under Hostile Scrutiny

Luke 14:1–6

If we are to understand what happened to Jesus it is essential to remember that the orthodox Jews of his day regarded him as a law-breaker. He healed on the Sabbath; therefore he worked on the Sabbath; therefore he broke the law. On this occasion a Pharisee invited him to a meal on the Sabbath. It is by no means impossible that the Pharisees 'planted' the man with the dropsy in this house to see what Jesus would do. They were watching him; and the word used for *watching* is the word used for *interested and sinister espionage*. Jesus was under scrutiny.

This passage tells us certain things about Jesus and his enemies.

(1) It shows us the serenity with which Jesus met life. There is nothing more trying than to be under constant and critical scrutiny. When that happens to most people they lose their nerve and, even more often, lose their temper. But even in things which would have broken most people's spirit, Jesus remained serene. If we live with him, he can make us like himself.

(2) It is to be noted that Jesus never refused anyone's invitation of hospitality. To the end he never gave up on people. To hope to change them or even to appeal to them might be the forlornest of forlorn hopes, but he would never let a chance go. He would not refuse even an enemy's invitation. It is as clear as daylight that we will never make our enemies our friends if we refuse to meet them and talk with them.

(3) The most amazing thing about the scribes and Pharisees is their staggering lack of a sense of proportion. They would go to endless trouble to formulate and to obey their petty rules and regulations; and yet they counted it a sin to ease a sufferer's pain on the Sabbath day. If we had only one prayer to pray we might well ask to be given a sense of proportion. The things which come between individuals and which destroy friendships are often little things to which sensible people, in their saner moments, would never allow any importance. The little things can bulk so large that they can fill the whole horizon. Only if we put first things first will all things take their proper place — and love comes first.

The Rarity of Gratitude

Luke 17:11–19

Jesus was on the border between Galilee and Samaria and was met by a band of ten lepers. We know that the Jews had no dealings with the Samaritans; yet in this band there was at least one Samaritan. Here is an example of a great law of life. A common misfortune had broken down the racial and national barriers. In the common tragedy of their leprosy they had forgotten they were Jews and Samaritans and remembered only they were men in need. If a flood surges over a piece of country and the wild animals congregate for safety on some little bit of higher ground, you will find standing peacefully together animals that are natural enemies and at any other time would do their best to kill each other. Surely one of the things which should draw all people together is their common need of God.

No story in all the gospels so poignantly shows human ingratitude. The lepers came to Jesus with desperate longing; he cured them; and nine never came back to give thanks. So often, once people have got what they want, they never come back.

(1) Often we are ungrateful to one another. Few of us have not at some time owed a great deal to another person. Few of us, at the moment, believed we could ever forget; but few of us in the end satisfy the debt of gratitude we owe. It often happens that a friend, a teacher, a doctor, a surgeon does something for us which it is impossible to repay; but the tragedy is that we often do not even try to repay it.

(2) Often we are ungrateful to God. In some time of bitter need we pray with desperate intensity; the time passes and we forget God. Many of us never even offer a grace before meals. God gave us his only Son and often we never give to him even a word of thanks. The best thanks we can give him is to try to deserve his goodness and his mercy a little better. 'Bless the Lord, O my soul, and do not forget all his benefits' (Psalm 103:2).

October 27

Light for the Blind Eyes

John 9:1–5

This is the only miracle in the gospels in which the sufferer is said to have been afflicted from his birth. If we read with care and attention, we will see the loveliest progression in the blind man's idea of Jesus. It goes through three stages, each one higher than the last.

(1) He began by calling Jesus a man. 'A man called Jesus opened my eyes' (cf. verse 11). He began by thinking of Jesus as a wonderful man. He had never met anyone who could do the kind of things Jesus did; and he began by thinking of Jesus as a uniquely gifted man. We do well sometimes to think of the sheer magnificence and greatness of Jesus. In any gallery of the world's heroes, he must find a place. In any anthology of the loveliest lives ever lived, his would have to be included. In any collection of the world's greatest literature, his parables would have to be listed.

(2) He went on to call Jesus a prophet. When asked his opinion of Jesus in view of the fact that he had given him his sight, his answer was: 'He is a prophet' (verse 17). Now a prophet is someone who brings God's message to men and women. 'Surely the Lord God does nothing,' said Amos, 'without revealing his secret to his servants the prophets' (Amos 3:7). A prophet is someone who lives close to God and has penetrated into his inner councils. When we read the wisdom of the words of Jesus, we are bound to say: 'This is a prophet!' Whatever else may be in doubt, this is true — if people followed the teachings of Jesus, all personal, all social, all national and all international problems would be solved. If ever anyone had the right to be called a prophet, Jesus had.

(3) Finally the blind man came to confess that Jesus was the Son of God. He came to see that human categories were not adequate to describe him. It is a tremendous thing about Jesus that the more we know him, the greater he becomes.

The trouble with human relationships is that often the better we know people, the more we know their weaknesses and their failings; but the more we know Jesus, the greater the wonder becomes; and that will be true, not only in time, but also in eternity.

314

The Resurrection and the Life

John 11:1–44

When Martha declared her belief in the orthodox Jewish belief in the life to come, Jesus suddenly said something which brought to that belief a new vividness and a new meaning. 'I am the resurrection and the life,' he said. 'He who believes in me will live even if he has died; and everyone who lives and believes in me shall never die.' What exactly did he mean? Not even a lifetime's thinking will reveal the full meaning of this; but we must try to grasp as much of it as we can. One thing is clear—Jesus was not thinking in terms of physical life; for, speaking physically, it is not true that those who believe in him will never die. Christians experience physical death just like other people.

We must look for a more than physical meaning.

(1) Jesus was thinking of the death of sin. He was saying: 'Even if people are dead in sin, even if, through their sins, they have lost all that makes life worth calling life, I can make them alive again.' In point of historical fact, that is abundantly true. People can become so selfish that they are dead to the needs of others.

They can become so insensitive that they are dead to the feelings of others. They can become so involved in the petty dishonesties and the petty disloyalties of life that they are dead to honour. People can become so hopeless that they are filled with an inertia, which is spiritual death. Jesus Christ can resurrect them. The witness of history is that he has resurrected millions and millions of people like them, and his touch has not lost its ancient power.

(2) Jesus was also thinking of the life to come. He brought into life the certainty that death is not the end. We call this world the land of the living; but it would in fact be more correct to call it the land of the dying. Through Jesus Christ, we know that we are journeying not to the sunset but to the sunrise; in truth we are resurrected, for we are freed from the fear which is characteristic of the godless life; we are freed from the frustration which is characteristic of the sin-ridden life; we are freed from the futility of the Christless life.

Life is raised from sin's death and becomes so rich that it cannot die but must find in death only the transition to a higher life.

October 29

The Man Who Would Not Be Silenced

Luke 18:35–43

The one thing which stands out in this story is the sheer, desperate persistence of the blind man. Jesus was on his way to Jerusalem to the Passover. At such a time pilgrims travelled in bands together. One of the commonest ways for a Rabbi to teach was to discourse as he walked. That was what Jesus was doing, and the rest of the pilgrim band were crowding close around him, not to miss anything that he might say. As such a pilgrim band passed through a village or a town those who themselves could not go to the feast lined the wayside to see the pilgrims pass and to bid them Godspeed on the way.

It was among the wayside crowd that the blind man was sitting. When he heard the murmur of the approaching throng he asked what was happening and was told that Jesus was passing by. Immediately he cried out to Jesus for help and healing. Thereupon everyone tried to silence him. The people round Jesus were missing what he was saying because of the clamour of this blind man. But the man would not be silenced. He shouted again.

This story tells us two things.

(1) It tells us something about the blind man. He was determined to come face to face with Jesus. Nothing would stop him. He refused to be silent and he refused to be restrained. His sense of need drove him relentlessly into the presence of Jesus. Whoever wants a miracle must show that spirit. A gentle, sentimental longing never really taps the power of God; but the passionate, intense desire of the very depths of the human heart will never be disappointed.

(2) It tells us something about Jesus. At that moment he was discoursing to the crowd like any Rabbi. But at the blind man's cry of need he stopped, the discourse forgotten. For Jesus it was always more important to act than to talk. Words always took second place to deeds. Here was a human soul in need. Speech must end and action begin.

316

October 30

The Way of the Fig Tree

Matthew 21:18–22

Few honest readers of the Bible would deny that this is perhaps the most uncomfortably difficult passage in the New Testament. If it is taken with complete literalism, it shows Jesus in an action which is an acute shock to our whole conception of him. It must, therefore, be approached with a real desire to find out the truth which lies behind it and with the courage to think our way through it.

Frequently the prophets made use of symbolic actions; when they felt that words would not penetrate, they did something dramatic to drive a lesson home. Let us suppose that some such symbolic action is at the back of this story. If this was a symbolic action, it was meant to teach something.

(1) It taught that uselessness invites disaster. That is the law of life. Anything which is useless is on the way to elimination; anything can justify its existence only by fulfilling the end for which it was created. The fig tree was useless; therefore it was doomed.

The nation of Israel had been brought into existence for one reason and one reason only—that from it there might come God's Anointed One. He had come; the nation had failed to recognize him; more, they were about to crucify him. The nation had failed in its function which was to welcome God's Son—therefore the nation was doomed.

(2) It taught that profession of faith without practice is condemned. The tree had leaves; the leaves were a claim to have figs; the tree had no figs; its claim was false; therefore it was doomed. The Jewish nation professed faith in God; but in practice they were unable to recognize God's Son; therefore they stood condemned.

Profession of faith without practice is something of which we are all more or less guilty. It does incalculable harm to the Christian Church; and it is doomed to disaster, for it produces a faith which cannot do anything else but wither away.

We may well believe that Jesus used the lesson of a diseased and degenerate fig tree to say to the Jews—and to us—that uselessness invites disaster, and profession of faith without practice is doomed.

October 31

The Universality of the Church

John 21:1–14

It was certainly someone who knew the fishermen of the Sea of Galilee who wrote this story. Night-time was the best for fishing. W. M. Thomson in *The Land and the Book* describes night fishing: 'There are certain kinds of fishing always carried on at night. It is a beautiful sight. With blazing torch, the boat glides over the flashing sea, and the men stand gazing keenly into it until their prey is sighted, when, quick as lightning, they fling their net or fly their spear; and often you see the tired fishermen come sullenly into harbour in the morning, having toiled all night in vain.'

In the Fourth Gospel everything is meaningful, and it is therefore hardly possible that John gives the definite number 153 for the fishes without meaning something by it. It has indeed been suggested that the fishes were counted simply because the catch had to be shared out between the various partners and the crew of the boat, and that the number was recorded simply because it was so exceptionally large. But when we remember John's way of putting hidden meanings in his gospel for those who have eyes to see, we must think that there is more to it than that.

Many ingenious suggestions have been made. The simplest of the explanations is that given by the fourth-century biblical scholar Jerome. He said that in the sea there are 153 different kinds of fishes; and that the catch is one which includes every kind of fish; and that therefore the number symbolizes the fact that some day all people of all nations will be gathered together to Jesus Christ.

We may note a further point. This great catch of fishes was gathered into the net, and the net held them all and was not broken. The net stands for the Church; and there is room in the Church for all people of all nations. Even if they all come in, the Church is big enough to hold them all.

Here, John is telling us in his own vivid yet subtle way of the universality of the Church. There is no kind of exclusiveness in her, no kind of prejudice or selectiveness. The embrace of the Church is as universal as the love of God in Jesus Christ.

Parables of God's Love

November 1

The Problem of the New Idea

Matthew 9:16–17

Jesus was perfectly conscious that he came to men and women with new ideas and with a new conception of the truth, and he was well aware how difficult it is to get a new idea into people's minds. So he used two pictures which any Jew would understand. 'No one', he said, 'takes a piece of new and unshrunken cloth to patch an old garment. If that happens, on the first occasion that the garment becomes wet, the new patch shrinks, and as it shrinks, it tears the cloth apart, and the rent in the garment gapes wider than ever.' The Jews were passionately attached to things as they were. It was the avowed object of the scribes and Pharisees 'to build a fence around the law'. To them, a new idea was not so much a mistake as a sin.

That spirit is by no means dead. Very often in a church, if a new idea or a new method or any change is suggested, the objection is promptly raised: 'We never did that before.' I once heard two theologians talking together. One was a younger man who was intensely interested in all that the new thinkers have to say; the other was an older man of a rigid and conventional orthodoxy. The older man heard the younger man with a kind of half-contemptuous tolerance, and finally closed the conversation by saying: 'The old is better.'

Throughout all its history, the Church has clung to the old. What Jesus is saying is that there comes a time when patching is folly, and when the only thing to do is to scrap something entirely and to begin again. There are forms of church government, there are forms of church service, there are forms of words expressing our beliefs, which we so often try to adjust and tinker with in order to bring them up to date; we try to patch them.

No one would willingly, or recklessly, or callously abandon what has stood the test of time and of the years and in which former generations have found their comfort and put their trust; but the fact remains that this is a growing and an expanding universe; and there comes a time when patches are useless, and when individuals and churches have to accept the adventure of the new, or withdraw into the backwater, where they worship not God but the past.

November 2

The Sower Went out to Sow

Matthew 13:1–9, 18–23

Here is a picture which anyone in Palestine would understand. If we take the parable as a warning to hearers, it means that there are different ways of accepting the word of God.

(1) There are the hearers with shut minds. There are people into whose minds the word has no more chance of gaining entry than the seed has of settling into the ground that has been beaten hard by many feet. There are many things which can shut people's minds. Prejudice can make them blind to everything they do not wish to see. The unteachable spirit can erect a barrier which cannot easily be broken down. It can be the result of pride which does not know that it needs to know; and it can be the result of the fear of new truth and the refusal to adventure on the ways of thought.

(2) There are the hearers with minds like the shallow ground. Some people are at the mercy of every new craze. They take a thing up quickly and just as quickly drop it. They must always be in fashion. It is possible to be like that with the word. When people hear it, they may be swept off their feet with an emotional reaction; but no one can live on an emotion. We all have minds, and it is a moral obligation to have an intelligent faith. Christianity has its demands, and these demands must be faced before it can be accepted.

(3) There are the hearers who have so many interests in life that often the most important things get crowded out. It is characteristic of modern life that it becomes increasingly crowded and increasingly fast. We become too busy to pray; we become so preoccupied with many things that we forget to study the word of God. We must be careful to see that Christ is not pushed into the sidelines of life.

(4) There are people who are like the good ground. In their reception of the word, there are four stages. Like the good ground, their minds are open. They are at all times willing to learn. They are prepared to hear. They have thought the thing out and know what this means for them, and are prepared to accept it. They translate their hearing into action. They produce the good fruit of the good seed. The real hearers are those who listen, who understand and who obey.

321

The Act of an Enemy

Matthew 13:24–30, 36–43

It may well be said that in its lessons this is one of the most practical parables that Jesus ever told.

(1) It teaches us that there is always a hostile power in the world, seeking and waiting to destroy the good seed. Our experience is that both kinds of influence act upon our lives—the influence which helps the seed of the word to flourish and to grow, and the influence which seeks to destroy the good seed before it can produce fruit at all. The lesson is that we must be forever on our guard.

(2) It teaches us how hard it is to distinguish between those who are in the kingdom and those who are not. Some people may appear to be good and may in fact be bad; and others may appear to be bad and may yet be good. We are much too quick to classify people and label them good or bad without knowing all the facts.

(3) It teaches us not to be so quick with our judgments. If the reapers had had their way, they would have tried to tear out the darnel and they would have torn out the wheat as well. Judgment had to wait until the harvest came. In the end, we will be judged, not by any single act or stage in our lives, but by our whole lives. No one who sees only part of a thing can judge the whole; and no one who knows only part of an individual's life can judge the whole person.

(4) It teaches us that judgment does come in the end. Judgment is not hasty, but judgment comes. It may be that, humanly speaking, in this life the sinner seems to escape the consequences—but there is a life to come. It may be that, humanly speaking, goodness never seems to enter into its reward—but there is a new world to redress the balance of the old.

(5) It teaches us that the only person with the right to judge is God. It is God alone who can discern the good and the bad; it is God alone who sees all of an individual and all of a person's life. It is God alone who can judge.

All in the Day's Work

Matthew 13:44

When we are dealing with any parable, the details are never meant to be stressed; the parable has one main point, and to that point everything else is subservient. In this parable, the great point is the joy of the discovery that made the man willing to give up everything to make sure beyond question that the treasure became his own. Nothing else in the parable really matters.

(1) The lesson of this parable is, first, that the man found the precious thing, not so much by chance, as in his day's work. It is true to say that he stumbled unexpectedly upon it, but he did so when he was going about his daily business. It would be a sad thing if it were only in churches, in so-called holy places and on so-called religious occasions that we found God and felt close to him.

There is an unwritten saying of Jesus which never found its way into any of the gospels, but which rings true: 'Raise the stone and you will find me; cleave the wood and I am there.' When the mason is working on the stone, when the carpenter is working with the wood, Jesus Christ is there.

(2) The lesson of this parable is, second, that it is worth any sacrifice to enter the kingdom. What does it mean to enter the kingdom? To enter the kingdom is to accept and to do God's will. Suddenly, as the man discovered the treasure, there may flash upon us, in some moment of illumination, the conviction of what God's will is for us. To accept it may be to give up certain aims and ambitions which are very dear, to abandon certain habits and ways of life which are very difficult to lay down, to take on a discipline and self-denial which are by no means easy—in a word, to take up our cross and follow after Jesus. But there is no other way to peace of mind and heart in this life and to glory in the life to come. It is indeed worth giving up everything to accept and to do the will of God.

November 5

The Catch and the Separation

Matthew 13:47–50

In Palestine, there were two main ways of fishing. One was with the casting-net, the *amphiblestron*. It was a hand-net which was cast from the shore. The second way of fishing was with the dragnet, the *sagene*, what we would call the seine-net or the trawl. This is the way referred to in this parable. The seine-net was a great square net with cords at each corner, and weighted so that, at rest, it hung, as it were, upright in the water. When the boat began to move, the net was drawn into the shape of a great cone and into the cone all kinds of fish were swept. The net was then drawn to land, and the catch was separated.

There are two great lessons in this parable.

(1) It is in the nature of the dragnet that it does not, and cannot, discriminate. It is bound to draw in all kinds of things in its course through the water. Its contents are bound to be a mixture. If we apply that to the Church, which is the instrument of God's kingdom upon earth, it means that the Church cannot be discriminative but is bound to be a mixture of all kinds of people, good and bad, useless and useful.

There have always been two views of the Church—the exclusive and the inclusive. The exclusive view holds that the Church is for people who are good, people who are really and fully committed, people who are quite different from the world. There is an attraction in that view, but it is not the New Testament view, because, apart from anything else, who is to do the judging, when we are told that we must not judge (Matthew 7:1)? It is not the place of any one of us to say who is committed to Christ and who is not. The inclusive view feels instinctively that the Church must be open to all, and that, like the dragnet, as long as it is a human institution it is bound to be a mixture. That is exactly what this parable teaches.

(2) But equally, this parable teaches that the time of separation will come when the good and the bad are sent to their respective destinations. That separation, however, certain as it is, is not our work but God's. Therefore it is our duty to gather in all who will come, and not to judge or separate, but to leave the final judgment to God.

Who Is My Neighbour?

Luke 10:25–37

When Jesus told this story, he was telling about the kind of thing that was constantly happening on the Jerusalem to Jericho road.

Let us look at the characters.

(1) There was the traveller. He was obviously a reckless and foolhardy character. People seldom attempted the Jerusalem to Jericho road alone if they were carrying goods or valuables.

(2) There was the priest. He hastened past. No doubt he was remembering that anyone who touched a dead man was unclean for seven days (Numbers 19:11). He could not be sure but he feared that the man was dead; to touch him would mean losing his turn of duty in the Temple; and he refused to risk that. He set the claims of ceremony above those of charity. The Temple and its liturgy meant more to him than human suffering.

(3) There was the Levite. He seems to have gone nearer to the man before he passed on. The bandits were in the habit of using decoys. One of their number would act the part of a wounded man; and when some unsuspecting traveller stopped over him, the others would rush upon him and overpower him. The Levite was a man whose motto was 'Safety first'. He would take no risks to help anyone else.

(4) There was the Samaritan. The listeners would obviously expect that with his arrival the villain had arrived. He may not have been racially a Samaritan at all. The Jews had no dealings with the Samaritans and yet this man seems to have been a kind of commercial traveller who was a regular visitor to the inn.

In John 8:48 the Jews call Jesus a Samaritan. The name was sometimes used to describe someone who was considered a heretic and a breaker of the ceremonial law. A heretic he may have been, but the love of God was in his heart. It is not uncommon to find the orthodox more interested in dogmas than in help and to find those whom the orthodox despise to be the ones who show the greatest love for others. In the end we will be judged not by the creed we hold but by the life we live.

November 7

Ask and You Will Receive

Luke 11:5–13

Travellers often journeyed late in the evening to avoid the heat of the midday sun. In Jesus' story just such a traveller had arrived towards midnight at this friend's house. In the Middle East hospitality is a sacred duty; it was not enough to set before a visitor a bare sufficiency; the guest had to be confronted with an ample abundance.

The lesson of this parable is not that we must persist in prayer; it is not that we must batter at God's door until we finally compel him for very weariness to give us what we want, until we coerce an unwilling God to answer. A *parable* literally means *something laid alongside*. If we lay something beside another thing to teach a lesson, that lesson may be drawn from the fact that the things are like each other or from the fact that the things are a contrast to each other. The point here is based, not on likeness, but on contrast. What Jesus says is, 'If a churlish and unwilling householder can in the end be coerced by a friend's shameless persistence into giving him what he needs, how much more will God who is a loving Father supply all his children's needs?' 'If you,' he says, 'who are evil, know that you are bound to supply your children's needs, how much more will God?'

This does not absolve us from intensity in prayer. After all, we can guarantee the reality and sincerity of our desire only by the passion with which we pray. But it does mean this, that we are not wringing gifts from an unwilling God, but going to one who knows our needs better than we know them ourselves and whose heart towards us is the heart of generous love.

If we do not receive what we pray for, it is not because God grudgingly refuses to give it but because he has some better thing for us. There is no such thing as unanswered prayer. The answer given may not be the answer we desired or expected; but even when it is a refusal it is the answer of the love and the wisdom of God.

The Place of Material Possessions in Life

Luke 12:13–34

It was not uncommon for people in Palestine to take their unsettled disputes to respected Rabbis; but Jesus refused to be mixed up in anyone's disputes about money. But out of that request there came to Jesus an opportunity to lay down what his followers' attitude to material things should be.

To those who had an abundant supply of possessions Jesus spoke this parable of the rich fool. Two things stand out about this man.

(1) He never saw beyond himself. There is no parable which is so full of the words *I, me, my* and *mine*. A schoolboy was once asked what parts of speech *my* and *mine* are. He answered, 'Aggressive pronouns'. The rich fool was aggressively self-centred.

(2) He never saw beyond this world. All his plans were made on the basis of life here. There is a story of a conversation between an ambitious youth and an older man who knew life. Said the young man, 'I will learn my trade.' 'And then?' said the older man. 'I will set up in business.' 'And then?' 'I will make my fortune.' 'And then?' 'I suppose that I shall grow old and retire and live on my money.' 'And then?' 'Well, I suppose that some day I will die.' 'And then?' came the last stabbing question. Those who never remember that there is another world are destined some day for the grimmest of grim shocks.

In Palestine wealth was often in the form of costly raiment; the moths could get at the fine clothes and leave them ruined. But if people clothe their souls with the garments of honour and purity and goodness, nothing on earth can injure them. If they seek the treasures of heaven, their hearts will be fixed on heaven; but if they seek the treasures of earth, their hearts will be bound to earth—and some day they must say goodbye to those things that were so precious, for, as the grim Spanish proverb has it, 'There are no pockets in a shroud.'

Be Prepared

Luke 12:35–48

This passage has two senses. In its narrower sense it refers to the second coming of Jesus Christ; in its wider sense it refers to the time when God's summons enters a person's life, a call to prepare to meet our God. No one can tell the day or the hour when eternity will invade time and summons will come. How, then, would we like God to find us?

In the second section of this passage Jesus draws a picture of the wise and the unwise steward. In the Middle East the steward had almost unlimited power. He was himself a slave, yet he had control of all the other slaves. A trusted steward ran his master's house for him and administered his estate. The unwise steward made two mistakes.

(1) He said, I will do what I like while my master is away; he forgot that the day of reckoning must come. We have a habit of dividing life into compartments. There is a part in which we remember that God is present; and there is a part in which we never think of him at all. We tend to draw a line between sacred and secular; but if we really know what Christianity means we will know that there is no part of life when the master is away. We are working and living forever in our great taskmaster's eye.

(2) He said, I have plenty of time to put things right before the master comes; there is nothing so fatal as to feel that we have plenty of time. Jesus said, 'We must work the works of him who sent me while it is day; night is coming when no one can work' (John 9:4).

The passage finishes with the warning that knowledge and privilege always bring responsibility. Sin is doubly sinful to those who knew better; failure is doubly blameworthy in those who had every chance to do well.

The Gospel of the Other Chance

Luke 13:6–9

Here is a parable at one and the same time lit by grace and closely packed with warnings.

(1) The fig tree occupied a specially favoured position. It was not unusual to see fig trees, thorn trees and apple trees in vineyards. The soil was so shallow and poor that trees were grown wherever there was soil to grow them; but the fig tree had a more than average chance, and it had not proved worthy of it. Repeatedly, directly and by implication, Jesus reminded people that they would be judged according to the opportunities they had.

(2) The parable teaches that uselessness invites disaster. It has been claimed that the whole process of evolution in this world is to produce useful things, and that what is useful will go on from strength to strength, while what is useless will be eliminated. The most searching question we can be asked is: 'Of what use were you in this world?'

(3) Further, the parable teaches that nothing which only takes out can survive. The fig tree was drawing strength and sustenance from the soil; and in return was producing nothing. That was precisely its sin. In the last analysis, there are two kinds of people in this world—those who take out more than they put in, and those who put in more than they take out.

(4) The parable tells us of the gospel of the second chance. A fig tree normally takes three years to reach maturity. If it is not fruiting by that time it is not likely to fruit at all. But this fig tree was given another chance. It is always Jesus' way to give us chance after chance. Peter and Mark and Paul would all gladly have witnessed to that. God is infinitely kind to those who fall and rise again.

(5) But the parable also makes it quite clear that there is a final chance. If we refuse chance after chance, if God's appeal and challenge come again and again in vain, the day finally comes, not when God has shut us out, but when we by deliberate choice have shut ourselves out. God save us from that!

The Empire of Christ

Luke 13:18–19

This is an illustration which Jesus used more than once, and for different purposes. There is much in Luke's conception that we would do well to learn.

(1) There is room in the kingdom for a wide variety of beliefs. No individual and no church has a monopoly of all truth. To think ourselves right and everyone else wrong can lead to nothing but trouble and bitterness and strife.

(2) There is room in the kingdom for a wide variety of experiences. We do infinite harm when we try to standardize Christian experience and insist that everyone must come to Christ in the same way. One person may have a sudden shattering experience and be able to point to the day and the hour, even the very minute, when God invaded his or her life. Another's heart may open to Christ naturally and without crisis, as the petals of a flower open to the sun. Both experiences come from God and both these people belong to God.

(3) There is room in the kingdom for a wide variety of ways of worship. One person finds contact with God in an elaborate ritual and a splendid liturgy; another finds him in the bare simplicities. There is no right or wrong here. It is the glory of the Church that within its fellowship somewhere each of us will find the worship that brings us to God. Let each of us discover it for ourselves, but let us not think our way the only way and criticize another's.

(4) There is room in the kingdom for all kinds of people. The world has its labels and its distinctions and its barriers. But in the kingdom there is no distinction between rich and poor, small and great, famous and unknown. The Church is the one place where distinctions have no legitimate place.

(5) There is room in the kingdom for all nations. In the world today are many national barriers; but none of them has any standing with God. There is room in the city of God for all the world and more.

The Leaven of the Kingdom

Luke 13:20–21

This is an illustration which Jesus took from his own home. In those days bread was baked at home. Leaven was a little piece of dough which had been kept over from the last baking and had fermented in the keeping. Jesus had seen Mary put a little bit of leaven in the dough and had seen the whole character of the dough changed because of it. 'That', he said, 'is how my kingdom comes.'

There are two interpretations of this parable. From the first the following points emerge.

(1) The kingdom of heaven starts from the smallest beginnings. The leaven was very small but it changed the whole character of the dough.

(2) The kingdom of heaven works unseen. We do not see the leaven working but all the time it is fulfilling its function. The kingdom is on the way. Anyone who knows a little history will be bound to see that. Seneca, the greatest of all Roman thinkers, could write, 'We strangle a mad dog; we slaughter a fierce ox; we plunge the knife into sickly cattle lest they taint the herd; children who are born weakly and deformed we drown.' In AD 60 that was the normal thing. Things like that cannot happen today because slowly, but inevitably, the kingdom is on the way.

The second interpretation of this parable insists that far from working unseen the work of the leaven is manifest to all because it turns the dough into a bubbling, seething mass. On this basis, the leaven stands for the disturbing power of Christianity. In Thessalonica it was said of the Christians, 'These people who have been turning the world upside down have come here also' (Acts 17:6). True religion is never dope, never sends people comfortably to sleep, never makes them placidly accept the evils that should be striven against. Real Christianity is the most revolutionary thing in the world; it works revolution in the individual life and in society.

The kingdom of heaven is the leaven which fills each of us at one and the same time with the peace of God and with the divine discontent which will not rest until the evils of earth are swept away by the changing, revolutionizing power of God.

The Necessity of Humility

Luke 14:7–11

Jesus chose a homely illustration to point out an eternal truth. If a quite undistinguished guest arrived early at a feast and annexed the top place, and if a more distinguished person then arrived, and the man who had usurped the first place was told to step down, a most embarrassing situation resulted. If, on the other hand, a man deliberately slipped into the bottom place, and was then asked to occupy a more distinguished place, his humility gained him all the more honour.

Humility has always been one of the characteristics of the truly great. When Thomas Hardy was so famous that any newspaper would gladly have paid enormous sums for his work, he used sometimes to submit a poem, and always with it a stamped and addressed envelope for the return of his manuscript should it be rejected. Even in his greatness he was humble enough to think that his work might be turned down.

How can we retain our humility?

(1) We can retain it by realizing the facts. However much we know, we still know very little compared with the sum total of knowledge. However much we have achieved, we still have achieved very little in the end. However important we may believe ourselves to be, when death removes us or when we retire from our position, life and work will go on just the same.

(2) We can retain it by comparison with the perfect. It is when we see or hear the expert that we realize how poor our own performance is. Many golfers have decided to burn their clubs after a day watching the professionals at golf's Open Championship. Many musicians have decided never to appear in public again after hearing a truly great performance. Many preachers have been humbled almost to despair when they have heard a real saint of God speak. And if we set our lives beside the life of the Lord of all good life, if we see our unworthiness in comparison with the radiance of his stainless purity, pride will die and self-satisfaction will be shrivelled up.

The King's Banquet and the King's Guests

Luke 14:15–24

In Palestine, when anyone made a feast, the day was announced long beforehand and the invitations were sent out and accepted; but the exact time was not announced; and when the day came and all things were ready, servants were sent out to summon the already invited guests. To accept the invitation beforehand and then to refuse it when the day came was a grave insult.

In the parable the invited guests made their excuses, and people's excuses do not differ so very much today.

(1) The first man said that he had bought a field and was going to see it. He allowed the claims of business to usurp the claims of God. It is still possible to be so immersed in this world that we have no time to worship, and even no time to pray.

(2) The second man said that he had bought five yoke of oxen and that he was going to try them out. He let the claims of novelty usurp the claims of Christ. It often happens that when people enter into new possessions they become so taken up with them that the claims of worship and of God get crowded out. It is perilously easy for a new game, a new hobby, even a new friendship, to take up the time that should be kept for God.

(3) The third man said, with even more finality than the others, 'I have married a wife, and I cannot come.' One of the wonderful, merciful laws of the Old Testament laid it down, 'When a man is newly married, he shall not go out with the army or be charged with any related duty. He shall be free at home one year, to be happy with his wife whom he has married' (Deuteronomy 24:5). No doubt that very law was in this man's mind. It is one of the tragedies of life when good things crowd out the claims of God. There is no lovelier thing than a home, and yet a home was never meant to be used selfishly.

They live best together who live with God; they serve each other best who also serve their neighbours; the atmosphere of a home is most lovely when those who dwell within it remember that they are also members of the great family and household of God.

November 15

On Counting the Cost

Luke 14:25–33

When Jesus said this he was on the road to Jerusalem. He knew that he was on his way to the cross; the crowds who were with him thought that he was on his way to an empire.

That is why he spoke to them like this. In the most vivid way possible he told them that those who followed him were not on the way to worldly power and glory, but must be ready for a loyalty which would sacrifice the dearest things in life and for a suffering which would be like the agony of a man upon a cross. We must not take his words with cold and unimaginative literalness. The language of the Middle East is always as vivid as the human mind can make it. When Jesus tells us to hate our nearest and dearest, he does not mean that literally. He means that no love in life can compare with the love we must bear to him.

There are two suggestive truths within this passage.

(1) It is possible to be a follower of Jesus without being a disciple; to be a camp follower without being a soldier of the king; to be a hanger-on in some great work without pulling one's weight. Once someone was talking to a great scholar about a younger man. He said, 'So and so tells me that he was one of your students.' The teacher answered devastatingly, 'He may have attended my lectures, but he was not one of my students.' It is one of the supreme handicaps of the Church that in it there are so many distant followers of Jesus and so few real disciples.

(2) It is a Christian's first duty to count the cost of following Christ. The tower which the man was going to build was probably a vineyard tower. Vineyards were often equipped with towers from which watch was kept against thieves who might steal the harvest. An unfinished building is always a humiliating thing.

It is so with the Christian way. But if we are daunted by the high demands of Christ let us remember that we are not left to fulfil them alone. He who called us to the steep road will walk with us every step of the way and be there at the end to meet us.

November 16

The Shepherd's Joy

Luke 15:1–7

The shepherd in Judaea had a hard and dangerous task. Pasture was scarce. The narrow central plateau was only a few miles wide, and then it plunged down to the wild cliffs and the terrible devastation of the desert. There were no restraining walls and the sheep would wander. George Adam Smith, an Old Testament scholar who travelled extensively in Palestine, wrote of the shepherd, 'On some high moor across which at night the hyaenas howl, when you meet him, sleepless, far-sighted, weather-beaten, armed, leaning on his staff and looking out over his scattered sheep, every one of them on his heart, you understand why the shepherd of Judaea sprang to the front in his people's history; why they gave his name to the king and made him the symbol of providence; why Christ took him as the type of self-sacrifice.'

The shepherd was personally responsible for the sheep. If a sheep was lost the shepherd must at least bring home the fleece to show how it had died. These shepherds were experts at tracking and could follow the straying sheep's footprints for miles across the hills. There was not a shepherd for whom it was not all in the day's work to risk his life for his sheep.

Many of the flocks were communal flocks, belonging, not to individuals, but to villages. There would be two or three shepherds in charge. Those whose flocks were safe would arrive home on time and bring news that one shepherd was still out on the mountainside searching for a sheep which was lost. The whole village would be upon the watch, and when, in the distance, they saw the shepherd striding home with the lost sheep across his shoulders, there would rise from the whole community a shout of joy and of thanksgiving. That is the picture Jesus drew of God; that, said Jesus, is what God is like. God is as glad when a lost sinner is found as a shepherd is when a strayed sheep is brought home.

God loves those who never stray away; but in his heart there is the joy of joys when a lost one is found and comes home.

The Coin a Woman Lost and Found

Luke 15:8–10

The coin in question in this parable was a silver drachma. It would not be difficult to lose a coin in a Palestinian peasant's house and it might take a long search to find it. The houses were very dark, for they were lit by one little circular window not much more than about eighteen inches across. The floor was beaten earth covered with dried reeds and rushes; and to look for a coin on a floor like that was very much like looking for a needle in a haystack.

There are two reasons why the woman may have been so eager to find the coin.

(1) It may have been a matter of sheer necessity. It was only one coin but it would have been worth more than a whole day's wage for a workingman in Palestine. The woman may well have searched with intensity because if she did not find the coin, the family would not eat.

(2) There may have been a much more romantic reason. The mark of a married woman was a headdress made of ten silver coins linked together by a silver chain. For years maybe a girl would scrape and save to amass her ten coins, for the headdress was almost the equivalent of her wedding ring. When she had it, it was so inalienably hers that it could not even be taken from her for debt. It may well be that it was one of these coins that the woman had lost, and so she searched for it as any woman would search if she lost her marriage ring. In either case it is easy to think of the joy of the woman when at last she saw the glint of the elusive coin and when she held it in her hand again. God, said Jesus, is like that.

No Pharisee had ever dreamed of a God like that. A great Jewish scholar has admitted that this is the one absolutely new thing which Jesus taught about God—that he actually searched for us. A Jew might have agreed that those who came crawling home to God in self-abasement and prayed for pity might find it; but he would never have conceived of a God who went out to search for sinners.

We believe in the seeking love of God, because we see that love incarnate in Jesus Christ, the Son of God, who came to seek and to save that which was lost.

The Story of the Loving Father

Luke 15:11–32

Under Jewish law a father was not free to leave his property as he liked. The elder son must get two-thirds and the younger one-third (Deuteronomy 21:17). It was by no means unusual for a father to distribute his estate before he died, if he wished to retire from the actual management of affairs. But there is a certain heartless callousness in the request of the younger son. He said in effect, 'Give me now the part of the estate I will get anyway when you are dead, and let me get out of this.' The father did not argue. He knew that if the son was ever to learn he must learn the hard way; and he granted his request. Without delay the son realized his share of the property and left home.

He soon ran through the money; and he finished up feeding pigs, a task that was forbidden to a Jew because the law said, 'Cursed is he who feeds swine.' Then Jesus paid sinning humanity the greatest compliment it has ever been paid. 'When he came to himself', he said. Jesus believed that being away from God prevented people from being truly themselves. That was only possible once they were on their way home. Beyond a doubt Jesus did not believe in total depravity. He never believed that you could glorify God by denigrating human beings; he believed that we are never essentially ourselves until we come home to God. So the son decided to come home and plead to be taken back not as a son but in the lowest rank of slaves, the hired servants.

This parable should never have been called the parable of the prodigal son, for the son is not the hero. It should be called the parable of the loving father, for it tells us rather about a father's love than a son's sin. The father must have been waiting and watching for the son to come home, for he saw him a long way off. When he came, he forgave him with no recriminations.

Once Abraham Lincoln was asked how he was going to treat the rebellious Southerners when they had finally been defeated and had returned to the Union of the United States. The questioner expected that Lincoln would take a dire vengeance, but he answered, 'I will treat them as if they had never been away.' It is the wonder of the love of God that he treats us like that.

A Bad Man's Good Example

Luke 16:1–13

This is a difficult parable to interpret. It is a story about as choice a set of rogues as one could meet anywhere. The difficulty of the parable is clearly seen from the fact that Luke attaches no fewer than four different lessons to it.

(1) In verse 8 the lesson is that the children of this world are wiser in their generation than the children of light. That means that, if only Christians were as eager and ingenious in their attempt to attain goodness as those with more worldly concerns are in their attempts to attain money and comfort, they would be much better people. If only people would give as much attention to the things which concern their souls as they do to the things which concern their business, they would be much better human beings.

(2) In verse 9 the lesson is that material possessions should be used to cement the friendships wherein the real and permanent value of life lies. How many of us are grateful to a better-off friend who has seen us through some time of need in the most practical way? Possessions are not in themselves a sin, but they are a great responsibility, and those who use them to help their friends have gone far to discharge that responsibility.

(3) In verses 10 and 11 the lesson is that the way of fulfilling a small task is the best proof of fitness or unfitness to be entrusted with a bigger task. That is clearly true of earthly things. But Jesus extends the principle to eternity. He says, 'Upon earth you are in charge of things which are not really yours. You cannot take them with you when you die. They are only lent to you. You are only a steward over them. They cannot, in the nature of things, be permanently yours. On the other hand, in heaven you will get what is really and eternally yours. And what you get in heaven depends on how you use the things of earth.'

(4) Verse 13 lays down the rule that no slave can serve two masters. Serving God can never be a part-time or a spare-time job. Once we choose to serve God every moment of our time and every atom of our energy belongs to God. God is the most exclusive of masters. We either belong to him totally or not at all.

November 20

The Punishment of the Man
Who Never Noticed

Luke 16:19–31

This is a parable constructed with such consummate skill that not one phrase is wasted. First, there is the rich man, usually called Dives, which is the Latin for *rich*. Every phrase adds something to the luxury in which he lived. He was clothed in purple and fine linen. That is the description of the robes of the high priests, and such robes were hugely expensive, costing many times the value of a workingman's daily wage. He feasted in luxury every day. The word used for *feasting* is the word that is used for a gourmet feeding on exotic and costly dishes.

In a country where the people were fortunate if they ate meat once in the week and where they toiled for six days of the week, Dives is a figure of indolent self-indulgence. Lazarus was waiting for the crumbs that fell from Dives' table. In that time there were no knives, forks or napkins. Food was eaten with the hands and, in very wealthy houses, the hands were cleansed by wiping them on hunks of bread, which were then thrown away. That was what Lazarus was waiting for.

What was the sin of Dives? He had not ordered Lazarus to be removed from his gate. He had made no objections to his receiving the bread that was flung away from his table. He did not kick him in the passing. He was not deliberately cruel to him. The sin of Dives was that he never noticed Lazarus, that he accepted him as part of the landscape and simply thought it perfectly natural and inevitable that Lazarus should lie in pain and hunger while he wallowed in luxury. As someone said, 'It was not what Dives did that got him into jail; it was what he did not do that got him into hell.'

The sin of Dives was that he could look on the world's suffering and need and feel no answering sword of grief and pity pierce his heart; he looked at a fellow human being, hungry and in pain, and did nothing about it. His was the punishment of the man who never noticed.

It is a terrible warning that the sin of Dives was not that he did wrong things, but that he did nothing.

November 21

Unwearied in Prayer

Luke 18:1–8

This parable tells of the kind of thing which could, and often did, happen.
There are two characters in it.

(1) The judge was clearly not a Jewish judge. All ordinary Jewish disputes
were taken before the elders, and not into the public courts at all. If, under
Jewish law, a matter was taken to arbitration, one man could not constitute a
court. This judge was one of the paid magistrates appointed either by Herod
or by the Romans. Such judges were notorious. Unless plaintiffs had influence and money to bribe their way to a verdict they had no hope of ever getting a case settled. These judges were said to pervert justice for a dish of meat.
People even punned on their title. Officially they were called *Dayyaneh Geze-
roth*, which means *judges of prohibitions or punishments*. Popularly they were
called *Dayyaneh Gezeloth*, which means *robber judges*.

(2) The widow was the symbol of all who were poor and defenceless. It was
obvious that she, without resource of any kind, had no hope of ever extracting
justice from such a judge. But she had one weapon—persistence. This parable
is like the parable of the friend at midnight. It does not liken God to an unjust
judge; it contrasts him to such a person. Jesus was saying, 'If, in the end, an
unjust and rapacious judge can be wearied into giving a widow justice, how
much more will God, who is a loving father, give his children what they need?'

That is true, but it is no reason why we should expect to get whatever we
pray for. Often a father has to refuse the request of a child, because he knows
that what the child asks would hurt rather than help. God is like that. We do
not know what is to happen in the next hour, let alone the next week, or month,
or year. Only God sees time whole, and, therefore, only God knows what is
good for us in the long run. That is why Jesus said we must never be discouraged in prayer. That is why he wondered if human faith would stand the
long delays before the Son of Man should come.

We will never grow weary in prayer and our faith will never falter if, after
we have offered to God our prayers and requests, we add the perfect prayer:
Your will be done.

November 22

The Sin of Pride

Luke 18:9–14

The devout observed two or three prayer times daily — in the morning and the evening and sometimes also at noon. Prayer was held to be specially efficacious if it was offered in the Temple and so at these hours many went up to the Temple courts to pray. Jesus told of two men who went.

(1) There was a Pharisee. He did not really go to pray to God. He prayed with himself. True prayer is always offered to God and to God alone. A certain American cynically described a preacher's prayer as 'the most eloquent prayer ever offered to a Boston audience'. The Pharisee did not really go to pray; he went to inform God how good he was.

(2) There was a tax collector. He stood afar off, and would not even lift his eyes to God.

This parable unmistakably tells us certain things about prayer.

(1) No one who is proud can pray. The gate of heaven is so low that none can enter it save upon their knees.

(2) No one who despises others can pray. In prayer we do not lift ourselves above others. We remember that we are one of a great army of sinning, suffering, sorrowing humanity, all kneeling before the throne of God's mercy.

(3) True prayer comes from setting our lives beside the life of God. No doubt all that the Pharisee said was true. He did fast; he did meticulously give tithes; he was not like other people; still less was he like that tax collector. But the question is not, 'Am I as good as my neighbour?' The question is, 'Am I as good as God?'

Once I made a journey by train to England. As we passed through the Yorkshire moors I saw a little whitewashed cottage and it seemed to me to shine with an almost radiant whiteness. Some days later I made the journey back to Scotland. The snow had fallen and was lying deep all around. We came again to the little white cottage, but this time its whiteness seemed drab and soiled and almost grey in comparison with the pure whiteness of the driven snow. It all depends what we compare ourselves with.

How to Forgive

Matthew 18:21–35

This parable teaches certain lessons which Jesus never tired of teaching.

(1) It teaches that lesson which runs through all the New Testament—we must forgive in order to be forgiven. Those who will not forgive others cannot hope that God will forgive them. 'Blessed are the merciful,' said Jesus, 'for they will receive mercy' (Matthew 5:7). As James had it: 'For judgment will be without mercy to anyone who has shown no mercy' (James 2:13). Divine and human forgiveness go hand in hand.

(2) Why should that be so? One of the great points in this parable is the contrast between the two debts. The first servant owed his master 10,000 talents—and a talent was the equivalent of fifteen years' wages. That is an incredible debt. It was more than the total budget of the ordinary province. The total revenue of the province which contained Idumaea, Judaea and Samaria was only 600 talents; the total revenue of even a wealthy province like Galilee was only 300 talents. Against that background, this debt is staggering. It was this that the servant was forgiven. The debt which a fellow servant owed him was a trifling thing; it was 100 denarii, and a denarius was the usual day's wage for a working man. It was therefore a mere fraction of his own debt.

The biblical scholar A. R. S. Kennedy drew this vivid picture to contrast the debts. Suppose they were paid in small coins (he suggested sixpences; we might think in terms of five-pence pieces or dimes). The 100-denarii debt could be carried in one pocket. The 10,000-talent debt would take an army of about 8,600 carriers to carry it, each carrying a sack of coins 60 pounds in weight; and they would form, at a distance of a yard apart, a line five miles long!

The contrast between the debts is staggering. The point is that nothing that others can do to us can in any way compare with what we have done to God; and if God has forgiven us the debt we owe to him, we must forgive our neighbours the debts they owe to us. Nothing that we have to forgive can even faintly or remotely compare with what we have been forgiven.

November 24

The Master Seeks His Workers

Matthew 20:1–16

This parable contains truth which goes to the very heart of the Christian religion. In it, there is the comfort of God. It means that no matter when people enter the kingdom — late or soon, in the first flush of youth, in the strength of the middle of the day, or when the shadows are lengthening — they are equally dear to God.

May we not go even further with this thought of comfort? Sometimes people die full of years and full of honour, with their day's work ended and their task completed. Sometimes young people die almost before the door of life and achievement has opened at all. From God, they will both receive the same welcome; for both, Jesus Christ is waiting, and in neither case, in the divine sense, has life ended too soon or too late.

Here also is the generosity of God. These men did not all do the same work; but they did receive the same pay. There are two great lessons here. The first is, God does not look on the amount of our service. As long as it is all we have to give, all service ranks the same with God. The second lesson is even greater — all God gives is of grace. We cannot earn what God gives us; we cannot deserve it; what God gives us is given out of the goodness of his heart; what God gives is not pay, but a gift; not a reward, but a grace.

Surely that brings us to the supreme lesson of the parable — the whole point of work is the spirit in which it is done. The servants are clearly divided into two classes. The first came to an agreement with the master; they had a contract; they said: 'We work, if you give us so much pay.' As their conduct showed, all they were concerned with was to get as much as possible out of their work. But in the case of those who were engaged later, there is no word of contract; all they wanted was the chance to work, and they willingly left the reward to the master.

We are not Christians if our first concern is pay. Christians work for the joy of serving God and others. That is why the first will be last and the last will be first. It is the paradox of the Christian life that those who aim at reward lose it, and those who forget reward find it.

November 25

The Better of Two Bad Sons

Matthew 21:28–32

The meaning of this parable is crystal clear. The Jewish leaders are the people who said they would obey God and then did not. The tax-gatherers and the prostitutes are those who said that they would go their own way and then took God's way.

But there are truths in this parable which go far beyond the situation in which it was first spoken. It tells us that there are two very common classes of people in this world. First, there are the people whose promises are much better than their practice. They will promise anything; they make great protestations of piety and fidelity; but their practice lags far behind. Second, there are those whose practice is far better than their promises. They claim to be tough, hardheaded materialists, but somehow they are found out doing kindly and generous things, almost in secret, as if they were ashamed of it. They profess to have no interest in the Church and in religion, and yet in reality they live more Christian lives than many professing Christians.

We have all of us met these people, those whose practice is far away from the almost sanctimonious piety of their professed beliefs, and those whose practice is far ahead of the sometimes cynical, and sometimes almost irreligious, declarations which they make about what they believe. The real point of the parable is that, while the second class are infinitely to be preferred to the first, neither is anything like perfect. The really good man or woman is the one in whom professed belief and practice meet and match.

Further, this parable teaches us that promises can never take the place of performance, and fine words are never a substitute for fine deeds. The son who said he would go, and did not, had all the outward marks of courtesy. In his answer, he called his father 'sir' with all respect. But a courtesy which never gets beyond words is a totally illusory thing. True courtesy is obedience, willingly and graciously given.

344

The Vineyard of the Lord

Matthew 21:33–46

This parable has much to tell us.

(1) It tells of God's trust in human beings. The owner of the vineyard entrusted it to the cultivators. He did not even stand over them to exercise a police-like supervision. He went away and left them with their task. God pays us the compliment of entrusting us with his work.

(2) It tells of God's patience. The master sent messenger after messenger. He did not come with sudden vengeance when one messenger had been abused and ill-treated. He gave the cultivators chance after chance to respond to his appeal. God bears with us in all our sinning and will not cast us off.

(3) It tells of God's judgment. In the end, the master of the vineyard took the vineyard from the cultivators and gave it to others. God's sternest judgment is when he takes out of our hands the task which he meant us to do. To become useless to God is to sink to the lowest level.

(4) It tells of the deliberateness of human sin. The cultivators carry out a deliberate policy of rebellion and disobedience towards the master. Sin is deliberate opposition to God; it is the taking of our own way when we know quite well what the way of God is.

(5) It tells of the claim of Jesus. It shows us quite clearly Jesus lifting himself out of the succession of the prophets. Those who came before him were the messengers of God; no one could deny them that honour; but they were servants; he was the Son. This parable contains one of the clearest claims Jesus ever made to be unique, to be different from even the greatest of those who went before.

(6) It tells of the sacrifice of Jesus. It makes it clear that Jesus knew what lay ahead. In the parable, the hands of wicked men killed the son. Jesus was never in any doubt of what lay ahead. He did not die because he was compelled to die; he went willingly and with open eyes to death.

Joy and Judgment

Matthew 22:1–14

This parable contains both a local and a universal lesson.

(1) The local lesson is this: Jesus has just said that the king, to supply his feast with guests, sent his messengers out into the highways and byways to gather people in. That was the parable of the open door. It told how the Gentiles and the sinners would be gathered in. This parable strikes the necessary balance. It is true that the door is open to everyone, but when people come they must bring a life which seeks to fit the love which has been given to them. Grace is not only a gift; it is a grave responsibility. We cannot go on living the life we lived before we met Jesus Christ. We must be clothed in a new purity and a new holiness and a new goodness. The door is open, but the door is not open for the sinner to come and remain a sinner, but for the sinner to come and become a saint.

(2) This is the permanent lesson. The way in which people come to anything demonstrates the spirit in which they come. If we go to visit in a friend's house, we do not go in the clothes we wear on the building site or in the garden. We know very well that it is not the clothes which matter to the friend. It is not that we want to put on a show. It is simply a matter of respect that we should present ourselves in our friend's house as neatly as we can.

So it is with God's house. This parable has nothing to do with the clothes in which we go to church; it has everything to do with the spirit in which we go to God's house. It is profoundly true that church going must never be a fashion parade. But there are garments of the mind and of the heart and of the soul—the garment of expectation, the garment of humble penitence, the garment of faith, the garment of reverence—and these are the garments without which we ought not to approach God.

Too often, we go to God's house with no preparation at all; if every man and woman in our congregations came to church prepared to worship, after a little prayer, a little thought and a little self-examination, then worship would be worship indeed—the worship through which things happen in the souls of men and women and in the life of the Church and in the affairs of the world.

The Fate of the Unprepared

Matthew 25:1–13

If we look at this parable with Western eyes, it may seem an unnatural and a 'made-up' story. But, in point of fact, it tells a story which could have happened at any time in a Palestinian village and which could still happen today. A wedding was a great occasion. The whole village turned out to accompany the couple to their new home, and they went by the longest possible road, in order that they might receive the glad good wishes of as many as possible.

The point of this story lies in a Jewish custom which is very different from anything we know. When a couple married, they did not go away for a honeymoon. They stayed at home; for a week they kept open house; they were treated, and even addressed, as prince and princess; it was the happiest week in all their lives. To the festivities of that week their chosen friends were admitted; and it was not only the marriage ceremony, it was also that joyous week that the foolish virgins missed, because they were unprepared.

The parable has at least two universal warnings.

(1) It warns us that there are certain things which cannot be obtained at the last minute. It is far too late for a student to be preparing when the day of the examination has come. It is too late to acquire a skill, or a character, if we do not already possess it, when some task offers itself to us. Similarly, it is easy to leave things so late that we can no longer prepare ourselves to meet with God. When the Queen of England, Mary of Orange, was dying, her chaplain sought to tell her of the way of salvation. Her answer was: 'I have not left this matter to this hour.' To be too late is always tragedy.

(2) It warns us that there are certain things which cannot be borrowed. The foolish virgins found it impossible to borrow oil when they discovered they needed it. We cannot borrow a relationship with God; we must possess it for ourselves. We cannot borrow a character; we must be clothed with it. We cannot always be living on the spiritual capital which others have amassed. There are certain things we must win or acquire for ourselves, for we cannot borrow them from others.

The Condemnation of the Buried Talent

Matthew 25:14–30

There can be no doubt that originally in this parable the whole attention is riveted on the useless servant. There can be little doubt that he stands for the scribes and the Pharisees, and for their attitude to the law and the truth of God. The useless servant buried his talent in the ground, in order that he might hand it back to his master exactly as it was. The whole aim of the scribes and Pharisees was to keep the law exactly as it was.

But there is much more in this parable than that.

(1) It tells us that God gives us differing gifts. One man received five talents, another two, and another one. It is not our talent which matters; what matters is how we use it. God never demands from us abilities which we have not got; but he does demand that we should use to the full the abilities which we do possess.

(2) It tells us that the reward of work well done is still more work to do. The two servants who had done well are not told to lean back and rest on their oars because they have done well. They are given greater tasks and greater responsibilities in the work of the master.

(3) It tells us that those who are punished are the people who will not try. The man with the one talent did not lose his talent; he simply did nothing with it. Even if he had adventured with it and lost it, it would have been better than to do nothing at all. It is always a temptation for the one-talent person to say: 'I have so small a talent and I can do so little with it. It is not worthwhile to try, for all the contribution I can make.' The condemnation is for anyone who, having even one talent, will not try to use it, and will not risk it for the common good.

(4) It lays down a rule of life which is universally true. It tells us that to those who have, more will be given, and those who have not will lose even what they have. The meaning is this. If we have a talent and exercise it, we are progressively able to do more with it. But, if we have a talent and fail to exercise it, we will inevitably lose it.

God's Standard of Judgment

Matthew 25:31–46

This is one of the most vivid parables Jesus ever spoke, and the lesson is crystal clear—that God will judge us in accordance with our reaction to human need. And there are certain things which this parable teaches us about the help which we must give.

(1) It must be help in simple things. The things which Jesus picks out—giving a hungry person a meal, or a thirsty person a drink, welcoming a stranger, cheering the sick, visiting the prisoner—are things which anyone can do. It is not a question of giving away huge sums of money, or of writing our names in the annals of history; it is a case of giving simple help to the people we meet every day. There never was a parable which so opened the way to glory to us all.

(2) It must be help which is uncalculating. Those who helped did not think that they were helping Christ and thus piling up eternal merit; they helped because they could not stop themselves. It was the natural, instinctive, quite uncalculating reaction of the loving heart. Whereas, on the other hand, the attitude of those who failed to help was: 'If we had known it was you we would gladly have helped; but we thought it was only some insignificant person who was not worth helping.' It is still true that there are those who will help if they are given praise and thanks and publicity; but to help like that is not to help, it is to pander to self-esteem. Such help is not generosity; it is disguised selfishness. The help which wins the approval of God is that which is given for nothing but the sake of helping.

(3) Jesus confronts us with the wonderful truth that all such help given is given to himself; in contrast, all such help withheld is withheld from himself. How can that be? If we really wish to bring delight to those who are parents, if we really wish to move them to gratitude, the best way to do it is to help their children. God is the great Father; and the way to delight the heart of God is to help his children, our fellow men and women.

When we learn the generosity which without calculation helps others in the simplest things, we too will know the joy of helping Jesus Christ himself.

DECEMBER

God with Us

What Jesus Did for Us

Revelation 1:1–6

Few passages set down with such splendour what Jesus did for us. He loves us, and he set us free from our sins at the cost of his own blood. The words *to wash* and *to set free* are very alike in Greek. *To wash* is *louein*; *to set free* is *luein*; and they are pronounced in exactly the same way. But there is no doubt that the oldest and best Greek manuscripts read *luein*. Again, *in his own blood* is a mistranslation. The word translated as *in* is *en*, which, indeed, can mean *in*; but here it is a translation of the Hebrew word *be* (the *e* is pronounced very short as in *the*), which means *at the price of*.

What Jesus did, as John sees it, was to free us from our sins at the cost of his own blood. This is exactly what he says later on when he speaks of those who were ransomed for God by the blood of the Lamb (5:9). It is exactly what Paul meant when he spoke of us being *redeemed* from the curse of the law (Galatians 3:13) and when he spoke of *redeeming* those who were under the law (Galatians 4:5). In both cases, the word used is *exagorazein*, which means *to buy out from*, to pay the price of buying a person or a thing out of the possession of the one who holds power over that person or thing.

There is another very significant thing here. We must note carefully the tenses of the verbs. John says that Jesus loves us and set us free. *Loves* is the present tense, and it means that the love of God in Christ Jesus is something which is continuous. *Set us free* is the past tense, the Greek aorist, which tells of one act completed in the past—and it means that in the one act of the cross our liberation from sin was achieved. That is to say, what happened on the cross was one act in time which was for our benefit and an expression of the continuous love of God.

December 2

The Coming Glory

Revelation 1:7

In this passage, John sets down his confidence in the triumphant return of Christ, which would rescue Christians in distress from the cruelty of their enemies.

(1) To Christians, the return of Christ is a promise on which to feed the soul. John takes as his picture of that return Daniel's vision of the four great beasts, the powers which have held the world in their grip (Daniel 7:1–14). There was Babylon, the power that was like a lion with eagle's wings (7:4). There was Persia, the power that was like a savage bear (7:5). There was Greece, the power that was like a winged leopard (7:6). There was Rome, a beast with iron teeth, beyond description (7:7). But the day of these bestial empires was over, and the dominion was to be given to a gentle power like a son of man. 'As I watched in the night visions, I saw one like a [son of man] coming with the clouds of heaven. And he came to the Ancient One and was presented before him. To him was given dominion and glory and kingship, that all peoples, nations and languages should serve him' (7:13–14).

It is from that passage in Daniel that there emerges the ever recurring picture of the Son of Man coming on the clouds (Mark 13:26, 14:62; Matthew 24:30, 26:64). When we strip away the purely temporary imagery—we, for instance, no longer think of heaven as a localized place above the sky—we are left with the unchanging truth that the day will come when Jesus Christ will be Lord of all. In that hope, there has always been the source of strength and the comfort of Christians for whom life was difficult and for whom faith meant death.

(2) To the enemies of Christ, the return of Christ is a threat. The day will come when all people, even those who crucified him, will look on him again; and, this time, he will not be a broken figure on a cross but a regal figure to whom universal dominion has been given. The day will come when those who disregarded and those who opposed Jesus Christ will find him the Lord of the universe and the judge of their souls.

The Picture of the Risen Christ (1)

Revelation 1:14–18

In this passage, John takes titles which in the Old Testament are descriptions of God and applies them to the risen Christ.

His head and his hair were white, as white wool, like snow. This, taken from the description of the Ancient One in Daniel 7:9, is symbolic of two things.

(1) It stands for great age; and it speaks to us of the eternal existence of Jesus Christ.

(2) It speaks to us of divine purity. The snow and the white wool are the emblems of stainless purity. 'Though your sins are like scarlet,' said Isaiah, 'they shall be like snow; though they are red like crimson, they shall become like wool' (Isaiah 1:18). Here we have the symbols of the pre-existence and the sinlessness of Christ.

His eyes were as a flame of fire. Daniel is always in John's mind, and this is part of the description of the divine figure who brought the vision to Daniel: 'His eyes like flaming torches' (Daniel 10:6).

His voice was as the sound of many waters. This is the description of the voice of God in Ezekiel 43:2. But it may be that we can catch an echo of the little island of Patmos. As H. B. Swete has it in his book *The Apocalypse of John*: 'The roar of the Aegean was in the ears of the seer.' Swete goes on to say that the voice of God is not confined to one note. Here, it is like the thunder of the sea; but it can also be like a still small voice (1 Kings 19:12) or, as the Greek version of the Old Testament has it, like a gentle breeze. It can thunder a rebuke; and it can sing softly with the soothing comfort of a mother over her hurt child.

He had seven stars in his right hand. Here again, we have something which was the prerogative of God alone. But there is also something lovely. When the seer fell in awed terror before the vision of the risen Christ, the Christ stretched out his right hand and placed it on him and told him not to be afraid. The hand of Christ is strong enough to uphold the heavens and gentle enough to wipe away our tears.

December 4

The Picture of the Risen Christ (2)

Revelation 1:14–18

There was coming forth from his mouth a sharp, two-edged sword. The sword referred to was not long and narrow like a fencer's blade; it was a short, tongue-shaped sword for close fighting. Again, the seer has searched the Old Testament for his picture. Isaiah says of God: 'He shall strike the earth with the rod of his mouth' (Isaiah 11:4); and of himself: 'He made my mouth like a sharp sword' (Isaiah 49:2). The symbolism tells us of the penetrating quality of the word of God. If we listen to it, no shield of self-deception can withstand it; it strips away our self-deludings, lays bare our sin and leads to pardon. 'The word of God is living and active, sharper than any two-edged sword' (Hebrews 4:12).

His face was as the sun shining in its strength. In Judges, there is a great picture which may well have been in John's mind. The enemies of God shall perish, 'but may your friends be like the sun as it rises in its might' (Judges 5:31). If that is true of those who love God, how much truer it must be of God's beloved Son. Swete sees something even lovelier here—nothing less than a memory of the transfiguration. On that occasion, Jesus was transfigured before Peter, James and John, 'and his face shone like the sun' (Matthew 17:2). No one who had seen that sight could ever forget the glow; and, if the writer of this book is that same John, perhaps he saw again on the face of the risen Christ the glory he had glimpsed on the Mount of Transfiguration.

When I saw him, I fell at his feet like a dead man. This was the experience of Ezekiel when God spoke to him (Ezekiel 1:28, 3:23, 43:3). But surely we can again find a memory of the gospel story. On that day in Galilee, when there was the great catch of fish and Peter glimpsed who Jesus was, he fell to his knees, conscious only that he was a sinful man (Luke 5:1–11). To the end of the day, there can be nothing but reverence in the presence of the holiness and the glory of the risen Christ.

December 5

The Picture of the Risen Christ (3)

Revelation 1:14–18

Stop being afraid. These were words which the disciples had heard more than once from the lips of Jesus. It was in this way that he spoke to them when he came to them across the water (Matthew 14:27; Mark 6:50); and it was above all in this way that he spoke to them on the Mount of Transfiguration, when they were terrified at the sound of the divine voice (Matthew 17:7). Even in heaven, when we come near the unapproachable glory, Jesus is saying: 'I am here; do not be afraid.'

I am the first and the last. In the Old Testament, this is nothing other than the self-description of God (Isaiah 44:6, 48:12). It is the promise of Jesus that he is there at the beginning and the end. He is there in the moment of birth and at the time of death. He is there when we set out upon the Christian way and when we finish our course.

I am the living one, although I was dead and I am alive forever and forever. Here is at once the claim and the promise of Christ, the claim of one who conquered death and the promise of one who is alive for evermore to be with his people.

I have the keys of death and Hades. Death has its gates (Psalm 9:13, 107:18; Isaiah 38:10); and Christ has the keys of these gates. There were those who took this claim—and some still do—as a reference to the descent into hell (1 Peter 3:18–20). There was a belief in the ancient Church that, when Jesus descended into Hades, he unlocked the doors and brought out Abraham and all God's faithful people who had lived and died in the generations before. But we may take it in an even wider sense; for we who are Christians believe that Jesus Christ has abolished death and brought life and immortality to light through the gospel (2 Timothy 1:10), that because he lives we too shall live (John 14:19), and that, therefore, for us and for those whom we love, the bitterness of death is forever past.

December 6

The Opening Heavens and the Opening Door

Revelation 4:1

In the early chapters of Revelation, there are three of the most important doors in life.

(1) There is the door of opportunity. 'Look,' said the risen Christ to the church at Philadelphia, 'I have set before you an open door' (Revelation 3:8). That was the door of the glorious opportunity by which the message of the gospel could be taken to the regions beyond. God sets before every one of us our own door of opportunity.

(2) There is the door of the human heart. 'Listen!' says the risen Christ, 'I am standing at the door, knocking' (Revelation 3:20). At the door of every heart there comes the knock of the nail-pierced hand, and we may open or refuse to open.

(3) There is the door of revelation. 'I looked, and there in heaven a door stood open,' says the seer. God offers to every one of us the door which leads to the knowledge of God and of life eternal.

More than once, the New Testament speaks of the heavens being opened; and it is of the greatest significance to see the object of that opening.

(1) There is the opening of the heavens for vision. 'The heavens were opened, and I saw visions of God' (Ezekiel 1:1). God sends to those who seek him the vision of himself and of his truth.

(2) There is the opening for the descent of the Spirit. When Jesus was baptized by John, he saw the heavens opened and the Spirit descending upon himself (Mark 1:10). When our minds and souls seek upwards, the Spirit of God descends to meet them.

(3) There is the opening for the revelation of the glory of Christ. It was the promise of Jesus to Nathanael that he would see the heaven open and the angels of God ascending and descending upon the Son of Man (John 1:51). Some day, the heavens will open to disclose the glory of Christ; and inevitably that day will bring joy to those who have loved him and amazement and fear to those who have despised him.

December 7

The Lamb

Revelation 5:1–8

Here is the supreme moment of this vision—the emergence of the Lamb in the scene of heaven. The Lamb is one of the great characteristic ideas of Revelation in which Jesus Christ is so named no fewer than twenty-nine times. The word that John uses for *Lamb* is *arnion*. This is the word that Jeremiah uses, when he says: 'I was like a gentle lamb led to the slaughter' (Jeremiah 11:19). By using *arnion* and using it so often, John wants us to see that this is a new idea which he is introducing.

(1) The Lamb still bears the marks of having been slain. There we have the picture of the sacrifice of Christ, still visible in the heavenly places. Even in the heavenly places, Jesus Christ is the one who loved us and gave himself for us.

(2) There is another side to this. This same Lamb, with the marks of sacrifice still on it, is the Lamb with the seven horns and the seven eyes.

(a) The seven horns stand for omnipotence, the possession of infinite power. Here is the great paradox: the Lamb bears the sacrificial wounds upon it; but at the same time it is clothed with the very might of God, which can now shatter its enemies. The Lamb has seven horns; the number seven stands for perfection; no one can withstand the power of the Lamb, which is perfect.

(b) The Lamb has seven eyes, and the eyes are the Spirits which are despatched into all the earth. The picture comes from Zechariah. There, the prophet sees the seven lamps which are 'the eyes of the Lord, which range through the whole earth' (Zechariah 4:10). It is an eerie picture; but quite clearly it stands for the omniscience of God, his infinite knowledge.

Here is a tremendous picture of Christ. He is the fulfilment of all the hopes and dreams of Israel, for he is the Lion of Judah and the Root of David. He is the one whose sacrifice was for the benefit of all people, and who still bears the marks of it in the heavenly places. But the tragedy has turned to triumph and the shame to glory; and he is the one whose all-conquering might no one can withstand and whose all-seeing eye no one can escape.

December 8

Fellowship with God

Revelation 21:1–4

Here is the promise of fellowship with God and all its precious consequences. The voice is that of one of the angels of the presence. God is to make his dwelling place with human beings. The word used for *dwelling place* is *skene*, literally a *tent*. Originally, in the wilderness, the tabernacle was a tent—the *skene* supreme. This, then, means that God is to make his tabernacle with men and women forever, to give his presence to them forever. Here in this world and amid the things of time, our awareness of the presence of God comes and goes; but in heaven we will be permanently aware of that presence.

God's promise to make Israel his people and to be their God echoes throughout the Old Testament. 'I will place my dwelling in your midst. . . . And I will walk among you, and will be your God, and you shall be my people' (Leviticus 26:11–12). In Jeremiah's account of the new covenant, the promise of God is: 'I will be their God, and they shall be my people' (Jeremiah 31:33). The promise to Ezekiel is: 'My dwelling-place shall be with them; and I will be their God, and they shall be my people' (Ezekiel 37:27). The highest promise of all is intimate fellowship with God, in which we can say: 'I am my beloved's and my beloved is mine' (Song of Solomon 6:3).

This fellowship with God in the golden age brings certain things. Tears and grief and crying and pain have gone. That, too, had been the dream of the prophets of past times. 'They shall obtain joy and gladness,' said Isaiah of the pilgrims of the heavenly way, 'and sorrow and sighing shall flee away' (Isaiah 35:10). 'I will rejoice in Jerusalem, and delight in my people; no more shall the sound of weeping be heard in it, or the cry of distress' (Isaiah 65:19). Death, too, shall be gone. That, too, had been the dream of the ancient prophets. 'He will swallow up death forever. Then the Lord God will wipe away the tears from all faces' (Isaiah 25:8).

This is a promise for the future. But, even in this present world, those who mourn are blessed, for they will be comforted, and death is swallowed up in victory for those who know Christ and the fellowship of his sufferings and the power of his resurrection (Matthew 5:4; Philippians 3:10).

December 9

All Things New

Revelation 21:5–6

For the first time, God himself speaks; he is the God who is able to make all things new. Again, we are back among the dreams of the ancient prophets. Isaiah heard God say: 'Do not remember the former things, or consider the things of old. I am about to do a new thing' (Isaiah 43:18–19). This is the witness of Paul: 'If anyone is in Christ, there is a new creation' (2 Corinthians 5:17). God can take people and re-create them, and will some day create a new universe for the saints whose lives he has renewed.

It is not God but the angel of the presence who gives the command to write. These words must be written down and remembered; they are true and absolutely to be relied upon. 'I am Alpha and Omega,' says God to John, 'the beginning and the end.' Again, John is hearing the voice that the great prophets had heard: 'I am the first and I am the last; besides me there is no god' (Isaiah 44:6). Alpha is the first letter of the Greek alphabet and omega the last. John goes on to amplify this statement. God is the beginning and the end. The word for *beginning* is *arche*, and means not simply first in point of time but first in the sense of the source of all things. The word for *end* is *telos*, and means not simply end in point of time but the *goal*.

John is saying that all life begins in God and ends in God. Paul expressed the same thing when he said, perhaps a little more philosophically: 'For from him and through him and to him are all things' (Romans 11:36), and when he spoke of 'one God and Father of all, who is above all and through all and in all' (Ephesians 4:6).

360

December 10

The Eternal Word

John 1:1–2

It is John's great thought that Jesus is none other than God's creative and life-giving and light-giving Word, that Jesus is the power of God which created the world and the reason of God which sustains the world come to earth in human and bodily form.

The Word was already there at the very beginning of things. John's thought is going back to the first verse of the Bible: 'In the beginning when God created the heavens and the earth' (Genesis 1:1). What John is saying is this—the Word is not one of the created things; the Word was there before creation; the Word is not part of the world which came into being in time; the Word is part of eternity and was there with God before time and the world began.

John was thinking of what is known as the pre-existence of Christ. In many ways, this idea of pre-existence is very difficult, if not altogether impossible, to grasp. But it does mean one very simple, very practical and very tremendous thing. If the Word was with God before time began, if God's Word is part of the eternal scheme of things, it means that God was always like Jesus. Sometimes we tend to think of God as stern and avenging; and we tend to think that something Jesus did changed God's anger into love and altered his attitude to human beings. The New Testament knows nothing of that idea. The whole New Testament tells us, this passage of John especially, that God has always been like Jesus. What Jesus did was to open a window in time that we might see the eternal and unchanging love of God.

John goes on to say that the Word was with God. What does he mean by that? He means that there has always been the closest connection between the Word and God. Let us put that in another and a simpler way—there has always been the most intimate connection between Jesus and God. That means no one can tell us what God is like, what God's will is for us, what God's love and heart and mind are like, as Jesus can.

December 11

Life and Light

John 1:3–4

The second of the great Johannine keywords which we meet here is the word *light*. 'I have come', said Jesus, 'as light into the world' (12:46). Let us see if we can understand something of this idea of the light which Jesus brings into the world. Three things stand out.

(1) The light Jesus brings is the light which puts chaos to flight. In the creation story, God moved upon the dark, formless chaos which was before the world began and said: 'Let there be light' (Genesis 1:3). The new-created light of God routed the empty chaos into which it came. So Jesus is the light which shines in the darkness (1:5). He is the one person who can save life from becoming a chaos. Left to ourselves, we are at the mercy of our passions and our fears.

(2) The light which Jesus brings is a revealing light. It is their condemnation that people loved the darkness rather than the light; and they did so because their deeds were evil; and they hated the light lest their deeds should be exposed (3:19–20). The light which Jesus brings is something which shows things as they are. It strips away the disguises and the concealments; it shows things in all their nakedness; it shows them in their true character and their true values. We never see ourselves until we see ourselves through the eyes of Jesus. We never see what our lives are like until we see them in the light of Jesus. Jesus often drives us to God by revealing us to ourselves.

(3) The light which Jesus brings is a guiding light. If people do not possess that light, they walk in darkness and do not know where they are going (12:36). When they receive that light and believe in it, they walk no more in darkness (12:46). One of the features of the gospel stories which no one can miss is the number of people who came running to Jesus asking: 'What am I to do?' When Jesus comes into life, the time of guessing and of groping is ended, the time of doubt and uncertainty and vacillation is gone.

The path that was dark becomes light; the decision that was wrapped in a night of uncertainty is illumined. Without Jesus, we are like people on an unknown road in the pitch dark. With Jesus, the way is clear.

December 12

The Hostile Dark

John 1:5

Here we meet another of John's keywords—*darkness* (*skotos*, *skotia*). This word occurs seven times in the gospel. To John, there was a darkness in the world that was as real as the light.

(1) The darkness is hostile to the light. The light shines in the darkness, but, however hard the darkness tries, it cannot extinguish it. John is saying: 'Into this world there comes Jesus, the light of the world; there is a darkness which would seek to eliminate him, to banish him from life, to extinguish him. But there is a power in Jesus that is undefeatable. The darkness can hate him, but it can never get rid of him.' As has been truly said: 'Not all the darkness in the world can extinguish the littlest flame.' The unconquerable light will in the end defeat the hostile dark. John is saying: 'Choose your side in the eternal conflict and choose aright.'

(2) The darkness stands for the natural sphere of all those who hate the good. It is those whose deeds are evil who fear the light (3:19–20). The person who has something to hide loves the dark; but it is impossible to hide anything from God. His searchlight sweeps the shadows and illuminates the skulking evils of the world.

(3) There are certain passages where the darkness seems to stand for ignorance, especially for that wilful ignorance which refuses the light of Jesus Christ. Jesus says: 'I am the light of the world. Whoever follows me will never walk in darkness' (8:12). Without Jesus Christ, we cannot find or see the way. It is like being blindfolded or even blind. Without Jesus Christ, life becomes lost.

Although some people did all they could to obscure and extinguish the light of God in Christ, they could not quench it. In every generation, the light of Christ still shines in spite of such efforts to extinguish the flame.

December 13

The Light of All People

John 1:9

In this verse, John uses a very significant word to describe Jesus. He says that Jesus was the real light. In Greek, there are two words which are very like each other. The Authorized Version and the Revised Standard Version use the word *true* to translate both of them; but they have different shades of meaning. The first is *alethes*. *Alethes* means *true* as opposed to false; it is the word that would be used of a statement which is true. The other word is *alethinos*. *Alethinos* means *real* or *genuine* as opposed to unreal.

So what John is saying is that Jesus is the real light that has come to bring enlightenment. Before Jesus came, there were other lights which were followed. Some were flickers of the truth; some were faint glimpses of reality; some were will o' the wisps which when followed led people out into the dark and left them there. It is still the case. There are still the partial lights; and there are still the false lights; and some people still follow them. Jesus is the only genuine light, the real light to guide us on our way.

John says that Jesus, by his coming into the world, brought the real light to everyone. His coming was like a blaze of light. It was like the coming of the dawn. A traveller tells how once in Italy he was standing on a hill overlooking the Bay of Naples. It was so dark that nothing could be seen; then all of a sudden there came a lightning flash and everything, in every detail, was lit up. When Jesus came into this world, he came like a light in the dark.

Further, Jesus is the light who lights everyone who comes into the world. The ancient world was exclusive. The Jews hated the Gentiles and held that they were created for no other purpose than to be fuel for the fires of hell. True, there was a lonely prophet who saw that Israel's destiny was to be a light to the Gentiles (Isaiah 42:6, 49:6), but that was a destiny which Israel had always definitely refused.

The Greek world never dreamed that knowledge was for everyone. The Roman world looked down on the barbarians, the uncultured peoples without the law. But Jesus came to be a light to all people. Only the God and Father of our Lord Jesus Christ has a heart big enough to hold all the world.

December 14

Unrecognized

John 1:10–11

In the end, God's creating and directing word did come into this world in the form of the man Jesus. John says that the word came to his own home and his own people gave him no welcome. What does he mean by that? He means that when God's word entered this world, he did not come to Rome or to Greece or to Egypt or to the Eastern empires. He came to Palestine; Palestine was specially God's land, and the Jews were specially God's people.

Jesus came to a land which was peculiarly God's land and a people who were peculiarly God's people. He ought, therefore, to have been coming to a nation that would welcome him with open arms; the door should have been wide open for him; he should have been welcomed like a traveller coming home; or, even more, like a king coming to his own—but he was rejected. He was received with hate and not with adoration.

We may put it in another way—a way that strikes home—that there are so few people who become what they have it in them to be. It may be through lethargy and laziness, it may be through timidity and cowardice, it may be through lack of discipline and self-indulgence, it may be through involvement in second bests and byways; but the world is full of people who have never realized the possibilities which are in them. We need not think of the task God has in store for us in terms of some great act or achievement of which everyone will know. It may be to fit a child for life; it may be at some crucial moment to speak that word and exert that influence which will save a life from ruin; it may be to do some quite small job superlatively well; it may be to touch the lives of many by our hands, our voices or our minds. The fact remains that God is preparing us by all the experiences of life for something; and many refuse the task when it comes and never even realize that they are refusing it.

There is all the pathos in the world in the simple saying: 'He came to his own home—and his own people gave him no welcome.' It happened to Jesus long ago—and it is still happening.

Children of God

John 1:12–13

There is a sense in which we are not naturally children of God. There is a sense in which we have to become children of God.

Children fall into two categories. There are those who never do anything else but make use of their home. All through their youth, they take everything that the home has to offer and give nothing in return. Their parents may work and sacrifice to give them every chance in life, and they take it as a right, never realizing what they are taking and making no effort to deserve it or repay it. When they leave home, they make no attempt to keep in touch. The home has served its purpose and they have finished with it. They are aware of no bond to be maintained and no debt to be paid. To their parents they owe their existence; and to their parents they owe what they are; but between children and parents there is no bond of love and intimacy. The parents have given all in love; but the children have given nothing in return.

On the other hand, there are children who are aware all their lives of what their parents are doing and have done for them. They take every opportunity to show their gratitude by trying to live up to the aspirations their parents have for them; as the years go on, they grow closer and closer to their parents; the relationship becomes the relationship of fellowship and friendship. Even when they leave home, the bond is still there and they are still conscious of a debt that can never be repaid.

It is the claim of John that we can enter into that true and real relationship only through Jesus Christ. When he says that it does not come from blood, he is using Jewish thought, for the Jews believed that a physical child was born from the union of the seed of the father with the blood of the mother. This relationship does not come from any human impulse or desire or from any act of the human will; it comes entirely from God. We cannot make ourselves children of God; we have to enter into a relationship which God offers us.

We can never enter into friendship with God by our own will and power; there is a great gulf fixed between the human and the divine. We can only enter into friendship with God when God himself opens the way.

The Word Became Flesh (1)

John 1:14

The word that John uses for *seeing* this word is *theasthai*; it is used in the New Testament more than twenty times and is always used of actual physical sight. This is no spiritual vision seen with the eye of the soul or of the mind. John declares that the word actually came to earth in the form of a man and was seen by human eyes. He says: 'If you want to see what this creating word, this controlling reason, is like, look at Jesus of Nazareth.'

To a Greek, this was the impossible thing. The one thing that no Greek would ever have dreamed of was that God could take a body. To a Greek, the body was an evil, a prison house in which the soul was shackled, a tomb in which the spirit was confined. Plutarch, the wise old Greek, did not even believe that God could control the happenings of this world directly; he had to do it by deputies and intermediaries, for, as Plutarch saw it, it was nothing less than blasphemy to involve God in the affairs of the world. Philo could never have said it. He said: 'The life of God has not descended to us; nor has it come as far as the necessities of the body.' The great Roman Stoic emperor, Marcus Aurelius, despised the body in comparison with the spirit: 'Therefore despise the flesh—blood and bones and a network, a twisted skein of nerves and veins and arteries. . . . The composition of the whole body is under corruption.'

Here was the shatteringly new thing—that God could and would become a human person, that God could enter into this life that we live, that eternity could appear in time, that somehow the Creator could appear in creation in such a way that he could actually be seen.

It may well be that we are often so eager to conserve the fact that Jesus was fully God that we tend to forget the fact that he was fully human. The word became flesh—here, perhaps as nowhere else in the New Testament, we have the full humanity of Jesus gloriously proclaimed. In Jesus we see the creating word of God, the controlling reason of God, taking human nature upon himself. In Jesus we see God living life as he would have lived it if he had been a man. Supposing we said nothing else about Jesus, we could still say that he shows us how God would live this life that we have to live.

December 17

The Word Became Flesh (2)

John 1:14

It might well be held that this is the greatest single verse in the New Testament. We have already seen how John has certain great words which haunt his mind and dominate his thought and are the themes out of which his whole message is elaborated.

(1) The first is *grace*. This word always has two basic ideas in it.

(a) It always has the idea of something completely undeserved. It always has the idea of something that we could never have earned or achieved for ourselves. The fact that God came to earth to live and to die for men and women is not something which humanity deserved; it is an act of pure love on the part of God. The word *grace* emphasizes at one and the same time our own helpless poverty and God's limitless kindness.

(b) It always has the idea of beauty in it. In modern Greek, the word means *charm*. In Jesus we see the loveliness of God. People had thought of God in terms of might and majesty and power and judgment. They had thought of the power of God which could crush all opposition and defeat all rebellion; but in Jesus we are confronted with the sheer loveliness of God.

(2) The second is *truth*. This word is one of the dominant notes of the Fourth Gospel. We meet it again and again. Here we can only briefly gather together what John has to say about Jesus and the truth.

(a) Jesus is the embodiment of the truth. He said: 'I am the truth' (cf. 14:6). To see truth, we must look at Jesus.

(b) Jesus is the communicator of the truth. He told his disciples that if they continued with him they would know the truth (8:31).

(c) The truth is what makes us free (8:32). There is always a certain liberating quality in the truth. The truth which Jesus brings liberates us from estrangement from God; it liberates us from frustration; it liberates us from our fears and weaknesses and defeats. Jesus Christ is the greatest liberator on earth.

The Word Became Flesh (3)

John 1:14

A lifetime of study and thought could not exhaust the truth of this verse. We have already looked at two of the great theme words in it; now we look at the third—*glory*. Again and again John uses this word in connection with Jesus Christ. We shall first look at what John says about the glory of Christ, and then we shall go on to see if we can understand a little of what he means.

(1) The life of Jesus Christ was a manifestation of glory. When he performed the miracle of the water and the wine at Cana of Galilee, John says that he manifested forth his glory (2:11). To look at Jesus and to experience his power and love was to enter into a new glory.

(2) The glory which he manifests is the glory of God. It is not from human beings that he receives it (5:41). He seeks not his own glory but the glory of him who sent him (7:18). It is his Father who glorifies him (8:50, 54). The glory that was on Jesus, that clung about him, that shone through him, that acted in him is the glory of God.

(3) Yet that glory was uniquely his own. At the end, he prays that God will glorify him with the glory that he had before the world began (17:5). He shines with no borrowed radiance; his glory is his and his by right.

(4) The glory which is his he has transmitted to his disciples. The glory which God gave him he has given to them (17:22). It is as if Jesus shared in the glory of God and the disciple shares in the glory of Christ. The coming of Jesus is the coming of God's glory among his people.

The glory of the Lord means quite simply the presence of God. John uses a homely illustration. A father gives to his eldest son his own authority, his own honour. The heir apparent to the throne, the king's heir, is invested with all the royal glory of his father. It was so with Jesus. When he came to this earth, the splendour of God was visible in him, and at the heart of that splendour was love.

When Jesus came to this earth, the wonder of God was visible in him, and the wonder was love. People saw that God's glory and God's love were one and the same thing.

December 19

The Inexhaustible Fullness

John 1:15–17

'From him we have received grace upon grace.' Literally the Greek means *grace instead of grace*. What does that strange phrase mean?

It may mean that in Christ we have found one wonder leading to another. Sometimes when we travel a very lovely road, vista after vista opens to us. At every view we think that nothing could be lovelier, and then we turn another corner and an even greater loveliness opens before us. When we embark on the study of some great subject, like music or poetry or art, we never get to the end of it. Always there are fresh experiences of beauty waiting for us. It is so with Christ. The more we know of him, the more wonderful he becomes. This phrase may be John's way of expressing the limitlessness of Christ. It may be his way of saying that those who keep company with Christ will find new wonders dawning upon their souls and enlightening their minds and capturing their hearts every day.

It may be that we ought to take this expression quite literally. In Christ, we find grace instead of grace. The different ages and the different situations in life demand a different kind of grace. We need one grace in the days of prosperity and another in the days of adversity. We need one grace in the sunlit days of youth and another when the shadows of age begin to lengthen. The Church needs one grace in the days of persecution and another when the days of acceptance have come. We need one grace when we feel that we are on top of things and another when we are depressed and discouraged and near to despair. We need one grace to bear our own burdens and another to bear one another's burdens. We need one grace when we are sure of things and another when there seems nothing certain left in the world.

The grace of God is never a static but always a dynamic thing. It never fails to meet the situation. One need invades life and one grace comes with it. That need passes and another need assaults us and with it another grace comes. All through life we are constantly receiving grace instead of grace, for the grace of Christ is triumphantly adequate to deal with any situation.

December 20

The Revelation of God

John 1:18

Here again, the keynote of John's gospel sounds: 'If you want to see what God is like, look at Jesus.' Why should it be that Jesus can do what no one else has ever done? Wherein lies his power to reveal God to men and women? John says three things about him.

(1) Jesus is *unique*. The Greek word is *monogenes*, which the Authorized Version translates as *only begotten*. It is true that that is what *monogenes* literally means; but long before this it had lost its purely physical sense, and had come to have two special meanings. It had come to mean *unique* and *specially beloved*. Obviously an only son has a unique place and a unique love in his father's heart. So this word came to express uniqueness more than anything else. It is the conviction of the New Testament that there is no one like Jesus. He alone can bring God to us and bring us to God.

(2) Jesus is God. Here we have the very same form of expression as we had in the first verse of the chapter. This does not mean that Jesus is identical with God; it does mean that in mind and character and being he is one with God. In this case, it might be better if we thought of it as meaning that Jesus is divine. To see him is to see what God is.

(3) Jesus is in the bosom of the Father. To be *in the bosom* of someone is the Hebrew phrase which expresses the deepest intimacy possible in human life. It is used of mother and child; it is used of husband and wife; a man speaks of the wife of his bosom (Numbers 11:12; Deuteronomy 13:6); it is used of two friends who are in complete communion with one another. When John uses this phrase about Jesus, he means that between Jesus and God there is complete and uninterrupted intimacy. It is because Jesus is so intimate with God that he is one with God and can reveal him to us.

In Jesus Christ the distant, unknowable, invisible, unreachable God has come to men and women; and God can never be a stranger to us again.

December 21

Creation and Re-Creation

Matthew 1:18–25

The Jews specially connected the Spirit of God with the work of creation. It was through his Spirit that God performed his creating work. In the beginning, the Spirit of God moved upon the face of the waters, and chaos became a world (Genesis 1:2). 'By the word of the Lord the heavens were made,' said the psalmist, 'and all their host by the breath of his mouth' (Psalm 33:6). (Both in Hebrew, *ruach*, and in Greek, *pneuma*, the word for *breath* and *spirit* is the same word.) 'When you send forth your spirit, they are created' (Psalm 104:30). 'The spirit of God has made me,' said Job, 'and the breath of the Almighty gives me life' (Job 33:4).

The Spirit is the Creator of the World and the Giver of Life. So, in Jesus there came into the world God's life-giving and creating power. That power, which reduced the primal chaos to order, came to bring order to our disordered lives. That power, which breathed life where there was no life, has come to breathe life into our weaknesses and frustrations. We could put it this way — we are not really alive until Jesus enters into our lives.

The Jews specially connected the Spirit not only with the work of creation but with the work of re-creation. Ezekiel draws his grim picture of the valley of dry bones. He goes on to tell how the dry bones came alive; and then he hears God say: 'I will put my spirit within you, and you shall live' (Ezekiel 37:14). The Rabbis had a saying: 'God said to Israel: "In this world my Spirit has put wisdom in you, but in the future my Spirit will make you to live again."' When people are dead in sin and in lethargy, it is the Spirit of God which can waken them to life anew.

So, in Jesus there came to this world the power which can re-create life. He can bring to life again the soul which is dead in sin; he can revive again the ideals which have died; he can make strong again the will to goodness which has perished. He can renew life when people have lost all that life means.

The Saviour's Entry into the World

Matthew 1:18–25

To our Western ways of thinking, the relationships in this passage are very bewildering. First, Joseph is said to be betrothed to Mary; then he is said to be planning quietly to divorce her; and then she is called his wife. But the relationships represent normal Jewish marriage procedure, in which there were three steps.

(1) There was the engagement. The engagement was often made when the couple were only children. It was usually made through the parents, or through a professional matchmaker. And it was often made without the couple involved ever having seen each other. Marriage was held to be far too serious a step to be left to the dictates of the human heart.

(2) There was the betrothal. The betrothal was what we might call the ratification of the engagement into which the couple had previously entered. At this point the engagement, entered into by the parents or the matchmaker, could be broken if the girl was unwilling to go on with it. But once the betrothal was entered into, it was absolutely binding. It lasted for one year. During that year, the couple were known as husband and wife, although they had not the rights of husband and wife. It could not be terminated in any other way than by divorce. It was at this stage that Joseph and Mary were.

(3) The third stage was the marriage proper, which took place at the end of the year of betrothal. If we remember the normal Jewish wedding customs, then the relationships in this passage are perfectly usual and perfectly clear.

So at this stage it was told to Joseph that Mary was to bear a child, that that child had been begotten by the Holy Spirit, and that he must call the child by the name Jesus. Jesus is the Greek form of the Jewish name Joshua, and Joshua means *Yahweh is salvation*. Long ago, the psalmist had heard God say: 'It is he who will redeem Israel from all its iniquities' (Psalm 130:8). And Joseph was told that the child to be born would grow into the Saviour who would save God's people from their sins.

Jesus was not so much the Man born to be King as the Man born to be Saviour. He came to this world, not for his own sake, but for us and for our salvation.

Born of the Holy Spirit

Matthew 1:18–25

If we come to this passage with fresh eyes, and read it as if we were reading it for the first time, we will find that what it stresses is not so much that Jesus was born of a woman who was a virgin, as that the birth of Jesus is the work of the Holy Spirit. What then does it mean to say that in the birth of Jesus the Holy Spirit of God was specially operative? Let us leave aside all the doubtful and debatable things, and concentrate on that great truth, as Matthew would wish us to do.

In Jewish thought, the Holy Spirit had certain very definite functions. We cannot bring to this passage the Christian idea of Holy Spirit in all its fullness, because Joseph would know nothing about that. We must interpret it in the light of the Jewish idea of the Holy Spirit, for it is that idea that Joseph would inevitably bring to this message, for that was all he knew.

According to the Jewish idea, the Holy Spirit was the person who brought God's truth to men and women. It was the Holy Spirit who taught the prophets what to say; it was the Holy Spirit who taught people of God what to do; it was the Holy Spirit who, throughout the ages and the generations, brought God's truth to men and women. So, Jesus is the one person who brings God's truth to them. Let us put it in another way. Jesus is the one person who can tell us what God is like and what God means us to be. In him alone, we see what God is and what we ought to be.

Before Jesus came, people had only vague and shadowy, and often quite wrong, ideas about God; they could only at best guess and grope; but Jesus could say: 'Whoever has seen me has seen the Father' (John 14:9). In Jesus we see the love, the compassion, the mercy, the seeking heart and the purity of God as nowhere else in all this world. With the coming of Jesus, the time of guessing is gone and the time of certainty is come.

Before Jesus came, people did not really know what goodness was. In Jesus alone, we see true humanity, true goodness and true obedience to the will of God. Jesus came to tell us the truth about God and the truth about ourselves.

A Wondrous Hymn

Luke 1:46–56

Here we have a passage which has become one of the great hymns of the Church—the Magnificat. It has been said that religion is the opiate of the people; but it has also been said that the Magnificat is the most revolutionary document in the world. It speaks of three of the revolutions of God.

(1) He scatters the proud in the plans of their hearts. That is a moral revolution. Christianity is the death of pride. Why? Because if people set their lives beside that of Christ, it tears away the last vestiges of their pride. Christ enables us to see ourselves. It is the deathblow to pride. The moral revolution has begun.

(2) He casts down the mighty—he exalts the humble. That is a social revolution. Christianity puts an end to the world's labels and prestige. Muretus was a wandering scholar of the Middle Ages. He was poor. In an Italian town he became ill and was taken to a hospital for waifs and strays. The doctors were discussing his case in Latin, never dreaming he could understand. They suggested that since he was such a worthless wanderer they might use him for medical experiments. He looked up and answered them in their own learned tongue, 'Call no man worthless for whom Christ died.' When we have realized what Christ did for each and every one of us, it is no longer possible to regard anyone as being beneath us. The social grades are gone.

(3) He has filled those who are hungry—those who are rich he has sent empty away. That is an economic revolution. A non-Christian society is an acquisitive society where people are out for as much as they can get. A Christian society is a society where no one dares to have too much while others have too little, where everyone must get only to give away.

There is loveliness in the Magnificat but in that loveliness there is dynamite. Christianity brings about a revolution in individuals and revolution in the world.

Journey to Bethlehem

Luke 2:1–7

In the Roman Empire periodical censuses were taken with the double object of assessing taxation and of discovering those who were liable for compulsory military service. The Jews were exempt from military service, and, therefore, in Palestine a census would be predominantly for taxation purposes. Regarding these censuses, we have definite information as to what happened in Egypt; and almost certainly what happened in Egypt happened in Syria, too, and Judaea was part of the province of Syria. The information we have comes from actual census documents written on papyrus and then discovered in the dustheaps of Egyptian towns and villages and in the sands of the desert. Such censuses were taken every fourteen years. And from AD 20 until about AD 270 we possess actual documents from every census taken. If the fourteen-year cycle held good in Syria this census must have been in 8 BC and that was the year in which Jesus was born.

The journey from Nazareth to Bethlehem was eighty miles. The accommodation for travellers was most primitive. The eastern khan was like a series of stalls opening off a common courtyard. Travellers brought their own food; all that the innkeeper provided was fodder for the animals and a fire to cook. The town was crowded and there was no room for Joseph and Mary. So it was in the common courtyard that Mary's child was born. Swaddling clothes consisted of a square of cloth with a long bandage-like strip coming diagonally off from one corner. The child was first wrapped in the square of cloth and then the long strip was wound round and round about him. The word translated *manger* means a place where animals feed; and therefore it can be either the stable or the manger which is meant.

That there was no room in the inn was symbolic of what was to happen to Jesus. The only place where there was room for him was on a cross. He sought an entry to the overcrowded hearts of those around him; he could not find it; and still his search—and his rejection—go on.

December 26

Shepherds and Angels

Luke 2:8–20

It is a wonderful thing that the story should tell that the first announcement of God came to some shepherds. Shepherds were despised by the orthodox good people of the day. They were quite unable to keep the details of the ceremonial law; they could not observe all the meticulous hand washings and rules and regulations. Their flocks made constant demands on them; and so the orthodox looked down on them. It was to simple men of the fields that God's message first came. But these were in all likelihood very special shepherds.

In the Temple, morning and evening, an unblemished lamb was offered as a sacrifice to God. To see that the supply of perfect offerings was always available the Temple authorities had their own private sheep flocks; and we know that these flocks were pastured near Bethlehem. It is most likely that these shepherds were in charge of the flocks from which the Temple offerings were chosen. It is a lovely thought that the shepherds who looked after the Temple lambs were the first to see the Lamb of God who takes away the sin of the world.

When a boy was born, the local musicians congregated at the house to greet him with simple music. Jesus was born in a stable in Bethlehem and therefore that ceremony could not be carried out. It is lovely to think that the minstrelsy of heaven took the place of the minstrelsy of earth, and angels sang the songs for Jesus that the earthly singers could not sing.

All through these readings we must have been thinking of the rough simplicity of the birth of the Son of God. We might have expected that, if he had to be born into this world at all, it would be in a palace or a mansion. There was a European monarch who worried his court by often disappearing and walking incognito among his people. When he was asked not to do so for security's sake, he answered, 'I cannot rule my people unless I know how they live.'

It is the great thought of the Christian faith that we have a God who knows the life we live because he too lived it and claimed no special advantage over ordinary people.

December 27

Gifts for Christ

Matthew 2:1–12

From very early times, the gifts the wise men brought have been seen as particularly fitting. Each gift has been seen as representing something which specially matched some characteristic of Jesus and his work.

(1) Gold is the gift of a king. Seneca, the Roman philosopher, tells us that in Parthia it was the custom that no one could ever approach the king without a gift. And gold, the king of metals, is the fit gift for a king. So, Jesus was 'the Man born to be King'. But he was to reign not by force but by love; and he was to rule over human hearts, not from a throne, but from a cross.

(2) Frankincense is the gift for a priest. It was in the Temple worship and at the Temple sacrifices that the sweet perfume of frankincense was used. The function of a priest is to open the way to God for men and women. The Latin word for *priest* is *pontifex*, which means a *bridge-builder*. The priest is the one who builds a bridge between human beings and God. That is what Jesus did. He opened the way to God; he made it possible for us to enter into the very presence of God.

(3) Myrrh is the gift for one who is to die. Myrrh was used to embalm the bodies of the dead. Jesus came into the world to die. Holman Hunt painted a famous picture of Jesus. It shows Jesus at the door of the carpenter's shop in Nazareth. He is still only a boy and has come to the door to stretch his limbs, which have grown cramped over the bench. He stands there in the doorway with arms outstretched, and behind him, on the wall, the setting sun throws his shadow, and it is the shadow of a cross. In the background there stands Mary, and as she sees that shadow there is the fear of coming tragedy in her eyes. Jesus came into the world to live for men and women, and, in the end, to die for them. He came to give for us his life and his death.

Gold for a king, frankincense for a priest, myrrh for one who was to die — these were the gifts of the wise men, and, even at the cradle of Christ, they foretold that he was to be the true king, the perfect high priest, and in the end the supreme Saviour of the world.

The Slaughter of the Children

Matthew 2:13–18

Herod was a past master in the art of assassination. He had no sooner come to the throne than he began by annihilating the Sanhedrin, the supreme court of the Jews. Later he slaughtered 300 court officers out of hand. Later still he murdered his wife Mariamne, and her mother Alexandra, his eldest son Antipater, and two other sons, Alexander and Aristobulus. And in the hour of his death he arranged for the slaughter of the notable men of Jerusalem.

It was not to be expected that Herod would calmly accept the news that a child had been born who was going to be king. He had carefully inquired of the wise men when they had seen the star. Even then, he was craftily working out the age of the child so that he might take steps towards murder; and now he put his plans into swift and savage action. He gave orders that every child under two years of age in Bethlehem and the surrounding district should be slaughtered.

There are certain critics who hold that this slaughter cannot have taken place because there is no mention of it in any writer outside this one passage of the New Testament. The Jewish historian Josephus, for instance, does not mention it. There are two things to be said. First, Bethlehem was a comparatively small place, and in a land where murder was so widespread the slaughter of twenty or thirty babies would cause little stir, and would mean very little except to the broken-hearted mothers of Bethlehem. Second, the nineteenth-century historian Thomas Macaulay, in his famous *History of England*, points out that John Evelyn, the well-known seventeenth-century diarist, who was a most assiduous and voluminous recorder of contemporary events, never mentions the massacre of Glencoe.

The fact that a thing is not mentioned, even in the places where one might expect it to be mentioned, is no proof at all that it did not happen. The whole incident is so typical of Herod that we need not doubt that Matthew is passing the truth down to us.

Return to Nazareth

Matthew 2:19–23

It was in Nazareth that Joseph settled, and it was in Nazareth that Jesus was brought up. It must not be thought that Nazareth was a quiet little backwater, quite out of touch with life and with events.

Nazareth lay in a hollow in the hills in the south of Galilee. But a young boy had only to climb the hills for half the world to be at his door. He could look west and the waters of the Mediterranean, blue in the distance, would meet his eyes; and he would see the ships going out to the ends of the earth.

He had only to look at the plain which skirted the coast, and he would see, slipping round the foot of the very hill on which he stood, the road from Damascus to Egypt, the land bridge to Africa. It was one of the greatest caravan routes in the world. It was the road by which, centuries before, Joseph had been sold down into Egypt as a slave. It was the road that, 300 years before, Alexander the Great and his legions had followed. It was the road by which, centuries later, Napoleon was to march. It was the road which, in the twentieth century, General Sir Edmund Allenby was to take. Sometimes it was called the Way of the South, and sometimes the Road of the Sea. On it, Jesus would see all kinds of travellers from all kinds of nations on all kinds of errands, coming and going from the ends of the earth.

But there was another road. There was the road which left the sea coast at Acre or Ptolemais and went out to the east. It was the Road of the East. It went out to the eastern bounds and frontiers of the Roman Empire. Once again, the cavalcade of the caravans and their silks and spices would be continually on it; and on it also the Roman legions clanked out to the frontiers.

Nazareth indeed was no backwater. Jesus was brought up in a town where the ends of the earth passed the foot of the hilltop. From his boyhood days, he was confronted with scenes which must have spoken to him of a world for God.

The Dawning Realization

Luke 2:41–52

A Jewish boy became a man when he was twelve years of age. Then he became a son of the law and had to take the obligations of the law upon him. So at twelve Jesus for the first time went to the Passover. We may well imagine how the holy city and the Temple and the sacred ritual fascinated him. When his parents returned he lingered behind. It was not through carelessness that they did not miss him. Usually the women in a caravan started out much earlier than the men, for they travelled more slowly. The men started later and travelled faster and the two sections would not meet until the evening encampment was reached. It was Jesus' first Passover. No doubt Joseph thought he was with Mary, Mary thought that he was with Joseph and not until the evening camp did they miss him.

They returned to Jerusalem to search for him. For the Passover season it was the custom for the Sanhedrin to meet in public in the Temple court to discuss, in the presence of all who would listen, religious and theological questions. It was there they found Jesus.

And now comes one of the key passages in the life of Jesus. 'Your father and I', said Mary, 'have been looking for you anxiously.' 'Did you not know', said Jesus, 'that I must be in my Father's house?' See how very gently but very definitely Jesus takes the name *father* from Joseph and gives it to God.

Here we have the story of the day when Jesus discovered who he was. And mark this—the discovery did not make him proud. It did not make him look down on his humble parents, the gentle Mary and the hard-working Joseph. He went home and he was obedient to them. The fact that he was God's Son made him the perfect son of his human parents.

Truly godly people do not despise earthly ties; rather because they belong to God they discharge human duties with supreme fidelity.

December 31

The Years Between

Jesus came into the world to be the Saviour of the world, and for thirty years he never moved beyond the bounds of Palestine, except to the Passover at Jerusalem. He died when he was thirty-three, and of these thirty-three years thirty were spent without record in Nazareth. To put it in another way, ten-elevenths of Jesus' life were spent in Nazareth. What was happening then?

(1) Jesus was growing up to boyhood, and then to manhood, in a good home; and there can be no greater start to life than that.

(2) Jesus was fulfilling the duties of an eldest son. It seems most likely that Joseph died before the family had grown up. Maybe he was already much older than Mary when they married. In the story of the wedding feast at Cana of Galilee there is no mention of Joseph, although Mary is there, and it is natural to suppose that Joseph had died. So Jesus became the village craftsman of Nazareth to support his mother and his younger brothers and sisters. A world was calling him, and yet he first fulfilled his duty to his mother and to his own family and to his own home.

(3) Jesus was learning what it was like to be a workingman. He was learning what it was like to have to earn a living, to save to buy food and clothes, and maybe sometimes a little pleasure; to meet the dissatisfied and the critical customer, and the customer who would not pay his debts. If Jesus was to help men and women, he must first know what their lives were like. He did not come into a protected, cushioned life; he came into the life that all must live. He had to do that, if he was ever to understand the life of ordinary people.

(4) Jesus was faithfully performing the lesser task before the greater task was given to him to do. The great fact is that, if Jesus had failed in the smaller duties, the mighty task of being the Saviour of the world could never have been given to him to do. He was faithful in little so that he might become master of much.

It is a thing never to be forgotten that in the everyday duties of life we make or mar a destiny, and we win or lose a crown.

Scripture Index

CPSIA information can be obtained
at www.ICGtesting.com
Printed in the USA
LVOW11s0626290617
539755LV00002B/396/P